MORNG
DEVOTIONS

366 Biblical Truths
for Your Daily Walk

DR. TOM WALLACE

FOREWARD:

The Importance of Daily Devotions

As Christians we carry the most revolutionary message in the world—the Gospel. We preach that Jesus changes lives and He does! We preach that Jesus fixes broken homes and He does! We preach that Jesus is the solution to the problems of the world and He is! The question must be asked, why are there still Christians with drug problems, addictions to sin, broken homes, and a country with more problems than we dreamed possible?

I firmly believe a relationship with God is the baseline of Christianity and that every aspect of the Christian's life flows from it. A weak walk produces a weak faith. Through daily time with God in prayer and Bible study, we can build a strong relationship with our Heavenly Father. The wonderful aspect of the Gospel is that through acceptance of it, we begin a relationship with God the Father through His Son.

Too many Christians have accepted Christ as their Saviour to gain Heaven and shun Hell, but have never experienced the power of this new relationship. I believe a failure to know the One who created us and saved us has left Christianity in the same snares as the world. While the moment of salvation frees us from the flames of Hell, our relationship with God is the only avenue we have to be freed from the chains of sin while on this earth.

Since the beginning of my ministry, I have stressed the importance of a daily walk and relationship with God. If I were to counsel a church member with a private sin problem, I would start with an assessment of their personal walk with God. If I were to spend time with a struggling married couple, we would begin by checking both spouses' time with God. In my pre-marital counseling, the opening session explains the foundation of a successful marriage is rooted in a strong walk with God. I do not believe that you can have a long term effective Christian life without a daily walk with God. You may be able to sustain Christian ministry and life for some time in your own strength, but I do not believe that long term faithfulness can be built without a daily dependence upon God.

Therefore, if Jesus can change lives, we should spend as much time with Him as we can. If Jesus can fix broken homes, then both spouses need to wake up every day and learn more about Him. If Jesus Christ and the Gospel are the solution to a nation in shambles from the sin of this world, we had better begin asking God to guide our lives every day.

The Gospel unlocks our relationship with God, but our relationship with God unlocks the blessings of God. We are the beneficiary of time spent with a powerful God. You will never know all that God has for you until you begin a wonderful daily time with Him.

With this in mind, it is my joy to have had a part in a resource like the one you hold in your hands. Whether you are a new Christian or a seasoned saint, the principles of God's Word expressed and illustrated in this book will help you develop a daily walk with God.

As a pastor, I am always looking for new resources to assist in the spiritual growth of every Christian. I am thankful for the vision and heart of Dr. Tom Wallace and the effort it takes to create something like this. I am excited to see and hear of all that God will do through Christians spending time with God. I believe it is what we need for this day and hour.

—Dr. Mike Norris, Pastor

What an honor, what a privilege
To meet with my God in prayer,
To share my very heart with Him
And to know that He is there.

I would like to hear His thinking
On decisions I must make today,
And talk with Him about direction
Then listen to what He'll say.

Since He lives within my heart
And He's never far away,
I can sense and feel His presence
In a really special way.

I have His words before me
In the Bible in my hand,
I can know right from wrong
And how to make my stand.

He promises to give me wisdom
And all I need do is ask,
I'll see things from His view point
To cope with my earthly task.

I get comfort when my thoughts
Turn toward the days ahead,
For my future destiny is settled
In the things that He has said.

With my Bible and devotion book
I will have my time God
Then go singing and praising
Along the path I'll trod.

Then if the rapture should come today
Or I go in some other way,
I'll be glad I had my daily devotions
Before I started my day.

JANUARY 1
Here We Go Again

There is something exciting about getting started in a new year. We have a new chapter in the book, and a new page on the calendar, twelve new months, fifty-two new weeks, and three hundred sixty-five new days. All of these untouched, unmarred, unscarred, unblemished, and of course, uncertain and unknown.

Charles Kettering said, "We should all be concerned about the future because we will have to spend the rest of our lives there."

Joshua reminds us that we ought to sanctify ourselves *"for ye have not passed this way heretofore"* and *"tomorrow the Lord will do wonders among you"* (Joshua 3:4-5).

David reminds us, *"Thou wilt shew me the path of life"* (Psalm 16:11).

Like Paul we can *"forget those things that are behind, and press toward the mark of the prize of the high calling of God in Christ Jesus"* (Phil. 3:13-14).

Dr. W.A. Criswell used to tell about the old cowpoke in West Texas who went to see his first silent movie. The villain dressed in black rode up to the hero dressed in white with the beautiful girl standing by his side. The villain reached down, grabbed the girl, pulled her kicking and screaming up onto his horse and rode away.

The cowpoke got so excited, he jumped up, hollered, "Hey, you can't do that!" pulled out his two six guns and put twelve bullet holes in the movie screen. That cowpoke wasn't going to just sit there and let that happen. It will be a good thing for all of us to get up, roll up our sleeves, and get into the new year with zeal and excitement, new vision, and a spring in our step.

As Pastor Mike Norris says, "Hurry up the Lord is coming."

JANUARY 2
Let Us Go On

"Therefore leaving the principles of the doctrine of Christ, let us go on unto perfection" (Heb 6:1).

The Bible constantly admonishes us to forget the past and set our sights on the future. This passage assumes that we have trusted Christ. We are now to concentrate on growth, maturity, and filling of the Holy Spirit. Some obviously spend time majoring on the minors, and minoring on the majors.

I. THINGS THAT ARE BEHIND US.

Our original and inherited sin problem is behind us. David referred to this when he said, *"In sin did my mother conceive me."* (Psa. 51:5). Paul touched on this when he said, *"By one man sin entered into the world, and death by sin…"* (Rom. 5:12). Our own sins that are the result of that inherited sinful nature is also under the blood. He has promised to not remember them again. As the children sing in Sunday School, "Gone, gone, gone; yes, my sins are gone."

II. THINGS THAT ARE BEFORE US.

We have no way of knowing what the future holds but we know who holds the future. We also know about the judgment seat of Christ, the marriage supper, the millennial reign on earth, the glorified bodies, the celestial city, and the glories of heaven for all of eternity.

III. THINGS THAT ARE WITHIN US.

We believers have Christ in us. Paul speaks of, *"Christ in you the hope of glory."* (Col. 1:27). We also have the Spirit of God in us. Our bodies are the temple of God, and the Spirit of God dwells in us. Our Bible says, *"We have this treasure in earthen vessels, that the excellency of the power might be of God and not of us"* (II Cor.4:7).

JANUARY 3
Answer from Heaven

Sometimes answers to prayer are almost unbelievable. We had purchased a camp in the Baltimore area with a $1,000 down payment and that in itself was a miracle of the Lord. What happened next was even more of a miracle.

The buildings were in good condition except for the roof of the big dining hall and our meeting room. We couldn't make payments without campers and we couldn't have camp until the hole in the roof was fixed. A number of us began to pray and share our problem with the Lord. A short time later a plane from the Martin-Marietta Corporation in the Baltimore area was flying a test run over our area and a piece of the plane fell off. You will not believe where it fell. It fell right through the hole in the roof of

7

that building. We called the airplane company to report the incident. They came immediately to investigate. They informed us that, of course they would make arrangements to put a new roof on our building.

Our prayer was answered, our problem was solved, and our faith was greatly increased.

John wrote, *"And this is the confidence that we have in him, that, if we ask any thing according to his will, he heareth us: And if we know that he hear us, whatsoever we ask, we know that we have the petitions that we desired of him"* (1 John 5:14-15).

It should not have been a surprise. Jesus said, "Ask and ye shall receive." Jeremiah tells us what the Lord promised, *"Call unto me, and I will answer thee, and shew thee great and mighty things, which thou knowest not"* (Jeremiah 33:3).

God works in marvelous ways, His wonders to perform.

JANUARY 4
Real Holy War

Sammy was born in Palestine. He had lived there all his life; and now that he was of age, he began to dream of going to America.

Some of his family had already migrated and had begun to be successful in business. The more he heard from his relatives, the more determined he was to go himself.

His opportunity finally came and he took it. His parents wanted a good education for their boy so they enrolled him in our Christian school. The messages in our chapel programs and Bible teaching in the classrooms soon brought strong conviction and then eventually conversion.

When Sammy told his parents, they were irate. They were practicing Muslims. A holy war broke out in the home. His dad was filled with anger and spit in his face and walked away. He was heartbroken, but the joy of his relationship to Christ caused him to be happy to realize that he was suffering for Christ. He set out to 'present himself as a living sacrifice' as Paul wrote in Romans 12:1. Then he found Galatians 2:20, *"I am crucified with Christ, nevertheless I live, yet not I, but Christ liveth in me."* Then, *"Commit thy way unto the LORD; trust also in him; and he shall bring it to pass"* (Psalm 37:5).

Sammy met a wonderful Christian girl and they were married. They have surrendered their lives to serve the Lord as missionaries to the thousands of Arabs in the United States. That calling now has a new meaning since the September 11th tragedy. Maybe this is what Jesus was saying when He said, *"So likewise, whosoever he be of you that forsaketh not all that he hath, he cannot be my disciple"* (Luke 14:33).

JANUARY 5
In That Casket

John Bailey had been a Christian for almost 60 years. I had talked with him a number of times about his faith in Christ, and we had prayed together often. When John died I was asked to preach his funeral. I preached on the text, *"Precious in the sight of the Lord is the death of His saints."*

Several days later I went by the house to see how Mrs. Bailey was coping with her sorrow. I noticed a teenage girl lying on the couch. Mrs. Bailey introduced her to me and said, "She is my granddaughter, Carol." I told Carol, I was happy to meet her and asked, "Carol were you at your grandfather's funeral?" She assured me that she was. I then asked, "Carol, if you had been in that casket instead of your grandfather, where would you be right now?" Her reply, "It wouldn't be so good with me."

I pulled up a footstool and sat by the couch and explained to her that she was born with a sinful nature and that she could not go to Heaven unless something was done about that. I then explained the death, burial, and resurrection of Jesus to her and how she could receive Christ as her personal Saviour right then and there if she would like to. She assured me that she would. She very sweetly put her faith in Christ and was saved.

That would be a good question for anybody. If you, dear friend, were in your casket right now, where would your soul be? Let's face it, we will all be in our caskets one day too soon. That would be a good thing to have settled.

JANUARY 6
Me Too, Please

Everyone listened intently as I gave examples in my sermon, one after another, of how people get saved. The occasion was a meeting at the Lighthouse Baptist Church in Florence, AL.

I explained that one of the greatest joys of the Christian life was helping someone establish their relationship to Christ. I read the words of Solomon, *"He that winneth souls is wise"* (Prov. 11:30). I then read to them the words, *"For the Son of man is come to seek and to save that which was lost,"* and that getting people saved was the closest things to the heart of God (Luke 19:10). I further emphasized that it did not take a Bible college graduate or a preacher to do this. I stated that the Lord would be delighted to use any of us, if we would allow ourselves to be used by Him.

The song leader was a city policeman and his wife was the pianist. They both excelled in their part of the service. When the invitation was given to come forward and tell the Lord that they would accept the challenge to go out and tell someone about Christ and help them get saved, they both responded to the invitation.

The policeman's wife had a burden for a lady that she worked with. She sought her out at lunch time and tenderly witnessed to her. She willingly accepted Christ right there at the table. Another lady sitting there at the same table listening to the conversation, suddenly interrupted and said, "I want to do that, too." She too was saved right there on the spot. What a radiant joy the policeman's wife had on her face as she gave testimony of the experience that night in our service.

JANUARY 7
Losing It

"But as one was felling a beam, the axe head fell into the water: and he cried, and said, Alas, master! for it was borrowed" (2 Kings 6:5).

The story is told of the man who was sitting on his porch when a truck pulled up in front of his house, a man got out of the truck and dug a hole, then got back in the truck.

A second man got out and filled the hole up. While the man on the porch watched, the other two men repeated the digging and filling up holes seven times.

Finally the man said to the two men, "Fellows, I don't want to meddle in your business, but would you mind telling me what you're doing?" The men said, "We're planting trees, but the man who puts the trees in the ground is sick today." They were just going through the motions.

I thought of the student in Elisha's school who was cutting down a tree. The axe head flew off the handle of his axe.

The axe handle represents the human part in the account while the axe head represents the power of God. What should a person do when he loses his power?

There are four things he could have done:

- He could have pouted and blamed the person who made the axe; it was their fault.

- He could have pitied himself. "Why do bad things always happen to me?"

- Then he might have pretended and just kept swinging an empty axe handle. The "thud" sound of an empty axe handle tells us something is wrong.

- Finally he could pray, and that's what he did. He cried out, *"Alas, master, for it was borrowed."*

We need a sharp edge if we are to accomplish anything for the Lord.

JANUARY 8
The Giants Keep Coming

In the Bible classic of David and Goliath we see right triumph over wrong. The guy in the white hat wins over the one in the black. The little with God's help wins over the one who depicts evil.

Even the kindergarten children begin to understand that we can overcome big obstacles and mountain-like problems when God is in it. Our Goliath is not a nine-foot giant Philistine. It may be cancer, the death of our mate, a wayward child, a suicide in the family, or some other tragic situation.

So many times however, we miss another great truth in this story. Little is said about the giant's four big brothers. After David's victory these brothers came one by one to avenge their brother's death. David was not able to handle these giants and had to depend upon his men to come to his aid. Each of the other giants was slain by someone else.

The Christian life is referred to in the Bible as a walk, a race, a pilgrimage, and even a fight. Paul said, *"I have fought a good fight."* Every believer is troubled by the giants of the world, the flesh, and the devil. We have trouble, too, with giant despair, pride, doubt, selfishness, jealousy, covetousness, and dozen other ancient sins as Dr. Lee Roberson put it, "that dog the steps of modern men."

Just about the time we get one problem solved, another one comes

11

charging over the hill. However, the Bible says, *"the battle is the Lords."* In His strength we can overcome the giant and all his brothers. With Paul we can say, *"I can do all things through Christ which strengtheneth me"* (Phil. 4:13).

JANUARY 9
The Unfriendly Bible

An old poem reads:
> This old book is my guide, tis a friend by my side.
> It will lighten and brighten my day,
> And each promise I find,
> Soothes and gladdens my mind,
> As I read it and heed it each day.

This ancient bestseller, the Bible, has been superior to any and all other books for thousands of years. It is an anvil that has worn out multitudes of skeptic hammers. Its literary excellence, its exhaustive wealth of truth, its minute accuracy of statements, its fullness of teaching, its eternal freshness, and its marvelous power to change lives makes it the book of books. It is filled with promises of great privileges and tremendous benefits for the Christian. It is an, "Open, sesame" to Ali Baba's cave to those who believe.

However it is not the same book to the unbeliever, the worldly mind, and the disobedient Christian. The truth of the Bible goes against the grain. It rubs the fur the wrong way for the person who is not walking in the light of its teachings.

It warns of accountability and judgment. Those who reject the creator God, refuse to accept the reality of Heaven, the awfulness of an eternal Hell, and the awesome length of eternity try in vain to dethrone God and seat themselves in His place.

We are taught that men do not come to the light because their deeds are evil. The old book can be the best friend a person ever had, giving understanding and comfort in times of need, or it can be an unfriendly volume on the library shelf warning of awful retribution. And as Dr. R. G. Lee so eloquently preached, "Payday Someday."

It refuses to go away.

JANUARY 10
Three Hundred Stitches

The young man lying in the hospital bed looked like he was wearing a football helmet, but it turned out to be a large head bandage. The last thing he remembered was speeding down the highway in his car. How did he get here in this hospital bed? What happened anyway?

They told him that that he had been there several days and that he had three hundred stitches in his head. It was a miracle that he had not died right there on the spot, and it's really a good thing that he didn't. Eternity is a long time without Christ. He could have been on a slab in the city morgue.

I sat down on the edge of his bed and talked with him about getting things squared away with the Lord. He listened carefully as I talked about the problem of original sin, and the awful judgment to follow at the end of a life without Christ.

After explaining how Christ died on the Cross, was buried in the ground, and then rose again on the third day to make a payment for our sin, and explaining to him how to receive the Lord into his heart, he readily opened his heart to the Lord.

That was a very close call. He could have died and gone out to meet the Lord unprepared. What a tragedy that would have been. Our Bible says, *"it is appointed unto men once to die but after this the judgment"* (Hebrews 9:27). We ought not wait for the accident, or the heart attack, or a stroke before getting around to getting this settled. *"Behold now in the accepted time; behold now is the day of salvation"* (2 Cor. 6:2).

JANUARY 11
Costly Mistakes

Dr. Jack Treiber of Santa Clara, CA tells of a young woman in his church who saved her money and bought a brand new car. She washed it every week, carefully vacuumed it on the inside, and drove it to the station and filled the gas tank every Saturday morning, without fail. It would seem that she had the best-cared-for car in the state of California.

Two years later and while she was driving down the road, smoke began to roll out from under the hood. It began to jump and sputter. The motor stopped and would not start again.

The mechanic checked everything out and gave her the verdict: there was no oil in the crank case. The motor had completely burned up. The girl did not realize that she was to get the oil checked and changed on a regular basis.

In this case ignorance was no excuse. The damage had been done. Many sincere well-meaning folks go to church, live their lives according to the golden rule, and keep things in order but have neglected to accept Christ as their personal Saviour and get born again.

The writer of the book of Hebrews makes it very plain, *"How shall we escape if we neglect so great salvation"* (Hebrews 2:3).

Paul advises the Christian also about this. He says, *"Neglect not the gift that is in thee, which was given thee by prophecy, with the laying on of the hands of the presbytery"* (1 Timothy 4:14).

Many are guilty of neglect in their devotions, and such matters as church attendance, Bible study, prayer life, giving tithes, and witnessing. Dr. Bill Rice said, "The road to Hell is paved with good intentions."

JANUARY 12
Caesar's Big Mistake

It was 44 AD. Julius Caesar's chariot rounded the corner where a small group of onlookers were gathered around a fallen statue. The head was broken off and so were the arms. It was a statue of the great emperor himself.

At his order, the driver pulled the chariot to a halt. Caesar walked into the crowd to check out the cause. Just then a loyal Roman handed him a small scroll. He tucked it into his robe, boarded his chariot and was quickly on his way. He didn't bother to read his message.

The knife that was driven into him just missed the small scroll. Later those who would examine him read the message intended for the great leader. A warning of the assignation was on the scroll giving the names of those involved. A few minutes to read and heed would have changed the history of the world; however, it was simply ignored.

How many folks have been given a tract with a message that would prevent them from experiencing eternal death, but they stuffed it in their pocket and didn't bother to check out the solemn warning.

Ezekiel the prophet gave a good word on this. He preached, *"He heard the sound of the trumpet, and took not warning; his blood shall be upon him. But he that taketh warning shall deliver his soul"* (Ezekiel 33:5). *"Therefore we ought to give the more earnest heed to the things which we have heard"* (Hebrews 2:1).

Paul the Apostle cautioned young Timothy, *"Take heed unto thyself, and unto the doctrine; continue in them: for in doing this thou shalt both save thyself, and them that hear thee"* (1 Timothy 4:16).

JANUARY 13
Little Biting Worms

A couple in Louisiana were having problems in their marriage. They decided to take their small boy to the river and go fishing. They helped him get line baited and thrown into the water; then they moved a short distance away. They threw their lines in the water too, but without worms. They wanted to talk, not fish.

A game warden came along and asked the small boy if he was catching any fish. "No," the boy said, "My fishing worms keep biting me." The warden looked at the "worms" and asked, "where did you get these?"

The boy pointed and said, "under that rock over there." The game warden picked up the boy and ran to his to parents. The "worms" were little copperhead snakes. They had bitten the boy numerous times. The little fellow died on the way to the hospital. This little fellow became the victim of those little poisonous snakes.

We can see a great truth is this account. We have all become victims of the tragedy of the fall of Adam and Eve in the garden of Eden. The wages of sin is death. Jesus Christ, God's son, is the only antidote for the curse of sin. He came to pay for our sin through His death, burial, and resurrection.

When the children of Israel had been bitten by snakes in the wilderness, the Lord told Moses to put a brass serpent on a pole and have the people come and look upon it. If they believed that the Lord would heal them, they lived. Many died because they did not believe. Jesus later said, *"As Moses lifted up the serpent, even so must the Son of man be lifted up."* By faith we look and live.

JANUARY 14
Answered Prayer

They insist that it is a true story. A couple in Charlotte, North Carolina, went out into their back yard and found their cat had climbed and was clinging to the top of a skinny sapling tree. It would not come down.

They tried everything to rescue the cat. They put a bowl of warm milk under the tree. That didn't work. They opened a can of cat food, heated it to make the aroma rise and lure the cat down. It would not budge.

In the past the man had done some cowboy tricks with a rope. He told his wife he was going to lasso the top of the tree and pull it down and she should be ready to grab the cat.

He caught the top of the tree with his first throw and gently pulled down the tree and the cat. Just as she reached to get the cat, the rope slipped off and the tree flew back and the cat went flying into the air and over the fence.

Next door an old couple were having a cookout with their little granddaughter from California. They asked her to ask the blessing on the hamburgers and hot dogs. She thanked the Lord for the food and then added, "Lord you know that I have been asking you for a kitty cat." Just at that moment the cat landed on the table. She took the cat into her arms thanking the Lord.

When the couple came through the gate to retrieve their kitten, they did not get the cat back. The girl took it home with her because God gave it to her.

"Call unto me, and I will answer thee, and shew thee great and mighty things, which thou knowest not" (Jeremiah 33:3).

JANUARY 15
Cop Saved

Joe Paisley was sitting in his squad car at 2:00 A.M. making sure the bad guys did not do bad things to the good guys. What happened next would change Joe's life forever.

Joe was my first cousin. It was quite a surprise when he showed up at my house with his fiancée and asked if I would perform their wedding ceremony. I asked him if he had ever received Christ as his Saviour. His answer was even more of a surprise.

"I sure have," he said. "You helped me get that settled." He went on to tell me that while sitting in the police cruiser, he was listening to rock music on his radio, and I came on with a closing thought for the day.

He said, "You asked, Is there anybody out there who would like to go to heaven, but you don't have the matter settled," He continued, "Then you said, Why don't you bow your head and ask the Lord Jesus to come into your heart right now and save your soul?"

"I did just that," Joe explained. "The Lord saved me then and there," he continued.

A short time later Joe died from cancer. What a blessing it was, when I looked at him in his casket, to know that he had put his trust in the Lord Jesus and now had gone to heaven.

"For whosoever shall call upon the name of the Lord shall be saved. How then shall they call on him in whom they have not believed? and how shall they believe in him of whom they have not heard? and how shall they hear without a preacher?" (Romans 10:13-14).

He heard. He believed. He called, and he got saved.

JANUARY 16
A Trouble-free Life

Are you weary? No need to be. Are you heavy-hearted? No need for that either. Do you have troubles? If so, there is something you can do about it.

Dr. Curtis Hutson used to say, "I am the only one who can mess up my day." He refused to allow health, finances, weather conditions, people, or any circumstances to rob him of God's blessings.

We can do that, too. Jesus spoke of *"being free indeed."* In John 14 there are four reasons given to enable me to do this.

First, we have peace. The Bible speaks of Peace with God, Jesus said, *"Peace I leave with you, my peace I give unto you: not as the world giveth, give I unto you. Let not your heart be troubled, neither let it be afraid"* (John 14:27).

Then there is peace of God. Paul explains this kind of peace when he said, *"Be careful for nothing; but in everything by prayer and supplication with thanksgiving let your requests be made known unto God. And the peace of God, which passeth all understanding, shall keep your hearts and minds through Christ Jesus"* (Phil. 4:6-7). This peace is available outside of an intensive care room, or by a casket at the funeral home.

Then, there is a place. Heaven. We have an inheritance, incorruptible, undefiled, that fadeth not away, reserved in heaven for us. Again, we have a promise. "I will come again." This is called the blessed hope of the believer. That thought turns mountains into molehills.

Then the person. Jesus is the only person qualified to get us into heaven. He is not a best way, or one of the ways; He is the way and also the only way.

JANUARY 17
Jesus—Judas

When Leonardo DaVinci painted *The Last Supper*, he used live models. It is said that he literally interviewed hundreds of young men before choosing an innocent-looking nineteen-year-old to model Christ. He spent months perfecting Christ on canvas, then seven additional years on the remaining apostles.

A search for a hard, calloused face that would represent Judas seemed impossible. At last in a dungeon in Rome, a man with all the marks of sin was found waiting on death row because of a life of crime. The king granted permission for the shaggy character to pose for the famous artist.

Each day for months he was brought to the studio. DaVinci kept noticing a strange familiarity about the hardened prisoner. As they talked, the man stated, "You should remember me. I posed for you seven years ago. You painted me as Christ."

Sin has done that to many a man. The sins of immorality, drunkenness, living in the drug culture, lying, killing, and stealing, develops hatred, malice, greed, selfishness, and corruption. These things turn a beautiful smile to an ugly frown. This is followed by bitterness, anger, and disappointment.

There are enemies out there bent on luring us to a life centered on the world, the flesh, and the devil. The Bible points out that these ideologies and philosophies manifest themselves in the lust of the flesh, the lust of the eyes, and the pride of life."

Those who wander down the broad road lose freedom, health, peace, and their life. The prophet Isaiah stated it well, *"There is no peace, saith my God, to the wicked"* (Isaiah 57:21).

With Christ that story can be reversed. He said, *"Peace I leave with you, my peace I give unto you: not as the world giveth. . ."* (John 14:27).

JANUARY 18
A Man with a Problem

A man went to a psychologist with his problem.

"All right, what is your problem?" asked the psychologist.

"Well," said the man, "I am married, I have three children, I have two houses, one in the city and one on the shore, two cars and a big boat."

"You don't seem to have much of a problem," interrupted the psychologist.

"Oh yes I have," explained the patient. "I only make $40.00 a week." His problem was very simple. The solution was a bit more of a problem. His income just did not reach.

This clearly illustrates a spiritual problem very common to a lot of people. Their spirituality just doesn't reach. The questions and problems mounted up while the spiritual income has steadily declined.

Our nation, our communities, and our homes are speeding downhill morally. Each month we have an increase in crime, unwed mothers, alcoholism, riots, strikes, confusion; there is corruption in government and society in general. At the same time there is less concern for church attendance and prayer, revival efforts, and recognition of God's promises and claims in the Bible. Our problem is evident. Our spirituality doesn't reach.

What shall we do about it? There seems to be two recommendations. Take some LSD and ignore the whole thing or repent and turn to Christ. We have freedom here. We are free to choose our pill, but we are not free to choose the results of that choice.

Solomon said, *"There is a way that seemeth right unto a man, but the end thereof are the ways of death"* (Proverbs 14:12). The Bible promises a home in Heaven, but it is contingent upon accepting Jesus as our Saviour. Then we are promised abundant life, and that is contingent upon putting our lives in His hands.

JANUARY 19
Good out of Bad

Traveling across the country in meetings has it blessings and benefits, but sometimes it has drawbacks. Going to new places and meeting new people can add so much to a person's life.

After being out on the road for six weeks, we returned home to find our house had been burglarized. We lost watches, rings, small radios, a few coins, and numerous other things. The Rolex watches that we paid only thirty-five dollars for in Indonesia and another in Tijuana, Mexico, were snatched up by the burglar thinking he had struck gold.

Some of the items were special to us because of sentimental reasons but not of much value at the pawn shop. We asked ourselves the age old question, "Why do bad things happen to good people?"

We made a list of the missing items and turned it in to our insurance company. The total was estimated at something near $1800.00. The insurance company paid in full.

If we had sold all those things at a yard sale we probably would not have received even one hundred dollars. I jokingly told my wife that we should arrange another break-in for next year. What seemed to be a really bad situation had turned out to be a blessing in disguise.

Someone has said, "Most clouds have silver linings." The Bible says, *"All things work together for good to them who love God..."* (Rom. 8:28). We would do well to look for the good things the Lord has for us in every situation that comes our way.

David said, *"Before I was afflicted I went astray: but now have I kept thy word"* (Psalm 119:67). The writer of Hebrews explains that things happen to us, *"For our profit, that we might be partakers of his holiness"* (Hebrews 12:10).

JANUARY 20
It's Just His Body

When our children were small, we decided to expose them to things relating to tragedy and death. We took our older two to the funeral home and explained about caskets, undertakers, flowers, etc. We hoped that when grandparents or uncles and aunts died, they would have their questions and curiosities settled. We accomplished our goal with the two older children, but we got busy and neglected the two younger ones. Before we got around to it, my grandfather died.

We brought the children together and explained that when we got to the funeral home we would see just Grandpop's body.

"His spirit and soul are in heaven with the Lord," we told them. "Do you understand?" we asked. They assured us that they did.

Everything went fine until we walked up to the casket. Our son Tim looked at Grandpop in the casket, and his eyes got big. He looked at me with a big question mark on his face. I asked him if something was wrong.

He whispered, "Dad, I thought you said just Grandpop's body would be in the casket."

"That's right," I told him, "just Grandpop's body."

"But Dad," he whispered out loud, "there's his head, his arms, and his legs." What I had been saying and what he was hearing were two different things.

When the Bible says we ought to present our bodies to the Lord, it is telling us that our feet ought to walk for Him, our hand ought to be serving Him, our mouth ought to speak out for Him, our mind ought to think about Him, and all of our body should be completely yielded to Him.

JANUARY 21
What about Death

Ten out of ten people die. There are no exceptions. All men are destined to "sleep with their fathers," "go the way of all the earth," and "give up the ghost."

The Bible says, "It is appointed unto man once to die." At the time of this writing, three close friends have *"walked through the valley of the shadow of death"* in the past week.

One of these fell from the roof of a tree house he was building for his grandchildren, one died from a brain tumor discovered just seven weeks before, and then one dear eighty-year-old great grandmother just sat down in her chair, closed her eyes, and *"was carried by the angels to Abraham's bosom."*

All of these had an unshakable faith in Christ and left no doubt in anybody's mind about their future destiny. They left their earthly body and were ushered into the presence of God in "a body not made with hands eternal in the heavens."

In a sense we all live on death row. Life can be described as "From the cradle to the coffin." Even Johnny Cash had it right when he sang about "The Long Black Train." Another pointed out that our life is the dash between the date of birth and death on our tombstone.

Death may come in a slow way, a sudden way, or even a strange way; but sooner or later death will come. One person said, "If I knew where I was going to die, I would never go there." For the Christian, death does not have to be feared, but it does need to be faced.

The main thing is to be sure we have made our reservation and that our name is written in the Book of Life.

JANUARY 22
Ken Jenkins

Ken Jenkins went to New Guiana with his wife and three children. He was doing an outstanding job, and then suddenly his wife died. He came home to bury her and brought the children.

He was anxious to get back to his new fledgling work; however, it was not going to be possible to take the children back without someone to care for them. He was really in a quandary.

He came before our mission board with an interesting request. A young woman had returned from a mission field in Africa. She had offered to go back with him and be a mother for the children and help him with the work. He could not take her back without marrying her and he requested our permission.

That board consisted of men like Dr. Lee Roberson, Dr. Harold Sightler, Dr. Jack Hudson, Dr. Dolphus Price, Dr. J.R, Faulkner, Dr. Don Sisk, myself, and several other well-known Christian leaders.

We asked Ken if he loved her. "I don't even know her," he said. "She is willing to go, and I desperately need her," he stated, and "I would like to take her back with me."

We asked him to wait outside with her, and we had a very interesting conversation. Finally someone made a motion that we grant the request. We got a second and a unanimous vote.

I went to visit them some time later and found them very much in love and enjoying a new baby that the Lord had given them. And as the old children's stories say it, "they lived happily ever after."

JANUARY 23
Liabilities and Assets

Bookkeepers have two columns in their ledger. One column is for the cash, accounts receivable, insurance, investments, equipment, and property values. The other column lists the mortgages, loans, depreciation, contracts to be fulfilled, etc.

I set up a ledger for my four children when they went off to college and recorded all the money that I had to advance them for expenses and needs while there. On birthdays, graduation, and weddings I subtracted money amounts from their debt column, and by graduation they were all out of debt.

I'm sure the Lord has plus and minus columns also in relation to His Children.

We had two fellows in our congregation who had the same name. One of them was faithful in attendance, a bus worker, and a faithful giver. He surrendered to the Lord and went to Bible College. He inherited a great deal of money and dropped checks in the offering for $30,000 on one occasion, and $40,000 on another. He told us there would $200,000 for the church in the next couple of years.

The other fellow stole equipment and tools on 21 occasions and sold them to a pawn shop. On another occasion he broke into our offices and robbed the petty cash drawer of several hundred dollars. He borrowed from our people for a long period of time. He left owing us a great deal of money.

One was an asset and a blessing, the other a liability and burden. It would be interesting to see how each of us shows up on God's ledger book. One day the books will be opened, and we will be judged according to our works.

"For we shall all stand before the judgment seat of Christ" (Romans 14:10).

JANUARY 24
Shake It Off

The story is told of a farmer and his mule. The mule fell into the farmer's well. The farmer heard the mule "braying"—or whatever mules do when they fall into wells. After carefully assessing the situation, the farmer sympathized with the mule but decided that neither the mule nor the well was worth the trouble of saving. Instead, he called his neighbors together and told them what had happened…and enlisted them to help haul dirt to bury the old mule in the well and put him out of his misery.

Initially, the old mule was hysterical! But as the farmer and his neighbors continued shoveling and the dirt hit his back. It suddenly dawned on him that every time a shovel of dirt landed on his back…he could shake it off and step up! This he did, blow after blow.

"Shake it off and step up…shake it off and step up!" he repeated to encourage himself. No matter how painful, or distressing the situation seemed, the old mule fought "panic" and just kept right on "shaking it off and stepping up!"

You're right! It wasn't long before the mule, battered and exhausted, stepped over the wall of that well! What seemed like would bury him, actually blessed him…all because of the manner in which he handled his adversity. That's life!

If we face our problems and respond to them positively, and refuse to give in to panic, bitterness, or self-pity… the adversities that come along to bury us usually have within them the potential to benefit and bless us!

Remember, forgiveness, faith, prayer, praise, and hope…all are excellent ways to "Shake it off and step up" out of the wells in which we find ourselves!

JANUARY 25
A Mad Dog

I read recently the account of a young man who was out for a walk. He noticed a vicious looking dog coming across the street toward him. The dog was showing his teeth and foaming at the mouth. Realizing the dog was mad and possibly infected with rabies, he started to retreat back the way he had come.

Suddenly the dog spotted some children playing in a vacant lot nearby. It turned and started running in their direction. Without thinking of his own safety, the young man quickly ran in front of the dog and started yelling to distract him.

The dog turned and attacked, seriously injuring him. He was rushed to a hospital for a long, slow period of healing. The parents and the children came to express their gratitude, the newspapers called him a hero, and the city officials gave him special recognition for endangering his life to save the children from a terrible fate.

This is just what Jesus did for every one of us. He saw that we were plagued with inherited sin and were in danger of an awful fate of eternal hell.

He stepped in and took the experience of judgment and death in our place. He was willing to be made a curse for us (Galatians 3:13). Peter says it well: *"Who his own self bare our sins in his own body on the tree, that we, being dead to sins, should live unto righteousness: by whose stripes ye were healed"* (1 Peter 2:24).

"Greater love hath no man than this, that a man lay down his life for his friends" (John 15:13).

"But God commendeth his love toward us, in that, while we were yet sinners, Christ died for us" (Romans 5:8).

JANUARY 26
The Open Mind

One Sunday morning I was returning from a hospital call and while coming around the Courthouse square in our town I noticed a new shop I had not seen before. Our town is a University town with almost 24,000 students. Someone had opened a shop to appeal to the students. It was called *"The Open Mind."*

I took a second look at a sign hanging across the middle of the door that said, "Closed." I chuckled and headed for church. I wondered as I drove along, how many people there will be sitting in our church today with their mind closed.

Seven different times in the second and third chapters of the book of Revelation the Lord said, *"He that hath an ear, let him hear what the Spirit saith unto the churches."* Jesus spoke also of *"Hearing they hear not and seeing they see not."* Isaiah the prophet was quoted saying, *"By hearing ye shall hear, and shall not understand; and seeing ye shall see, and shall not perceive."*

Hundreds of times the Bible says, *"The word of the Lord came unto them saying..."* Woe unto any who does not tune in to what the Lord has to say.

Several years ago in a church in Philadelphia I noticed a little boy causing distraction on the second row. I went over and sat beside him and started to talk with him. He stuck his fingers in both ears and closed his eyes. "case closed".

A lot of people have come to the place where they have their mind made up and they don't want to be confused with the facts.

The truth of the gospel and the wonderful message of Jesus Christ will change the world if we can get it past the ears and into the heart.

JANUARY 27
Five Husbands and a Lover

"The water that I shall give him shall be in him a well of water springing up into everlasting life" (John 4:14b).

One of the most interesting conversion stories in the Bible is the story of the Woman at the Well. While Jesus waited for His disciples to return from a shopping trip, a woman of Samaria came to draw water from Jacob's well. When Jesus asked her for a drink of water, it really took her by surprise.

"How is it that you, being a Jew, would ask me, a Samaritan, for water?" she asked.

There were at least three reasons for surprise.

First, she was a woman and He a man. Men just did not talk with strange women in public.

Second, she was a Samaritan and He a Jew. The Jews had no dealings with the Samaritans.

Then, thirdly, she was immoral and He the sinless Son of God.

Jesus then announced that, if she knew of the water that He could give her, she would be asking Him for water, rather than the other way around. When He spoke of the water turning into eternal life, she realized that He was talking about religion.

She quickly began to make excuses. "I go to church at Sychar, and You at Jerusalem," she declared. With that, Jesus assured her it was not a denominational matter, or race, but simply a relationship with God.

As He shared with her that He knew all about her sinful background, she was greatly convicted and gave her all to God. She was saved on the spot.

Immediately, she began to share the excitement of her conversion, and a number of people came to the Lord as a result of her testimony.

JANUARY 28
If Two Shall Agree

Jesus said, *"Again I say unto you, That if two of you shall agree on earth as touching any thing that they shall ask, it shall be done for them of my Father which is in heaven"* (Matthew 18:19).

I once knew of a Bible teacher who1 taught that each verse of Scripture in the Bible had a primary interpretation and sometimes more than one application.

The application of this verse emphasizes the strength and possibility of a man and wife who are in harmony when praying for their children or when two believers are praying for some need in their church.

The interpretation of the verse seems to be showing the power and strength in prayer when the two natures in each believer are in harmony.

We have two natures. The first is the nature of Adam that we are born with. The new nature comes at the time of new birth, or our salvation experience. The new nature is Christ Himself who is sinless. His desires, ambitions, and motives are always right and pure.

Our old nature is self-centered, carnal, and asks and prays for things that we may consume upon our own lusts (James 4:3). If we can get our body and mind in subjection to our new nature and bring it into subjection as Paul taught in I Corinthians 9:27, then we can have two praying in harmony and be assured that all our prayers can be answered.

Think of the awesome possibility, that we could get one hundred percent of our prayers answered. Jesus did exactly that. According to I John 5:14-15, if He hears our prayer, we will get what we ask for. Jesus said, *"I know that thou hearest me always"* (John 11:42).

JANUARY 29
Are You Listening

I included a funny story in my sermon while preaching to a large Spanish congregation in Cuernavaca, Mexico. Bro. Mike Patterson, the missionary pastor, was interpreting my message.

He is one of the world's best interpreters. He told the folks in Spanish, "Bro. Wallace is telling a funny story and it's not funny in Spanish, so when I give you the signal, I want you to laugh real loud for his benefit." They did and later when he told me what he had done, I laughed real loud too.

Getting what is in one's heart into one's head and out one's mouth, into other people's ears, then into their head, and then into their heart is not as easy as it may seem. Some hear only what they want to hear and what they agree with. The Bible speaks of those with itching ears.

The Bible says seven times in two chapters of the book of Revelation, *"He that hath an ear, let him hear what the Spirit saith unto the churches; To him that overcometh will I give to eat of the tree of life, which is in the midst of the paradise of God"* (Rev. 2:7).

One Sunday I had been especially hard on my folk in the morning service and had also kept them longer than I intended. I apologized on both accounts, asked the folks to forgive me, then told them I wanted them to go eat a good Sunday dinner, get an afternoon nap, then return for the evening service. I closed the service, and went to the back door to shake hands. One of our older ladies with great sincerity said, "Oh, Pastor, you don't need to apologize to us; we don't never pay no attention to anything you say."

JANUARY 30
The Gun Failed

The poor girl had so many problems that killing herself seemed like the only way out. She was at the end of her rope. This was the last straw. She nervously put the gun to her head, closed her eyes, and pulled the trigger. Nothing happened. She was confused and tormented with guilt. The memory of being abused as a child would not go away. Nothing seemed to work for her. Even the gun would not cooperate. Her dad had fired that gun hundreds of times, and it never failed.

When she came to me, I suggested that she needed to establish a relationship with someone who understood how she felt and knew what she had been through. She was ready to listen.

Instead of digging around in her past causing her to relive the old and bad experiences, I told her how much God loved her and how He would like to help with the problem. I carefully explained when Christ comes into our heart, He not only forgives our sin, but comes into our body to become a part of our life.

She got hold of the truth that the Lord would be there for her. She would not need to carry the guilt and burden alone. I showed her Psalm twenty-three, verse four where David said, *"Thou art with me; thy rod and thy staff they comfort me."*

She responded to the old story of the gospel and accepted Christ as Saviour. The beautiful healing process began. She even got up enough nerve to make it public before the church family and be baptized.

That father has fired that gun many times since that. As far as we know that's the only time that gun ever misfired.

JANUARY 31
Open Gate

I thought we were going to crash right into the gate but just seconds before we reached it, it opened for us and we went speeding through.

My host had picked me up at Reagan Airport in Washington and we were speeding down Route 66 into Virginia. We came upon a line of cars slowly working their way through the toll booths.

Without slowing down, my driver swerved to an outside lane and headed toward a gate. I was just ready to yell, "Look out" when the gate swung open. I looked back as we sped away to see the gate close behind us. My driver smiled and explained that he had a sensor on his windshield that he paid a fee each month to keep current.

I thought about the many folks who will approach the gate of heaven and go right in because they have Christ as their Saviour and the account is paid in full. It may not be the same for others.

It also brought to my mind the time when my first cousin Jerry Wallace took me to visit the nuclear plant at Three Mile Island at Peach Bottom, Pennsylvania.

We passed through several check points and each time he showed his identification and explained who I was. We were cleared each time, and I enjoyed looking over that vast facility. Without Jerry I would have been turned away immediately.

Jesus said, *"I am the door: by me if any man enter in, he shall be saved"* (John 10:9). He also said, *"I am the way...no man cometh unto the Father but by Me"* (John 14:6). Some will hear these terrible words, *"Depart from me, ye cursed, into everlasting fire, prepared for the devil and his angels"* (Matthew 25:41).

FEBRUARY 1
Too Busy

Talk about busy. George Mueller of Bristol, England, read the Bible through over 100 times. He must not have had anything else to do.

To the contrary, for over 40 years he averaged over 30,000 letters per year. He had nine assistants working in a dozen languages. He was the pastor of 1200 believers; had the oversight of five large orphanages and a huge publishing house; printed and distributed millions of books, tracts, and Bibles. He said, "I never think of going to my work without first having a good season of time with God and my Bible."

Dr. John Rice tells of riding a train to a meeting. A young man was asking him how he could get so much done. Bro. Rice said," I wrote two chapters of a book while he was asking me questions."

In a like manner Martin Luther said, "I have so many thing to do each day, if I did not spend at least three hours in prayer each morning I never would be able to get all my work done."

Dr. Dallas Billington while pastoring the largest church in the world his church was responsible for helping over two hundred churches get started said, "Plan your work and work your plan."

Basically all these men were putting their all into their life for Christ. So much of the time we make excuses for not spending more time with God. We could learn a lot from these men. Paul spoke of *"Redeeming the time, because the days are evil"* (Ephesians 5:16). (Or taking advantage of the time we have).

He also wrote, *"The time is short: it remaineth, that both they that have wives be as though they had none"* (1 Corinthians 7:29).

FEBRUARY 2
Unclaimed

I read in my Bible that the word of the Lord was of no profit to the Israelites in their journey out of Egypt because it was not mixed with faith (Heb. 4:2). Believing is everything. Jesus taught that *"And all things, whatsoever ye shall ask in prayer, believing, ye shall receive"* (Matthew 21:22).

Suppose someone wanted to be an encouragement and a blessing to a troubled young person. This person goes to Wal-Mart, K-Mart, or Toys-R-Us, selects an expensive bicycle, pays for it, then explains to the clerk that the bike is for this certain young man.

He then sends word about the bike and asks that the boy go by the store and pick it up. If the boy does not believe it is really there, or for some reason he doesn't want it, he will not go by to accept it. If he believes the word of the benefactor, it is a sure thing that he will find a way to get there to receive the bike.

John wrote, *"But as many as received him, to them gave he power to become the sons of God, even to them that believe on his name....Every good gift and every perfect gift is from above, and cometh down from the Father of lights"* (James 1:12, 17).

Even though the bike is bought and paid for, the boy will get no benefit from it until he believes and receives it as a gift.

Salvation is the same, and many will never go to heaven for the same reason. *"He that believeth on him is not condemned: but he that believeth not is condemned already, because he hath not believed in the name of the only begotten Son of God"* (John 3:18).

FEBRUARY 3
Up In Smoke

At the close of World War II, the Japanese had retreated from one of the islands of the Philippines. The air force had bombarded the island, and the naval ships had pulverized it with their big guns.

A company of young soldiers was then ordered to clean out the stragglers who might be left there. They invaded the area and were surprised to find that the Japanese had slipped away during the night. They were ordered then to gather the weapons and munitions left behind by the fleeing enemy.

One of our men told of finding a building covered with heavy tar paper and sealed with a protective cover. There was a big padlock on the door. One of the soldiers used his machine gun and blew the lock off the door. The young soldiers were amazed at the contents of the building. Inside there were hundreds of crates of Japanese yen. There were billions and billions of dollars in currency for future use by the Japanese.

They had planned to invade the West coast, then continue across America and take control of the USA. The money was to fund this.

The young soldiers took a few of the bills for souvenirs and set the building on fire and watched it all go up in smoke. Two weeks later the commanding officer announced to their group that they were to be transferred to mainland Japan. The people there were using that same currency in the stores there. One soldier remarked, "We could have bought Tokyo." They were rich and did not realize it.

Many Christians are just like that. The Bible teaches that we are *"... heirs of God, and joint-heirs with Christ"* (Romans 8:17). I'm afraid that many of us do not realize what we have.

FEBRUARY 4
Oh Yuck

All of us have heard our kids say, when they looked at turnip greens, green beans, or broccoli, "Yuck! I don't like that." We ask, "Have you ever tasted it?"

How do they know whether they like it or not? They are prejudging without facts. Thank the Lord most kids grow out of this stage.

In the present day society in which we live, not only our kids but everybody in society is exposed to teaching of secularism and humanistic philosophy in all levels of schooling, especially in state universities. Christianity is ridiculed and forbidden in government-funded institutions.

By the time a young person has been exposed to this philosophy for twelve to sixteen years the majority look upon Christianity as Yucky! This is also true of Hollywood movies and the secular media. Some commentators call it "the drive-by media."

It is one thing when a child calls carrots and peas yucky, but a bit more serious when non-Christians, in danger of losing their eternal soul, are exposed to Christianity and salvation, and they say, "Oh yuck! I don't want to be a Christian." How would they know, if they had never experienced it?

The book of Hebrews speaks of tasting of "the Heavenly gift." the good word of God, and the powers of the world to come" (Hebrews 6:4-5). After David tasted it, he said it was sweet as honey (Psalm 119:103). The psalmist said, *"O taste and see that the Lord is good"* (Psalm 34:8).

The devil would like for people to turn off Jesus and Bible Christianity without ever trying it. We hope they will grow out of that attitude before it costs them their soul.

FEBRUARY 5
God's Provision

Dr. Lee Roberson employed me to visit for the Highland Park Baptist Church while I was in college. My classes were arranged for the morning hours. I visited during the afternoon. What studying I was able to do was done late at night.

After studying into the wee hours of the morning for an important test, I got four or five hours sleep and headed off to an early class. On the way, I fell asleep and wrecked my car. The car still ran fine but it looked terrible. The fender and door were badly damaged. I was embarrassed to drive it, knowing that I not only represented the Lord but Dr. Roberson as well.

The estimate for getting the car fixed was over my head. One of the older students had been trained in body work and offered to fix it for $125.00 by using parts from a salvage yard. The $125.00 seemed like $1,000.00.

One of the deacons in our church was a dentist. He offered to clean and fix my teeth at no cost because I was a student. While in the dental chair, he asked about my car. I told him the whole story; he then pointed to a vase on a table and told me that any money received from walk-in patients who had no appointments was put in that jar for special needs of the Lord's people. He invited me to check out the contents and use it to help get my car fixed. The amount in the jar was $125.00. My car soon looked like new. My heart was filled with joy and my faith was greatly increased.

Philippians 4:19 states *"But my God shall supply all your need according to his riches in glory by Christ Jesus."*

FEBRUARY 6
Valley Full of Bones

The prophet Ezekiel had a very difficult job. God put him in a valley filled with dry bones. They were disjointed, scattered, and dead. This was a graveyard turned upside down. Many preachers have been called to challenge and stir dead and bored congregations. None could beat this crowd. "Preach to them," the Lord told Ezekiel. He did just that!

The reaction was a strange sight. The bones began to move about and join together. The result was unity. The bones came together and assembled like a church congregation on Easter Sunday morning. However something still was missing. There was no "life."

I suppose this is true of multitudes of congregations. Ezekiel preached again from the Word of the Lord and the breath of God came into these lifeless corpses. Ears began to hear, eyelids began to flutter, eyes began to see, color came back into cheeks, hearts began to beat, lungs began to breathe, hands began to move, lips began to speak, blood began to flow in veins, and suddenly they were very much alive.

Surely one of our greatest needs in this day of dead, lifeless religion where formality and meaningless procedure prevails is for the breath of God to come and give life.

It is not God that is dead, but people. The problem is that there are no Ezekiels to preach to the bones. The modern substitution for this old-time problem seems to be to have a dance, a jazz program, or a "pot" party. These things might arouse the boneyard for a little rattling and moving around, but it will not breathe unto them the breath of life.

Let's get back to preaching the gospel that is the *"power of God unto salvation to everyone that believeth"* (Romans 1:16).

FEBRUARY 7
Napoleon

When Napoleon invaded Russia, the battle raged fierce. In one city the great French conqueror became separated from his personal guards. He was spotted and recognized by some Russian soldiers who made chase.

He ran for his life, through the streets, up an alley, around a corner, and into a furrier shop. He pleaded with the furrier to hide him. The shop owner sat him down in a corner and covered him with a pile of furs and skins.

The soldiers burst through the door demanding, "Where is he? We saw him come into this shop." They tore the place apart and ran swords through the furs, missing the great soldier by inches.

Napoleon's own soldiers soon came to the rescue. The furrier asked the general, "How did it feel for such a great world leader to be in such danger and so close to death?"

He raised himself up to his full height and commanded, "Arrest this man, take him to the street, blindfold him, and assemble the firing squad, and shoot him. I will give the order myself."

They quickly obeyed. The man was stood against a wall. The order was given. The man heard the guns being raised at Napoleon's order. "Ready, aim..." The man stood in terror and fear. Then the command was given: "Take away the blindfold. Now you know how it feels," said the general.

There is no way for us to understand how Jesus felt when He hung on the cross enduring the sin of the world. We do know that He became a man and lived among us. He knows how we feel. *"[He] was in all points tempted like as we are"* (Hebrews 4:15).

FEBRUARY 8
Handling Pressure

Everybody experiences pressure. It may come in the form of financial stress, or physical needs, then problems with people, schedule complications, family pressure, and a number of other factors.

Jesus said, *"In the world ye shall have tribulation: but be of good cheer; I have overcome the world"* (John 16:33). My pastor recently had us turn in our Bibles to the writings of Solomon. He wrote *"Trust in the LORD with all thine heart; and lean not unto thine own understanding. In all thy ways acknowledge him, and he shall direct thy paths"* (Proverbs 3:5-6).

Those who are under pressure and will apply the truth of these verses to their situations will find that their problem can be solved quickly.

These verses tell us four things to do. First, Trust God entirely. We are to trust Him with, *"all our heart."* This means to really put ourselves into it. We learn that when we walk through the valley of the shadow of death, He is with us and His rod and staff will comfort us.

Then, second, we are to trust Him exclusively. He says, *"lean not on thine own understanding."* Instead of, "I think," "I believe," or "this is the way I look at it," we must say, "this is what the Bible tells me about that."

Then he tells us to trust Him extensively. That is, *"in all our ways acknowledge him."* If only I could realize that the Lord is interested in all my ways. He cares about my health, my family, my job, my house, and all the others of my life.

Finally the verse advises me about the end result of trusting Him. It says, *"He will direct thy path."* He has a will about every aspect of our lives. He says, *"Be careful (anxious) for nothing"* (Phil. 4:6).

FEBRUARY 9
The Talking Dead

Jim Gervatt is in Heaven. He died of a heart attack. A big beautiful new educational wing was dedicated to his memory in Glendola, New Jersey. I was invited to be guest speaker for this dedication service.

Jim's widow was there and so was his son and his granddaughter. His mother and his 92-year-old grandmother were also there. A great crowd had come to honor his memory. A beautiful bronze plaque was placed on the wall along with his picture.

A time of testimony was held. One by one people rose to give testimony to how Jim had touched their lives. Some stated he had won them to Christ. Others told how Jim had helped them get back in church. Still others said he helped them through the hard places.

They spoke of love and concern for the individual. He had visited the sick, encouraged the backsliding and comforted the wounded and hurt. Now suddenly he was gone!

It was all so hard to understand but nobody questioned God. It was so obvious that even though he was gone his influence was still very much alive. I remembered the verse, *"He being dead yet speaketh"* (Hebrews 11:4).

Obviously Jim had thought on and applied the truth of Jesus' words, *"Let your light so shine before men, that they may see your good works, and glorify your Father which is in heaven"* (Matthew 5:16).

Maybe we should give some thought to how much influence we can leave behind. My message was a challenge for folk to renew themselves to keeping his memory alive by making a commitment to rededicate themselves to the Lord and live like Jim Gervatt had lived. A good number of people promised that they would.

FEBRUARY 10
Little Is Much

Most of us know and love the truth in the song, "Little is much when God is in it." That same thought is found in the principle of wrong-doing and sin. Little is too much when we are speaking of sin.

One of Satan's subtle suggestions is "It's no big deal." He got Eve to eat forbidden fruit with that approach. Saul did not consider it a big thing to spare Agag the Amalekite king when God had said, "Slay utterly," but he lost his kingdom over it. When David insisted that the people of Israel be numbered against the advice of Joab, it did not appear to be much of an issue but thousands of people died because of it.

It is the little foxes that spoil the vines. Ninety-nine percent cold fresh water and one percent arsenic will make one, one hundred percent dead. There is no harm in the ninety-eight percent corn meal in rat poison but the two percent arsenic will ruin his day.

Ananias and Sapphira did not see that the little lie they told Peter was a big deal, but God saw it quite differently. There is no such thing as a little white lie.

A classic illustration of this truth is the death of Uzza who innocently touched the ark to keep it from falling. He was instantly killed. He violated a basic law of God.

Just slacking off a little bit in our Bible reading, in our praying, in our church attendance, in our tithing, and in our witnessing is a much bigger issue than we may think. The results will be much more damaging than we thought. Maybe the old adage "An inch is as near as a mile if you miss" is worth considering.

FEBRUARY 11
A Million Dollars

While visiting with my younger brother in the Villages near Ocala, Florida, we went golfing on one of the thirty golf courses that have been built there. Retirees from all over the country and around the world have bought and built expensive homes tucked away around the lakes, golf courses, restaurants, medical facilities, and malls. Most of the homes were in the $250,000 price range.

One very beautiful and expensive home located by a lake and on one of the golf courses was in the $750,000 bracket. The owner had operated a large dairy farm in the Indiana area for years; then oil was discovered on his property. As the oil was pumped out, the money flowed in. He moved to Florida to enjoy retirement. A realtor told him, "I can get you a million dollars for your house." The retired man replied, "What would I want with a million dollars?" I suppose it would be nice to come to that place in one's life.

It brought to mind a sermon I used to preach entitled, "How to have the benefits of a million dollars without having all the headaches that would go along with it." Bible Christians know that satisfaction and fulfillment do not come with money. Kraft, Penney, Wannamaker, Hughes, and others have testified to that.

Jesus promised that all things would be added to those who seek first the kingdom of God and His righteousness (Matthew 16:33). True riches are found in spiritual values and not material things. Someone said, "Men search through the books on the shelves of the town library trying to discover the secrets of a fulfilled life, and the janitor sweeping the floor has found it long ago in Jesus Christ."

FEBRUARY 12
Million-Dollar Formula

Wouldn't it be wonderful if a person could get all of the benefits of a million dollars without having all the headaches that would go along it? Most folks think they would like to have a million; but if they just knew what it would entail, they would probably decline the generous offer.

Suppose someone gave you a million late this evening. You would not be able to get it to the bank. You would need to sit up all night and guard it. Every noise would shake you up and make you think a burglar was after it. You have already lost a night's sleep and you are a nervous wreck and the excitement of the plans that you are making would have your emotions keyed to the breaking point.

The next day you will begin to face reality. The income tax will be somewhere around 70% and your tithe is $100,000.00 Now you have less than half of the million left and all the community clubs and drives will approach for a liberal contribution. All your relatives will be around to insure their standing. People will be extra friendly; and you know it is the money and not you, and you will be suspicious of everybody. A few days of this, and you will cry out, "I wish I had never seen a million dollars!"

On the other hand it is possible to have all the benefits that we think would be ours without the million. Peace, security, contentment and all the rest will never come with money. These come from God, and provision has been made through Jesus Christ and revealed to us through our Holy Bible. They are ours just for the taking. *"Possess ye your possessions"* (Joshua 1:11).

FEBRUARY 13
The Reason To Love

A Christian woman once asked Dr. Jack Hyles if he might give her some counsel. When he told her that he would be happy to do so, she shared with him that she had asked her husband if he loved her. He answered, "Of course I do." She then asked him why he loved her.

Hoping he would say because she was beautiful, intelligent, or pleasant and a joy to be around, she was wounded when he said, "I love you because the Bible tells me that I should."

She confessed to Dr. Hyles that she didn't want him to love her because the Bible told him to, but because she was special in all the areas mentioned. Dr. Hyles in his wisdom explained that if he loved her for her beauty or sweet spirit or any of these reasons, they might change when she got older and lost those qualities.

Her beauty would fade, and she might become fussy and hard to get along with, and her memory would fail, then he might no longer love her. However since the Bible does not change, it would still command the husband to love her in spite of an ill temper, or cantankerous spirit because of arthritis or some other physical problem.

She smiled and said, "Well, I never thought of it that way," and that wonderful lady went away as happy as a child with a new toy.

Paul wrote in Romans 8:35-39 about nine things that would not be able to keep us from God's love. We might add to that list ugliness, moodiness, fussiness, forgetfulness, and many other things that will not keep my mate from loving me if he or she cares about what the Bible says. Dr. Hyles was wise.

FEBRUARY 14
It's Who You Are

When taking advantage of curb-checking of my luggage at the Raleigh-Durham airport in Raleigh, North Carolina some time ago, I jokingly said to the young agent, "Fellow, could you get me a lower-numbered boarding pass?" They have A, B, and C sections with sixty in each group. I had a C - 20, which meant that I would be the one hundred fortieth person to board the plane. That almost guarantees that you will have to sit in a middle seat in the back section between two big fat folks. He looked at me with a grin and said, "Man, you is who you is."

One pastor in a daily devotional book wrote referring to Colossians 3:3, that says, *"For ye are dead and your life is hid with Christ,"* that it is not what you are doing but who you are that matters.

Many are struggling with pride and see themselves on a perch of self-satisfaction and self-importance. Others feel that they have come to the bottom of the ditch of despair.

Somewhere along the path to maturity, we need to recognize that this is not about me, but Christ in me, the hope of glory (Col. 1:7).

Several times in the New Testament, reference is made to Jesus knowing what people were thinking and what they had been doing.

When we stand before Him at the judgment seat, He will know everything we have ever said or done and He will judge us accordingly. He also sees and knows every thought, motive, act, and the thoughts and intents of our heart here and now. He knows who we are.

It's not who we were or who we will be in the future, but who we are right now. "We is who we is."

FEBRUARY 15
The Living Dead

Dr. Lee Roberson, the founder of the Tennessee Temple University of Chattanooga, Tennessee, and pastor of Highland Park Baptist Church for so many years, gave a message entitled, "Dead at 25, Buried at 72." He was referring to the aimless, purposeless people with no vision, no goal or dream that motivates them to make things happen.

As one old man stated it, "I don't know and I don't care; all I want is my rocking chair." An old preacher on the radio out of Detroit used to say, "Anything that is dead ought to be buried." He was referring to formal, dead, lifeless religion and reminded his listeners that Jesus was the way, the truth, and the life.

My friend, Bill Webb, preached a message in a meeting in the Cincinnati, Ohio, area called "Living Until You Die," He said Christ was the source of his life, the strength of his life, the satisfaction of his life, the standard of his life and the subject of his life. He closed with a quotation from Paul the apostle, "For me to live is Christ." Jesus said, *"I am the resurrection and the life: he that believeth in me though he were dead, yet shall he live"* (John 11:25).

Paul also said Christ is the hope of glory (Col. 1:27). The Psalmist wrote, *"Where there is no vision the people perish"* (Proverbs 29:18).

Many are floating down the river of life going wherever the current takes them. Death will not be a pleasant experience to the multitudes who have no satisfaction for having accomplished their goal and ambitions. It is time for all of us to say with the Apostle Paul, when he got up off his face on the Damascus road, *"Lord, what wilt thou have me to do?"*

FEBRUARY 16
Your Appointment

Occasionally my secretary calls to remind me that I have an appointment with my doctor or dentist. I appreciate the call. With my busy life, I might have forgotten and would be billed anyway.

I am sending you a call today to remind you that you have an appointment with God. The Bible reminds us that *"It is appointed unto men once to die, after this the judgment"* (Hebrews 9:27). Job spoke twice calling it an appointment. *"For I know that thou wilt bring me to death, and to the house appointed for all living"* (Job 30:23). Again, *"His days are determined, the number of his months are with thee, thou hast appointed his bounds that he cannot pass."* (Job 14:5). The Bible calls it, "gathering to the Father," "our long home," "giving up the ghost," and many other names.

Some say the only sure things in life are death and taxes. Some even find ways to avoid the taxes, but nobody beats death. It claims all ages, all races, all religions, and all economic levels. It doesn't matter how powerful or weak, how wealthy or how poor, how educated or how ignorant, how popular or otherwise. Everybody must go and leave it all behind. Judgment follows death just as sure as night follows day.

Three souls die each second, 180 souls die each minute, 10,800 souls die each hour, 260,000 souls die each day and approximately 10 million souls die each year and most die without Jesus Christ as their Saviour.

Ray Charles was quoted as having said, "Live every day as if it is your last. Because one of these days, it will be." There are no exceptions to the rule! Be reminded that you do have an appointment.

FEBRUARY 17
Muslim Hell

"**O**h, if I did that I would go straight to Hell."

These words came from a young stewardess on a Northwest Airline flight between Tokyo, Japan, and Detroit, Michigan.

She talked freely about a marriage to a non-Muslim that brought the wrath of her parents and a divorce from her mate. The two children were awarded to him by the court and broke her heart. She wanted to marry again, but even though she and her boyfriend were very much in love, they called it off rather than risk another break-up.

I suggested that what she really needed was to put her faith in Jesus Christ and let Him give her some peace and direction. That is when she blurted out, "Oh, if I did that I would go straight to Hell."

How sad! She had been taught that. She really believed that Christ was a deceiver and that it would be a mortal sin for her to accept Him as Saviour. Jesus came to keep people out of Hell not send them there. *"But there were false prophets also among the people, even as there shall be false teachers among you, who privily shall bring in damnable heresies, even denying the Lord that bought them, and bring upon themselves swift destruction"* (2 Peter 2:1).

This is so sad and millions will miss out on Heaven. Paul spoke of being, *"Carried away unto these dumb idols even as ye were led."* How we need to gather up children and bring them to Sunday School. We need to teach them that Jesus loves them and wants to save their soul and take them to Heaven before they get exposed to and taught some contrary thinking like this poor girl.

FEBRUARY 18
Doing More

Could I do bigger and better things for the Lord? Most of us probably believe we are doing about all we can for the cause of Christ. If we just had more time or more talent or more money, we could and certainly would do more to further the cause of Christ. We could get more people saved and get more of our prayers answered.

Maybe we could learn from the weight lifter. He does not wait for more strength to lift more weight; he lifts more weight to get more strength. The weight lifter lifts weight beyond his capacity and then develops muscle power that he did not have before.

We don't wait to get more strength for praying. We pray more; then we get more strength. We don't get more effective in witnessing by waiting or hoping; we witness and become more efficient as we do it. We do our giving by faith, and the Lord increases our faith to do more giving next time. We give even that which we do not have and that brings God's blessings upon us. We end up getting more in order to give more.

When I plant a grain of corn, I get an ear of corn. The same with wheat. Sitting around waiting for an ear of corn will not bring me corn. The miracles from God come when I give Him an occasion.

Why not launch into something over your head and then look up to God for some supernatural intervention. As Jesus said to Simon, *"Launch out into the deep, let down your nets for a draught"* (Luke 5:4).

FEBRUARY 19
Breakthrough

For years I've been counseling people to get a breakthrough every day, but I have never heard anyone ever mention it before. A breakthrough is a "lift" or "a battery charge." It's something like pushing a reset button or flipping the breaker in your fuse box. It might be compared to starting your car and putting it in gear, taking off down the road.

Sometimes it comes when reading the Bible. Other times when praying. God comes on the scene. His presence is real. His still, small voice is loud and clear. I've had it come when encouraging a patient in the hospital or when helping a person receive Christ as Saviour.

I've had several breakthroughs that have been life-changing. After being witnessed to for a couple of weeks at my job, I invited Christ into my heart; and life has never been the same.

On another occasion I felt that the Lord was calling me into His service and wanted me to be a preacher. This meant a new direction. My vision for the future was redirected. From a career with General Motors to being a pastor meant quitting my job, selling our house, and going to Bible college.

Another time there was the call to pastor a church, then a second church, and again a third. Each time there was a new beginning and an excitement with beginning again.

One thing to understand is that like manna in the wilderness, yesterday's breakthrough will not meet today's need. If you have not had a breakthrough yet today, take some time out to get one.

FEBRUARY 20
Drinking Drano

Our story today comes from Morrisville, Illinois.

My sister, a nurse, told of a man brought into the hospital where she worked. The poor guy must have been the most miserable man in the world to do what he did. I couldn't believe that anyone would ever come to the point where he would drink Drano.

Of course, he was trying to kill himself, but it didn't work out the way he planned. He did enough damage to himself to require them to remove his stomach and his esophagus. His mouth and throat were also destroyed.

The Drano left him unable to speak or swallow.

Had he succeeded with his plan, he would have only gotten himself out of the frying pan and into a real fire. Hell would have been a lot worse than what he going through here and now.

My friend, Pastor Lew Hunter, Sr., went by to see him at the hospital and gave him the gospel message from the Word of God. The poor fellow received Christ as his Saviour.

I went by and talked with him a few days later, and found him in a new state of mind. He gave a good testimony of his faith in Christ.

Oh, if he could have come to Christ a few days before, instead of turning to Drano. Drano might unclog a sink, but it will not solve a sin problem . . . that takes Christ.

Most people would not think of drinking Drano, but multitudes do try to solve their problems with alcohol, drugs, sex, sports, and a lot of other things. *"I am the way, the truth, and the life"* (John 14:6).

"Come unto me, all ye that labour and are heavy laden, and I will give you rest" (Matthew 11:28).

FEBRUARY 21
Faith Exercised

By faith I boarded a plane. The ticket promised that the pilot would deliver me to Pittsburgh, Pennsylvania. I trusted the pilot and the plane to get me there. It did and right on time. I stopped at a gas station and believed that gasoline was flowing from the pump into my tank and not buttermilk or lemonade. Most of us work all week believing that our employer will give us a salary check as promised. We drop our letters in a mailbox on a back street believing they will be delivered to the person we have addressed it to halfway around the world.

There are many ways that we have learned to live by faith. We have God's promise that He will let us into heaven if we accept the payment Jesus Christ made for us on the cross and allow Him to come into our heart. We must take Him at His word believing He will keep His promise.

The Bible says, *"By grace are ye saved, through faith. . ."* It also says, *"But without faith it is impossible to please him: for he that cometh to God must believe that he is, and that he is a rewarder of them that diligently seek him"* (Hebrews 11:6).

God has made a lot of promises to us in the Bible. He said on one occasion, *"Whatsoever ye shall ask, believing, ye shall receive"* (Matt. 21:22).

Even though it is not likely, it is possible to get every one of our prayers answered. According to 1 John 3:22, anything we ask believing, we receive, because we keep His commandments and do the things that are pleasing in His sight.

Dear reader, if you have not exercised faith in Christ yet, why not trust Him now.

FEBRUARY 22
The Paralysis of Fear

I've met a lot of men who claim to be tough as shoe leather and hard as nails. They boast that they fear neither man or beast. But when it comes to openly receiving and professing Christ as Saviour, they wilt like cowards and they shrink in fear.

The concern for what other men will think and say about them has cost many a person his eternal soul. This is also true of thousands of teenagers who allow pressure from their peers to cause them to reject Christ as Saviour and rob them of heaven.

A story is told of a mouse who greatly feared cats until a magician turned him into a cat. That took care of that until he was chased by a dog. The magician obliged him by turning him into a dog, but then he encountered a tiger. The mouse turned cat turned dog turned tiger appealed again to the magician, but the magician wisely told him, "You have the body of a tiger, but you still have the heart of a mouse," and he turned him once again into a mouse.

An old German proverb says, "Fear makes the wolf bigger than he is." The ten spies feared the inhabitants of Canaan and saw them as giants. Someone said, "He who fears death will not enjoy life."

"The fear of man bringeth a snare: but whoso putteth his trust in the Lord shall be safe" (Proverbs 29:25). This condition of fear can be easily overcome by heeding the advice of the Lord to Joshua, *"Have not I commanded thee? Be strong and of good courage, be not afraid neither be thou dismayed: for the Lord thy God is with thee whithersoever thou goest"* (Joshua 1:9).

FEBRUARY 23
Guilty But Justified

A man in a small town known as Mose was arrested and accused of stealing a pig. His trial date arrived, and he was brought into court.

The judge knew he had the pig, the jury knew, the prosecuting attorney knew, the defense attorney knew, and he knew he had the pig, but none of them could prove it.

The case was presented; the jury was dismissed and soon returned with a verdict. The slip of paper was handed to the bailiff who gave it to the judge. The judge then announced, "Mose, I am happy to announce that you have been exonerated." Mose then said, "Thank you, Judge, what do that mean? Do I have to give the pig back?"

This is one of the best descriptions of justification I have ever heard. We are all guilty. The Bible says that *"all have sinned and come short of the glory of God"* (Romans 3:23). *"For there is not a just man upon earth, that doeth good, and sinneth not"* (Ecclesiastes 7:20).

We are also under the condemnation of God. *"He that believeth not is condemned already, because he hath not believed in the name of the only begotten Son of God"* (John 3:18).

However, thank God the penalty has been paid. *"But God commendeth his love toward us, in that, while we were yet sinners, Christ died for us"* (Romans 5:8). *"There is therefore now no condemnation to them which are in Christ Jesus, who walk not after the flesh, but after the Spirit"* (Romans 8:1).

"For what saith the scripture? Abraham believed God, and it was counted unto him for righteousness" (Romans 4:3).

When we put our faith in Christ and believe or trust in Him, like Abraham, we are exonerated.

FEBRUARY 24
An Intellectual Got Saved

Warren was handsome, sharp, and as smart as they come; but he was also lost in sin and needed to be saved. The only reason he came to our church was because he had fallen in love with a beautiful girl who attended every service with her parents. He felt he was far above this religious bit, and my simple, plain preaching just didn't challenge his mental capacity.

When Dr. Monroe Parker came to hold a meeting in our church, Warren came along with Pat every night. Dr. Parker's illustrations and material from a long background of science, law, government, Bible, and education really intrigued young Warren.

Dr. Parker gave a scholarly presentation of Creation versus Evolution, and summed it up with David's statement, *"The fool hath said in his heart, There is no God"* (Psalm 14:1). "What a person is really saying," explained Bro. Parker, "is there is no God for me."

That got through to Warren. Down the aisle he came to receive Christ as his Saviour and get things settled in his heart with the Lord.

After I led him to the Lord at the altar, he began to grow and mature under my plain preaching. Warren, like hundreds of other converts in Dr. Monroe Parker's meetings, gave himself to serve the Lord in a full-time capacity.

Just as Jesus said, *"Except a man be born again, he cannot see the kingdom of God"* (John 3:3).

FEBRUARY 25
Winning a Specialist

A man came into my office wearing the most expensive sports coat I have ever seen. His pants matched his coat, and his alligator shoes and tie blended together perfectly. His million-dollar smile and warm handshake outshined his clothes.

He extended his hand and remarked, "Preacher, don't try to tell me how to make money. I've got money in twelve banks." He continued, "Don't try to advise me on building apartments. I've built ten of them in this area, and you can't help me with managing them either, because I manage over three hundred of them myself."

Then he stated, "But in this religion business, would you get me started in the kindergarten?" He was so sincere. I smiled and said, "With all due respect, fellow, you are not ready for the kindergarten, you need to start out in the maternity ward. You will need to get born again."

He laughed out loud. He thought that was so unique. "Tell me how to do that," he said. I took my Bible and in a very simple way showed him how to be born again. In just a few moments, he was born into God's family. He broke into a big smile when I read him Peter's words about "desiring the sincere milk of the word that we might grow thereby."

He extended his big hand to me again and said, "Sunday morning I will meet you in the baptistry." He did just that.

There are multitudes of people who are really sharp in their field, but are below kindergarten in understanding what it takes to be saved.

Paul said, *"the natural man receiveth not the things of the Spirit of God neither can he know them, for they are spiritually discerned"* (2 Cor. 2:14).

FEBRUARY 26
Two Doctors And The Great Physician

Dave and Peggy asked for an appointment. They were both university students in their mid-twenties. I was sure they had come to talk about marriage plans, but not so. They shared with me that they had been attending a Bible study at the university, and the instructor had advised them not to get married yet.

When I inquired as to his reason, they said they should get "born again" first. Dave looked at me and asked, "Do you know anything about being born again?"

"A little," I told him.

"Would you help us to get born again?" they asked. I led them through the simple plan of salvation. They listened like children.

When I inquired whether they would like to invite Christ into their heart and lives, they assured me that they would. I led each of them through a simple prayer. They both trusted Christ. When I asked if they really believed they were saved, they assured me that they were.

That's when I asked them what they were studying at the university. Dave told me he was getting his PhD in Psychology next month. Peggy was getting a PhD also in Psychology. Needless to say, I was shocked.

Both of them were baptized and became very active in our church, and Dave taught for us in our Christian school for a while. They both are now practicing in their field and are very active in a good church in a northern city.

I'm so glad I didn't know they were PhD's or I would have been over in Ezekiel trying to lead them to Christ around all those fiery wheels. As Peter told Cornelius, *"Of a truth I perceive that God is no respecter of persons"* (Acts 10:34).

FEBRUARY 27
No Longer an Atheist

I recently had the opportunity to speak to a Spanish group through an interpreter at a church in Florida. I gave a simple message on the text, *"The steps of a good man are ordered by the Lord: and he delighteth in his way"* (Psalm 37:23).

Verse 31 also states that none of his steps shall slide or be skipped. I pointed out that the Lord was watching to see if we skipped any of the steps.

My message emphasized the difference between the successful church at Jerusalem and the steps that made it successful and the church full of problems at Corinth and what caused the problems.

I explained how this also would apply to the individual life, or even a home, as well as a church. There were seven steps mentioned in Acts two.

They were assurance of salvation, baptism, church, Bible study, prayer, giving, and witnessing. I warned that to skip one of the steps would bring serious consequences and a loss of God's blessings.

A man who claimed to be an atheist but had been attending several Sundays, came up after the message and said, "I stepped on that first step today and I am ready now to start up the rest of the stairs."

I checked him out, and he had the matter settled in his heart. He was saved and sure of it. *"So then faith cometh by hearing and hearing by the word of God"* (Romans 10:17). *"For it is the power of God unto salvation to every one that believeth"* (Romans 1:16).

The atheist heard, believed, and became a believer. He began to see things he had never seen. He heard things he had never heard. He felt things he had never felt.

FEBRUARY 28
Wrong Mr. Green

Mr. Green was dying. He had terminal cancer. He was a patient in our local hospital, and a friend had asked me to go by and see if I might win him to Christ. I went by the very next day. I found his room and in just a few minutes had helped him establish a new relationship with the Lord. I was a bit confused though, because Mr. Green was not sick. In fact he was about to be discharged and was looking forward to going back to his job as soon as he was released.

At church the next Sunday the friend who had asked me to go by the hospital declared, "Did you hear about Mr. Green? He died last night."

"Oh, no, he got better and went home," I told the friend.

"No he never left the hospital; he was too sick," the friend stated. "I hope you were able to help him get saved."

The next day when I went back to the hospital and checked the records. There were two Mr. Greens. I obviously had won the wrong Mr. Green. I am afraid that the other Mr. Green missed heaven.

I'm sure the Lord knew the difference. Maybe the Lord knew something I didn't know. I will always wonder if the original Mr. Green had refused the Lord too many times and sinned away his day of grace.

"Seek ye the Lord while he may be found, call upon him while he is near" (Isaiah 55:6).

"He that hath ears to hear, let him hear" (Matthew 11:15).

FEBRUARY 29
Kings or Shepherds

Recently in a conference in Michigan I heard the gifted singer Lonnie Moore pointing out that Saul the son of Kish was a humble and faithful servant willing to spend several days looking for some lost donkeys. One might have thought he was looking for thoroughbred horses or some lost black-angus cattle instead of lowly donkeys.

The point of this account is that he was diligent and faithful to his father's wishes. Jesus touched on this truth when He said, *"He that is faithful in that which is least is faithful also in much"* (Luke 16:10).

He put further emphasis on this when He said, *"Thou hast been faithful over a few things, I will make thee ruler over many things"* (Matthew 25:21). Once Saul became King, things began to change. He became proud, self-centered, jealous, and disobedient to the Lord's commands.

This happened to Nebuchadnezzar, the Pharaoh of Egypt, as well as Herod in the days of Jesus. It also happens to a lot of preachers and church workers. Position produces pride if we are not careful.

I heard another message by Dr. Norris Belcher of Westminster, Maryland, and he pointed out that James and John, two very important

51

disciples of Jesus wanted to sit on His right and left hand when He came into His kingdom. A few days later Jesus needed two men to go into Bethany and get a lowly colt or donkey for Him to ride into Jerusalem to fulfill the scriptures. I think he chose these same two to get the message to them.

We need to be busy finding donkeys and bringing them to Jesus. He needs servants not kings.

MARCH 1
An Awesome Experience

Do you plan to see God some day? Jesus said in the famous Sermon on the Mount, *"Blessed are the pure in heart: for they shall see God."*

This surely will be one of the most awesome experiences that any of us has ever had. John said, "No man hath seen God at any time, but the Son of God hath declared Him."

In the Old Testament several people did see God, but in angelic form; and it truly was an awesome experience. Each time someone had a heavenly visitor, he fell to his knees or on his face because of the overcoming awe of the experience.

What does it mean to be "pure in heart"? Possibly it means to be made pure by being washed in the blood of Jesus Christ. That, of course, refers to being saved. Also, it might mean to be pure in motive and intent which would lead to pure lives and clean bodies.

The dictionary says that pure means to be single-minded or unmixed with any other. That would mean allowing my interest and goals to be totally centered on my relationship to God as Jesus said, *"Seek ye first the kingdom of God and his righteousness; and all these things shall be added unto you"* (Matthew 6:33).

Since we exist in a different dimension, there is no way for us to picture what things will be like at the throne in His presence. Paul quoted Isaiah the prophet and said, *"But as it is written, Eye hath not seen, nor ear heard, neither have entered into the heart of man, the things which God hath prepared for them that love him"* (1 Cor. 2:9).

Seeing God is an experience that we really can be looking forward to.

MARCH 2
Get the Kid on a Bike

When our bus workers at the church went out visiting their bus routes on Saturday morning, we instructed them to make "quickie" visits. Spending more than two or three minutes at one door was an unpardonable sin. It had been proven over and over that the ones who visited the most homes had the most riders. Soul-winning visitation and bus visitation are two different things. Since we also put strong emphasis on soul-winning, the workers began to feel a conflict.

To overcome this, one Saturday morning I challenged the workers to do their quick visits and cover all the ground possible, but watch for a kid on a bicycle. Once you spot the kid, forget quick visiting and try to win that kid to Christ.

At our prayer meeting on that Saturday night, sixteen out of forty-two men reported that they had won someone on a bike. The next Saturday we looked for a bald-headed man and I'm sure the angels wondered why so many bald-headed men were getting their names in the book of life that day.

After that, each Saturday we looked for a guy with a blue shirt, a girl wearing red, or a man with a beard, a man with a baseball cap on his head, and so on.

For the next several weeks we made hundreds of "quickie" visits then stopped in our tracks when we spotted our target for the day.

The fresh new approach resulted in a great number of souls getting into the kingdom of God.

I don't know if the old adage, "Variety is the spice of life," is true or not but variety sure put new life into our soul-winning program.

MARCH 3
He Got In Under The Wire

Some time ago I went to the hospital to pray for a man who was to have a limb removed. His other leg had already been taken off because of a diabetic problem. His family had been called to the hospital because of the seriousness of the matter. He wanted to see a preacher before going to surgery. They called me, and I was happy to go.

I asked the man, "If some complications should develop in the operating room, would everything be all right with your soul?"

"I'm afraid not," he answered.

"Would you like me to pray for you to help get the matter settled?"

"Yes, I would," he answered. I gave him the beautiful account of how God Himself came to earth and took on a body and became a man, the Lord Jesus. I mentioned the miracles and parables of Jesus and shared with him the gospel of the death, burial, and resurrection of Jesus Christ.

He told me he believed what the Bible said about that. We prayed together, he opened his heart, and Jesus Christ came into his life right then and there. His family was very touched about his decision.

The nurses and orderlies soon arrived to take him to surgery. He said goodbye to the family. He thanked me for helping him get this settled. Soon they had rolled him down the hall and were gone. He went to the operating room but never came back. A few days later I preached his funeral service and a number of people expressed to me how grateful they were that I had helped him give his life to the Lord. The Bible says, *"For whosoever shall call upon the name of the Lord shall be saved"* (Romans 10:13).

MARCH 4
It Just Evolved

Sir Isaac Newton sat at this desk buried in a book. The door opened and a scientist friend who was an avid evolutionist walked in. Sitting on Sir Isaac's desk was a replica of the solar system with planets revolving around the sun and moons revolving around the planets.

The scientist was fascinated by the model. He turned the crank and watched the heavenly bodies orbit around one another in perfect precision and order.

"What an exquisite thing this is," he said. "Who made it?"

Without looking up from his book, Newton answered, "Nobody."

Turning to Newton, his friend said, "Evidently you did not understand my question. Who made this model of the universe?"

Looking up, Newton insisted, "Nobody made this. It just happened to come together by chance and went into motion all on its own."

"You must think I'm some kind of fool. Of course somebody made it," said the friend, "and whoever did is a genius."

Laying his book aside, Newton arose and answered, "This is just a puny imitation of the real thing, our solar system. I cannot convince you that this toy does not have a designer and maker, yet you profess to believe that the original from which this model is taken with its massive and complex orbital motion has come into being without a designer and a maker. Now, tell me, what sort of reasoning makes you come to such a conclusion?"

So it is with all the reasoning of evolutionists. Genesis 1:1 says *"In the beginning God created the heaven and the earth."*

"All things were made by him; and without him was not anything made that was made" (John 1:3).

"The fool hath said in his heart, There is no God" (Psalm 14:1, 53:1).

MARCH 5
Can You Imagine?

Back in the early 30's, life was different. We used kerosene lamps. We called them "coal oil" lamps. We had no electricity, no telephones or televisions. We carried water from a well and from the creek when Mom washed clothes. We had no inside toilets, and we took a weekly bath in a number two wash tub. Everybody used the same water.

There were no McDonalds, Wendys, Burger Kings, or Wal-Marts. We had no electric washers, dryers, refrigerators, toasters, sweepers, CD's, DVD's, computers, laptops, iPhones, and a lot of other things.

Grass was something we cut, not smoked. Coke was soda pop. Pot was something you cooked in. No one had aids except deaf people. We had horses and wagons, model T cars, LP records, and 78 rpms.

The milkman put bottles of milk on the porch, and the bread man and ice man delivered these item to our house. There were no credit cards, ballpoint pens, or pantyhose. We never saw guys with earrings, or girls with rings in their eyebrows or diamond pins in her nose.

In a similar way, we will see some changes in the next hundred years. Mail service will be replaced by internet and e-mail. Landline phones will be phased out by cell phones. Checking at the bank will be replaced by transfer programs. We will have a cashless society.

Newspapers and books will be an audio download. Facebook, Twitter, and Google will eliminate privacy. Go a step farther and think about being in Heaven in glorified bodies.

Paul spoke of this saying, *"Eye hath not seen, nor ear heard, neither have entered into the heart of man, the things which God hath prepared for them that love Him"* (I Cor. 2:9).

MARCH 6
The Alamo

March sixth marks the anniversary of the fall of the Alamo outside of San Antonio, Texas, back in 1836. For more than 13 days, 186 brave and determined patriots withstood Santa Anna's seasoned army of over 4,000 troops. To a man, the defenders of that mission fort knew they would never leave alive. They had several opportunities to leave and live. Yet, they chose to fight and die. How foolish they must look to this generation of Americans.

It is difficult to recall that stouthearted men such as Davy Crockett (a nationally-known frontiersman and former Congressman), Will Travis (only-26-years old with a little baby at home), and Jim Bowie (a wealthy landowner with properties on both sides of the Rio Grande) really existed.

These were real men with real dreams and real desires. Real blood flowed through their veins. They loved their families and enjoyed life as much as any of us do. However, there was something different about them. They possessed a commitment that transcended personal safety and comfort.

This reminds us of what Jesus did when He gave His life that we might be really free. Our Bible says, *"If the Son therefore shall make you free, ye shall be free indeed"* (John 8:36).

Early in the siege, Travis wrote these words to the people of Texas:

> *"Fellow citizens and compatriots: I am besieged by a thousand or more of the Mexicans under Santa Anna...The enemy has demanded a surrender at discretion...I have answered the demand with a cannon shot and our flag still waves proudly from the walls. I shall never surrender or retreat...Victory Or Death!*
>
> *P.S. The Lord is on our side..."*

The apostle said, *"...I die daily"* (I Cor. 15:31). He also said, *"Stand therefore, having your loins girt about with truth."*

MARCH 7
Inward Beauty

When Dr. John Rice grew old, his skin wrinkled, he had bags under his eyes, bushy eyebrows, and a long double chin. He was quite homely; however, one would have to search far and near to find a man with a sweeter spirit, purer heart, and cleaner lifestyle.

On one occasion when he came to our home for dinner, I asked him to sit in our family room with my four small children while I helped Mrs. Wallace put the final touches to our meal.

I returned shortly to find two of the children sitting on his lap and the other two sitting right up against him with his arms around all of them. They were captivated by him. That was the real Dr. Rice.

One little girl said to him, "Bro. Rice, you are so handsome, except in the face." The apostle Paul spoke a great truth when he said, *"…though our outward man perish, yet the inward man is renewed day by day"* (2 Cor. 4:16).

The development and growth of the inward man prepares the believer for the time when the flesh fails. Solomon in his wisdom and Shakespearean terminology gives us a whole chapter in Ecclesiastes twelve on preparing for dark days ahead when clouds move in and the body begins its trip to the grave.

Peter pressed this issue when he stated, *"Whose adorning let it not be that outward adorning of plaiting the hair, and of wearing of gold, or of putting on of apparel; But let it be the hidden man of the heart, in that which is not corruptible, even the ornament of a meek and quiet spirit, which is in the sight of God of great price"* (1 Peter 3:3-4).

MARCH 8
Shields Of Brass

When Solomon built the temple, he had his craftsmen make three hundred shields of gold and used three pounds of gold in each shield. Everything in and about the temple was overlaid with pure gold. Impressive to say the least. When the queen of Sheba came to visit, she said, "Wow, the half has not been told."

After Solomon died, Rehoboam, his son, drifted away from the Lord and lost His blessing. He woke up one morning to find twelve hundred chariots, sixty thousand horsemen, and an innumerable mass of soldiers at his gate. They took away the shields of gold.

Rehoboam, to save face, had craftsmen to mold three hundred shields of brass and set in the place of the gold ones. They were fakes. He hoped the people would not notice the difference. The people building the tower of Babel used brick in place of stone and slime for mortar (Genesis 11:3).

In each of these accounts we have a substitute for the real thing. People are still doing the same in our day and time. Some substitute baptism or church membership for salvation. Many feel that giving a little something as one is able is just as good as tithing. Some say memorized or formal prayers in place of effectual and fervent praying. Others read a little devotion instead of studying to shew themselves approved of God, or mediating therein day and night. A lot of folk give a couple dollars to missions when a missionary speaker comes to present his work instead of making a faith promise commitment and giving every week. On and on it goes.

The shields looked the same on the surface and fooled the people;, but God was not fooled. and He is not fooled now either.

MARCH 9
A Shot in the Arm

Everybody's heart went out to the little elderly lady who hobbled through the waiting room of one of our local doctors. She was bent over like a horseshoe. A short cane kept her from toppling over. Her face bore the burden of her bent body. In just a few minutes she came out with a big smile beaming on her face. Her joy was evident. She walked tall with shoulders erect.

"Amazing," said one.

"A miracle," said another.

The next person called in asked, "Doctor, we all saw that poor old woman go in there all bent over and then we all saw her come out straightened up, walking briskly with that big smile. What did you do to her?"

"I really didn't do much for her," the doctor stated. "I just gave her a longer cane."

Jesus did that to just about everybody He met. He gave a blind man sight. To a dead girl it was life. A lunatic boy got a sound mind. At a wedding he turned water to wine. A bunch of weary discouraged fishermen, were amazed and delighted when he filled their nets with fish. On and on it goes. He is still doing that today.

He works now through His children and His servants. He gives salvation through our witnessing. He gives encouragement and hope to others. Our world is filled with people bent and burdened by the effects of sin.

The little short cane of religion and good works of a social gospel is not getting it done. Paul said it well, *"Christ in you, the hope of glory"* (Colossians 1:27). In another place Paul said, *"But thanks be to God, which giveth us the victory through our Lord Jesus Christ"* (1 Cor. 15:57).

MARCH 10
Facts And Principles

The Bible is an amazing book. To the unregenerate mind it is complicated and closed. To the believer it is an open book. To the Spirit-filled believer it is even easier to understand.

Jesus told Nicodemus that unless he was born again, he could not see (understand) the kingdom of God. Paul wrote, *"But the natural man receiveth not the things of the Spirit of God: for they are foolishness unto him: neither can he know them, because they are spiritually discerned"* (1 Cor. 2:14).

In spite of the fact that every color has a meaning, every number is suggestive, and the simple stories or parables have application and truth that is confusing to many, these same things are kindergarten level to others.

Paul also wrote, *"But I fear, lest by any means, as the serpent beguiled Eve through his subtilty, so your minds should be corrupted from the simplicity that is in Christ"* (2 Cor. 11:3).

In its simplest form the Bible is a book of facts and principles. The classics such as Noah's ark, Daniel and the lion's den, the Hebrew children in the furnace, have many facts but usually just one principle. While reading one of these accounts a few of the facts will stick in the mind, and the principle will be lightly impressed subconsciously upon the mind.

Hearing a sermon, listening to a Sunday School lesson, or reading it again will give me more of the facts and impress the principle a little deeper into the mind. The more exposure, the more scriptural I will become. The more scriptural I get, the more spiritual I will be. The more spiritual I am, the more fulfilled I will become. *"For to be spiritually minded is life and peace"* (Romans 8:6).

MARCH 11
Tuned In

"He that hath an ear, let him hear what the Spirit saith unto the churches"
—Revelation 2:7a.

This phrase is given seven times in chapters two and three of Revelation. There is an indication that some have ears while others do not. Paul spoke of the natural man who *"...receiveth not the things of the Spirit of God...because they are spiritually discerned"* (I Cor. 2:14).

There are hundreds of different signals around us at all times such as radio frequencies, telephone signals, and many others. We are not aware of these unless we have a receiver tuned to their frequency.

When a person receives Christ as his Saviour, he has the Holy Spirit dwelling in him and thus is able to tune in to God's frequency. The Bible says *"God heareth not sinners"* (John 9:31).

It is also important to fine tune the frequency. After a time of exposure to daily schedules, problems, people, and circumstances, e become occupied and our signal get bombarded with other signals of worldliness, carnality, and self-interests. It is vital that we take time for God and fine tune our signal each morning with our Bible and prayer to prevent the other powerful signals from crowding out and confusing our signal. We need to turn up the volume and give our whole-hearted attention to what God is saying to us.

Solomon said, *"...of making many books there is no end"* (Eccl.12:12). He was referring to the writings of Plato, Aristotle, Socrates, Darwin, Lenin, Marks, and many other secularists whose philosophy is bombarded continually in the education and media worlds around us.

Paul advised believers to *"Mediate upon these things; give thyself wholly to them"* (I Timothy 4:15). He was referring to the spiritual signal from the throne of God.

MARCH 12
Faith for Now

When Jesus came to comfort Martha and Mary because of the death of their brother Lazarus, Martha came to Him and blurted out in her grief, "If you had been here, my brother would not have died." She seems to be blaming Jesus for the situation. To comfort her, Jesus said, "Your brother will rise again." Martha responded, "I know He will rise in the resurrection." Then Jesus gave her one of the greatest promises in the Bible. *"I am the resurrection, and the life: he that believeth in me, though he were dead, yet shall he live"* (John 11:25).

Martha had faith for the past. She believed that Jesus could have kept Lazarus from dying. She also had plenty of faith for the future. She said, *"I know that he shall rise again in the resurrection at the last day"* (John 11:24). Her problem was that she had no faith for the present.

Looking back I can remember some of the insurmountable problems of my life and ministry and the way the Lord worked them out. It looks so simple and easy now that they are behind me. At the times when I had come to my "wits end", there was no light at the end of the tunnel.

I am the same about the future. I can see myself being resurrected, standing at the judgment seat of Christ, sitting at the marriage supper table, participating in the thousand-year millennium, and enjoying my glorified body.

On the other hand I'm struggling with what I'm going to do about some of the problems I am facing right now, today. I guess it's time to sing the old chorus "Everything's All Right in my Father's House."

MARCH 13
Friday the Thirteenth

Today is Friday and it is also the thirteenth day of the month. We are facing all kinds of scary possibilities. What if I walk under a ladder today, or a black cat crosses my path, or what do I do if I find I am the 13th person to walk into a room? Is my day going to be ruined if I am booked in room thirteen in a motel, or seated in the thirteenth row of an airplane?

These are real fears many entertain when the 13th day of the month falls on Friday. Some won't drive cars or eat in restaurants on this day;

others won't even leave the "safety" of their happy home.

This superstition traces its roots all the way back to the Garden of Eden. It was on a Friday, supposedly, that Eve ate the fruit that plunged humanity into the curse. Further, every judgment (Noah's flood, Babel, even the crucifixion) are said to have occurred on a Friday.

Should I give any weight to these ideas? Maybe it is better to stay safe than be sorry. John, the Revelator, in his first epistle wrote, *"There is no fear in love; but perfect love casteth out fear: because fear hath torment. He that feareth is not made perfect in love"* (1 John 4.18).

Three hundred and sixty-five times the Bible says, "Fear Not." I like the way Spurgeon explains this verse, "Fear dwells upon the punishment deserved, and so has no rest. When perfect love assures the soul of pardoned sin, the heart has joyful rest."

So, we must decide not to focus on the fear, but on the One who saved us from the penalty and curse of sin. What a salvation! What a Saviour!

MARCH 14
Around Forever

Mrs. Wallace was sitting in the reception area of a well-known mission agency waiting on me to wrap up a committee meeting when she heard one of three ladies talking with the receptionist ask, "Who is that lady?"

The receptionist replied, "Oh, that's Mrs. Tom Wallace; her name is Mary."

"Oh," remarked one of the women, "he's been around forever."

I had been a part of that mission organization for almost 50 years, but that's a long way from forever. In fact, I've been around for a total of 86 years when my birthday rolls around in August. That too is a long time but also a long way from forever.

Thinking back to what the woman said gave me great joy to realize that starting at my new birth experience in 1950, I received eternal life, and that will keep going as long as God lives. I'm going to be around forever. I have the promise of Jesus that I will never die.

He said *"Whosoever liveth and believeth in me shall never die"* (John 11:26) and, *"if a man keep my sayings he shall never see death"* (John 8:52). He also stated, *"I give unto them eternal life and they shall never perish"* (John 10:28).

The Lord gives us eternal life or everlasting life as a free gift, (Romans 6:23) and we will then be around forever. Nobody but God knows how many grains of sand are on the seashores of this world, nor the number of stars in the universe, and if we could total these up and allow each to represent a thousand years, it would only be just the beginning of eternity. In Heaven eternity will always be "now."

Just think: perfect love, peace, and joy forever.

MARCH 15
A Look at God

Like many others, I get an abundance of articles by e-mail every day. Many of them are junk, but occasionally one comes through that really says it all. Such a one is this. It was sent to me by Pastor Ivan Casteel of Oklahoma City, OK.

Suppose a killer should kidnap your only son, treat him shamefully, then kill him. What would your reaction be?

Someone has pointed out that we would have four options.

First, you could hunt him down and kill him using, "An eye for an eye, and a tooth for a tooth" philosophy. Many would agree with this approach and encourage you to give it your best shot (no pun intended).

Second, one might ignore the matter and just pretend that it never happened. You would need to clean out pictures, possessions, and anything else that constantly brings back memories and feelings.

Third, you could call 911, make a police report, aid in the investigation, until he is found and arrested, tried in a court of law, sentenced to prison or to the death chamber. This would give closure and a sense of having done the right.

Fourth, you could locate him, forgive him, adopt him into your family as your own son, make out your will and give your son's inheritance to him.

It is natural to think that no one could possibly do such a thing as that, but that is exactly what God did for us. *"And if children, then heirs; heirs of God, and joint-heirs with Christ; if so be that we suffer with him, that we may be also glorified together"* (Romans 8:17).

"But God commendeth his love toward us, in that, while we were yet sinners, Christ died for us" (Romans 5:8).

MARCH 16
Who Knows When

What do James Martin, Sonny Buchman, Premkumar Walakar, Sarah Ramos, Lori Rivera, Paschal Meyers, Kenneth Bridges, Linda Franklin, and Conrad Johnson have in common? We've all heard these names, but I doubt if very many can tell who they are or what they have in common.

These are nine of the thirteen people that were gunned down by a sniper around the Washington beltway area and died from a bullet fired by John Allen Muhammad and John Lee Malvo. The shooting spree in October of 2002 took the lives of ten people and left three seriously wounded. Their lives were taken unexpectedly with no warning. There was no time to prepare for a meeting with God.

No one knows the day or the hour of their death. We do know that it is appointed unto man once to die and then the judgment. The prophet Amos gives good advice when he says, *"Prepare to meet thy God"* (Amos 4:12).

At the time of this writing, my good friend Jim Breene, a former deacon of my church and a member of the board of directors of Wallace Ministries, Inc. is lying in his casket and waiting to be buried.

He went for hip replacement surgery, and developed blood clots. The clots went to his lungs and killed him. He and his wife Bettye had expected to be killed together in an accident on the highway or raptured at the coming of the Lord. His death caught us all by surprise.

How wise it is to get this matter settled while there is still breath in the body and opportunity to do something about it. How foolish to put this off and gamble with the most valuable possession one has, his eternal soul.

MARCH 17
St. Patrick the Baptist

Each year on this day people around the world remember the anointed missionary to Ireland by eating corned beef and cabbage, wearing shamrocks, Irish crosses and carrying walking sticks.

A legend exists that he was attacked by snakes during a time of fasting on top of a hill, and he banished snakes into the sea; thus no snakes in Ireland to this day.

There is also attention given to the fact that he was much more Baptist than Catholic. During the last half of the fifth century and at the age of sixteen, Patrick was kidnapped from his home in Britain by pirates and carried away as a slave to Ireland.

He was converted while alone caring for sheep. After six years he claims to have heard a voice telling him to escape and catch a ship home. Later he felt the call of God to return to Ireland as a missionary.

History records credit him for baptizing 120,000 converts, starting 365 churches and ordaining pastors for each. He only baptized believers by immersion with no mention of baptizing infants. He was independent of creed, catechisms, counsels, and popes.

In doctrine he was a Baptist. In the Lord's supper he rejected transubstantiation, the Catholic teaching that the actual blood of Christ is present. He accepted the Bible as the sole authority rather than the church or the pope. There is no mention of purgatory, Mariolatry, or submission to a pope. He recognized the work of the Holy Spirit in conversion and in intercession to God for the believer. There is no mention of priestly intercession or confession to a priest. He stood exactly where Martin Luther stood on justification by faith.

He died on March 17th.

MARCH 18
Coping with Critics

"Head and shoulders above the rest."
"The best man for the job."

That's what they were saying about Saul the son of Kish. He was to be their first king in Israel. Samuel agreed. *"See ye him whom the LORD hath chosen, that there is none like him among all the people"* (1 Samuel 10:24).

He was God's choice too. *"Thou shalt anoint him to be captain over my people Israel"* (1 Samuel 9:16). But, not everyone agreed. The opposition party filibustered and campaigned against him. They said, *"How shall this man save us, and they despised him"* (I Samuel 10:27).

There will always be critics, but look at how Saul reacted. *"He held his peace"* (I Samuel 10:27). Criticism is always directed at leadership.

Leaders should discipline themselves to listen only to constructive criticism. They must not waste valuable time responding to opposition. Leaders do not have time to come down from the wall to meet with the Sanballats, the Tobiases, and the Geshems in the plain of Ono. We cannot take time to listen to the Gashmus. We must focus on the job at hand. Because Saul did right, the Bible says, *"the Spirit of God came upon Saul when he heard those tidings"* (1 Samuel 11:6).

We can also learn from Saul that jealousy can consume and destroy all that we have accomplished. Dr. Lee Roberson gave me good advice in my early ministry.

"Tom, keep your eyes off of people and on the Lord." David paid very little attention to Goliath's size; he was thinking of how the Lord had killed the bear and the lion for him. Like Peter, never look at the waves, but keep looking to Jesus the author and finisher of our faith.

MARCH 19
Kill the Spider

Dr. Vance Havner used to say, "We spend much time sweeping spider webs when we ought to do something about the spider."

His statement brought to mind the thousands of times I have counseled with people who told me through tears and red faces about their awful sins of lying, stealing, cheating, adultery, murder, and other things that are hard to imagine.

Almost every time I would respond with, "When are we going to talk about your real problem?" Each time they would tell me that they had embarrassed themselves terribly by sharing their foul deeds. I always answered, "You have not even touched on your problem, you have been telling me about the results of your problem;"

The believer's problems come in two areas. The first are the sins of omission, and the second, the sins of commission. To omit, is to leave undone what I ought to do, while the sins of commission is to do what I ought not to do.

If one omits his Bible study, prayer, faithful church attendance, giving, and witnessing, he will become weak spiritually and will be vulnerable to temptation, lusting, covetousness, and other fleshly sins.

We need to daily spend time with God. About 90 to 95 % of our sins are omission, but we blame our failure 90 to 95% of the time on the sins of commission. It is the little foxes that spoil the vines. (Song of Sol. 2:15).

Whether it is a sin of omission or a sin of commission, we have a great promise from the Word of God, *"If we confess our sins, he is faithful and just to forgive us our sins, and to cleanse us from all unrighteousness"* (I John 1:9).

MARCH 20
Pruning the Vines

"Every branch in me that beareth not fruit he taketh away: and every branch that beareth fruit, he purgeth it, that it may bring forth more fruit"
(John 15:2).

One of our missionaries recently wrote from Africa and gave the following account of fruit-bearing.

"Our home has been blessed with orange, coconut, mango, and lemon trees that have been growing ever so steadily over the last few years. Although we were thankful for their provision of shade during the dry season I was frustrated with all of these trees because they failed to produce any fruit. I spoke with one of our church men (who is a farmer) about coming over and properly pruning my trees so they would start producing some fruit. I was shocked as I came home and saw our beautiful trees hacked down to an almost unrecognizable state. I told him "thank you" for his work but thought, "this faithful man just ruined all our trees!"

However a little while ago I was pleasantly surprised to collect over 150 oranges from one tree with 50 more still waiting to become ripe. Our lemon trees have begun flourishing and providing us with many lemons and I have been thrilled with the coconut milk and fresh coconut from our 2 coconut trees as well.

This influx of fruit came only after some maturity and the obvious pruning. None of us like the purging and the cutting away of the excess; It would serve us well to realize that the things God allows to come into our lives is pruning.

"Let us lay aside every weight, and the sin which doth so easily beset us, and let us run with patience the race that is set before us" (Hebrews 12:1).

MARCH 21
A Delightful Surprise

It really pays to give out tracts. Of course there is no way to know the long-range results of handing out gospel literature on the street, but sometimes the Lord allows us to see some immediate and delightful results.

Mrs. Wallace and I were passing out an attractive little booklet called "The Bridge of Salvation." Four cruise ships had docked at the harbor in Grand Cayman. Thousands of people were milling around the shops and attractions.

After giving away several hundred of these on four or five other occasions we decided to go on the submarine cruise. We were shocked at the price of $75.00 per person and decided to settle for the glass bottom boat ride at $34.00 each.

I explained to Sarah, the girl selling tickets, that we could not afford the submarine cruise and that we would settle for the less expensive glass bottom boat tour. I smiled and handed her one of our tracts. When we lined up to board the boat, Sarah came out and asked if we would come in and see her after our boat ride.

The trip was delightful; then we checked with her as we left, and she handed us two free tickets to the submarine ride. It was leaving in twenty minutes. She explained that they allowed her four free tickets each month and she wanted us to have two of hers.

We felt that the Lord was telling us that He was pleased with us for giving out tracts. Because this was a mission trip and I was filling in for a missionary who had to go home for a month, an airline stewardess had given us two of her vouchers that took care of the plane fare for us. The missionary had filled his car with gas and told us to help ourselves to anything we found to eat in their refrigerator and freezer.

Paul said, *"My God shall supply all your need according to his riches in glory in Christ Jesus"* (Phil. 4:19).

MARCH 22
Cleaning Up the Church

Someone said, "There is nothing better than a good king, and there is nothing worse than a bad one."

It was written of Uzziah one of the good kings of Judah, that he did that which was right in the sight of the Lord. His influence for good on Judah lasted for fifty-two years, then was carried over into the reign of his son Jotham for sixteen more years, then the next sixteen years of the reign of his grandson Ahaz, and on into twenty-nine years of his great grandson, Hezekiah.

In his first year Hezekiah opened the doors of the house of the Lord, repaired them, and called for the priests to sanctify themselves, clean out the filthiness of the holy place, and set things in their proper order (2 Chron. 29:5). The wrath of God had fallen on Jerusalem and Judea. (v. 8) Their fathers had been slain in battle, and their sons, daughters, and wives had been taken into captivity (v. 9).

Hezekiah's message needs to be heard again today. The filthiness of homosexual clergy, molestation of children by priests, acceptance of Christian rock music, the falling of preachers and Christian workers through pornography and the emphasis upon the social gospel, ministry needs to be carried forth out of the local church.

Could the tragedy of 911, Hurricane Katrina, deadly tornados, killer waves and other such natural disasters be the voice of God's judgment? It is time to set things in the house of the Lord (v. 35).

"But if I tarry long, that thou mayest know how thou oughtest to behave thyself in the house of God, which is the church of the living God, the pillar and ground of the truth" (1 Timothy 3:15).

MARCH 23
God Is Looking

We are bothered that airport screeners make such a fuss over a set of small fingernail clippers, or refuse to allow a white-haired grandmother to take her knitting needles with her on the plane. It's a bother, but we all know that it's for our good.

Long before airports and government buildings installed security checkpoints, God had screening devices in place. The psalmist wrote, *"O Lord, thou hast searched me and known me"* (Psalm 139:1).

David wrote in another place, *"His going forth is from the end of the heaven, and his circuit unto the ends of it: and there is nothing hid from the heat* (x-ray) *thereof"* (Psalm 19:6).

Solomon wrote, *"The eyes of the LORD are in every place, beholding the evil and the good"* (Proverbs 15:3). Even Job commented on this, *"For his eyes are upon the ways of man, and he seeth all his goings"* (Job 34:21).

David was aware that the Lord knew everything that was in his heart and his mind. His motives, his desires, his ambitions, his goals, and all his thoughts were laid out for display as goods on a vendor's table at a convention.

The pride, malice, anger, jealousy, envy, are like an open book to the Lord. Old time writers spoke of "seven deadly sins." As Dr. Roberson once called them, "Ancient sins that dog the steps of modern men." These are all known and seen by the Lord.

We, like David, would do well to realize that God is looking and listening, and pray as he prayed, *"Search me, O God, and know my heart: try me, and know my thoughts: And see if there be any wicked way in me, and lead me in the way everlasting"* (Psalm 139:23-24).

MARCH 24
Him and Them

Recently I heard a sermon in a conference by Dr. Scott Caudill, director of Macedonia Baptist Missions from the account of the miracle of the healing of two blind men in Matt. 20:29-34.

These two men were blind beggars. Their condition was desperate. They were in great need. In a like manner all of us have been blinded by the god of this world and also have a great need to have our spiritual eyes opened (2 Cor. 4:4).

The Lord Jesus told Nicodemus that he would not be able to see the kingdom of God unless he was born again. Once Jesus comes into our hearts, we will begin to notice the blind ones around us, and we also will have compassion on them.

There are spiritually blind people all around us but we will not see their need or care about them until we look through the eyes of Jesus.

Jesus had compassion on these men and gave them their sight. The crowd, including some religious people, rebuked them for crying out to the Saviour. They were unmoved and untouched by the pitiful cry of these needy men. Because they had no real understanding and relationship to Jesus, they had no concern and compassion for these blind men.

When we see Him, then we will see them. It is only when we are close to the Lord that we will share His concern for people on the mission fields of the world. When we love Him, then we will love them.

Jesus said, *"As the Father hath loved me, so have I loved you: continue ye in my love"* (John 15:9).

He is saying, "To the same level the Father loved me, and I loved you, I want you to love one another, and also to love sinners."

MARCH 25
It's Friday but Sunday's Coming

A pastor in New Jersey gave this title to his sermon at a Good Friday service. He said "It Is Friday but Sunday's Coming." His topic, of course, was when Jesus is dead, our hopes are gone; everything is bad; woe is me!

Of course, he hit a chord in almost everybody's life. As one person said, we ought to be good to everybody because everybody is having a tough time of it with divorces, wayward children, financial pressures, problems in the home, and problems on the job. Everybody is hoping for Sunday!

The preacher declared that all this was going to change. The resurrection is coming! Jesus is going to come forth, and He will be very much alive. Everything will be OK.

That is true in a lot of areas of our life, if we will just believe. Believing is the key to getting saved. Jesus said, *"Whosoever believeth in him shall not perish, but have everlasting life"* (John 3:16). Believing is the secret to getting our prayers answered. Jesus said again, *"Whatsoever ye shall ask in prayer, believing, ye shall receive."* (Matthew 21:22)

Most of us have been through a lot of experiences where there didn't seem to be any light at the end of the tunnel, but so far we have been able to come through every one of them. This, of course, is also true of the troubles we are going through right now.

We need to realize that Sunday is coming and everything is going to be great! It is time to rejoice in the future in the Lord. We are going to have glorified bodies, live on the earth during the millennial reign and enjoy the celestial city. What more could we ask? It may be Friday, but Sunday is coming!

MARCH 26
My Sheepskin Prayer Rug

When Sheffey the circuit riding preacher in the Bob Jones University film took his sheepskin from the back of his saddle and spread it on the ground under a big tree, we all expected to see an answer to his prayer.

You can imagine the delight and emotion in the service when a pastor friend of mine presented the three keynote speakers at his annual Independent Baptist conference with a beautiful sheepskin to use as a prayer rug. He had them laid out on a table at the front of the large new eight hundred seat auditorium that was filled to capacity and asked all the pastors, missionaries, and leaders from all over the region to sign the back of them.

I brought mine home and laid it on the floor in the corner of our sunroom where I pray. My thoughts always go immediately to the fact that the lamb had to give its life and shed its blood to provide me with this prayer rug.

Immediately my mind goes to John 1:29 where they said of Jesus, *"Behold the Lamb of God, which taketh away the sin of the world"*

I think too of the words, *"And almost all things are by the law purged with blood; and without shedding of blood is no remission"* (Hebrews 9:22).

After praising Him for His attributes, wonderful works, benefits, and blessings, I give Him my petitions. *"Forasmuch as ye know that ye were not redeemed with corruptible things, as silver and gold, from your vain conversation received by tradition from your fathers; But with the precious blood of Christ, as of a lamb without blemish and without spot"* (1 Peter 1:18-19).

MARCH 27
He Is Risen

"Fear not ye: for I know that ye seek Jesus, which was crucified. He is not here: for he is risen, as he said. Come, see the place where the Lord lay. And go quickly, and tell his disciples that he is risen from the dead; and, behold, he goeth before you into Galilee; there shall ye see him: lo, I have told you" (Matthew 28:5b-7).

Jesus is no longer on the cross, so take Him off. He is no longer in the tomb, so let Him out. However, He is here in the person of the Holy Spirit, so let Him in. Let Him into your life to take control and guide you into the riches of Christ.

There was a time when Easter was all about wearing a new hat or a new dress, or a new suit and fortunately that emphasis seems to have passed. Today I'm not sure what the emphasis is. More and more people are simply passing it up and going on what is called "spring break."

Since our government schools can no longer offer up anything of a religious nature to release the students for a few days, they have now introduced "the spring break," which has caused a mass migration to the beaches of Florida.

As we turn our thought to Christ and His resurrection, I'm reminded of the scoffer who tried to dampen a little girl's belief in Christ.

He said to her, "My poor little girl, you don't know what you believe. There have been many Christs; Which of them do you believe in?"

The little girl thought for a moment and said, "I believe in the Christ who died on the cross and rose from the dead." The scoffer was speechless.

MARCH 28
Seeking Jesus

"Behold, thy father and I have sought thee sorrowing. And he said unto them, How is it that ye sought me? wist ye not that I must be about my father's business?" (Luke 2:48-49).

They were very busy in religious matters. For days now they had been involved in the Passover activities. In the midst of the busy church activities, they had lost Jesus. Now really, Jesus wasn't lost. It was they who were lost. To be without Christ, one is lost indeed. They had been around Him since His birth. They just took for granted that He was with them.

In many a home, children have been surrounded by Him. Christian parents have taught their boys and girls the stories of the miracles and parables of Jesus. They've had them learn and repeat prayers such as, "Lord bless Mommy, Daddy, Grandpa, and Grandma, and our preacher." Long before these little ones learned about Peter Rabbit and Mr. McGregor's garden, Little Red Riding Hood, Little Bo Peep, Snow White and the seven dwarfs, Jack and the bean stalk, and Tom Thumb, they had learned to sing "Jesus love me, this I know, for the Bible tells me so."

But now they, supposing Him to be in their company, have lost Him at college through some agnostic professor, or on the job through the influence of a mocking co-worker, or someone in the gang who laughed at his or her faith and said, "Come on; Let's loosen up and have some fun."

They need to seek Him, sorrowing, until they find Him and begin to realize just who He is. They found Him in the temple. Church is a place where He is likely to be found. He Himself said, *"Seek and ye shall find"* (Matthew 7:7).

MARCH 29
Something Missing

I remember a professor in Bible college telling us that one of the ways to study our Bible was by comparing Scripture with Scripture.

Recently reading 1 Thess. 1:3, *"Remembering without ceasing your work of faith, and labour of love, and patience of hope in our Lord Jesus Christ, in the sight of God and our Father."* I thought of Revelation 2:2 which says, *"I know thy works, and thy labour, and thy patience."* Then in verse 4, it says, *"Nevertheless I have somewhat against thee, because thou hast left thy first love."*

In comparing these two passages we note that the same three words, work, labour, and patience are used, however the words faith, love and hope are missing in the second list and the Lord tells them that they have left their original position.

They have lost something. They were still working but not in faith. They were still laboring, but not in love. They were still being patient, but the hope was missing. It seems they were going through the motions, and covering their base, but their heart was not in it.

As in 2 Kings 6:5, their axe head has fallen off their axe, yet they are still chopping away at the tree trunk with an empty axe handle. Many are still preaching sermons, teaching lessons, singing songs, playing an instrument, running a bus route, serving as a deacon, etc. but the ring is not in the bell, and the spring is no longer in their step.

Solomon gave some good advice on this in Ecclesiastes 9:10, *"Whatsoever thy hand findeth to do, do it with thy might."* And Paul added, *"Whether therefore ye eat, or drink, or whatsoever ye do, do all to the glory of God"* (1 Cor. 10:31).

MARCH 30
Unprepared

How sad it was to hear the news of the Oakland Raiders linebacker Marquis Cooper and his three fellow football players being involved in a boating accident thirty-five miles off the Florida coast. The accident took the lives of Marquis and two of his friends. It was even more sad to learn that a friend had encouraged Cooper to install a GPS unit on his boat that would automatically send a distress signal if the boat should be overturned. The signal could easily be picked up by the Coast Guard and lead them to the accident scene.

Cooper acknowledged the need of such a device but told his friend he was planning to do it later. He did not realize there would not be a next time. They were unprepared for the tragic event.

Multitudes of people make this same mistake when it comes to preparing to meet God. A lot of folks plan to do something about the salvation of their soul, but as Felix told Paul, *"When I have a convenient season, I will call thee."*

They put off till tomorrow what they need to do today. Dr. Bill Rice used to say, "The road to Hell is paved with good intentions."

Think of standing before God and saying, "I was planning to do it, Lord; I just didn't get around to it." At the age of twelve, I learned the boy scout motto, "Be prepared."

Our Bible says, *"To him that knoweth to do good and doeth it not to him it is sin."* Many times, as in this case, it is also tragic.

Paul the apostle, quoting the wise words of Isaiah the prophet, said, *"Behold, now is the accepted time, behold, now is the day of salvation"* (2 Cor. 6:2).

MARCH 31
The Tale of Two Churches

Years ago in high school I was given an assignment to read a book called *The Tale of Two Cities.* I do not remember a lot about that book, but as I was reading the Bible in preparation for a sermon I was reminded of it as I compared the account of two churches. The first of these was the church in Jerusalem, the second the church of Corinth.

The church in Jerusalem was what I called the king Midas church. Everything they touched turned to gold. They held a ten-day prayer meeting and one hundred and ten people came and stayed the whole time. They had a service and three thousand were saved; then a few days later five thousand more were saved. When they held their baptismal service, every one of them submitted to baptism and were added to the church. When they encountered a need, people sold their possessions and gave it in the offering. In their visitation program, instead of going out once a week they went every day from house to house. Luke wrote that they gathered in one accord and were filled with the Holy Spirit. Wow, what a great church!

As I progressed to the book of First Corinthians, I found a second church. This one was filled with trouble. The first chapter tells of "contentions" among the believers. Next they were heeding the wisdom of men rather than the wisdom of God. Then there was carnality in chapter three. In chapter four there were stewardship problems, then immorality in chapter five. Every chapter tells of problems.

I have found this to be true also of many homes as well as individual lives. We must decide whether we want a Jerusalem life or a Corinthian life.

APRIL 1
Two Legs and a Piece of an Ear

There is a unique story in our Bible about a shepherd who discovered that one of his sheep was missing. He searched everywhere and finally, behind a big pile of brush, he found all that was left of the lamb: two legs and a piece of an ear. A lion had devoured his lamb and left behind the helpless legs and the useless piece of an ear (Amos 3:12).

There were no ears left to hear God, no eyes to see His handiwork, no mouth to sing or praise, no legs to walk with God, and no mind to mediate on the goodness of God.

This story is not about an ordinary sheep but one of God's children that He calls, "My sheep" in John 10:27. This is no ordinary lion either. This is the devil spoken of as a roaring lion seeking whom he may devour in 1 Peter 5:8. This is no ordinary shepherd but the shepherd spoken of in Psalm 23:1, "The Lord is my shepherd."

The devil is certainly after God's children. He wants to rip and tear them limb from limb and leave them helpless and hopeless. Like the lamb in our story, many believers have no mind left to meditate in the Word of God, or eyes to see the workings of the hand of God, or ears to hear the voice of God, or mouth to speak for God, or heart to feel the moving of God, and feet to walk in the pathways of God.

Many have fallen prey to the devil and been left helpless and worthless to the cause of Christ. We must learn to submit ourselves to God, resist the devil; and he will flee from us (James 4:7).

APRIL 2
Living On after Death

Someone published a book sometime ago entitled *Seven Men Who Rule the World from the Grave*. The book mentioned Charles Darwin, father of the theory of evolution; Karl Marx, the father of communism; Julius Wellhausen, father of higher criticism also referred to as "Christian communism;" John Dewey, father of progressive education, (the teaching of ideas and methods instead of truth); Sigmund Freud, father of the philosophy that propagates that sex drive determines human life and should not be suppressed, resulting in x-rated movies, pornographic literature, rape, incest, lust, etc.

Then there was John Maynard Keynes, father of modern economics or government give away programs. This fostered Roosevelt's "New Deal,' Johnson's "Great Society," and our modern welfare programs. Then, Soren Kirkenguard, father of Neo- Orthodox Religion, resulting in the Charismatic movement based on feelings, experience, and extra-Biblical revelation instead of the true teaching of the Bible.

We might add Elvis Presley, father of rock and roll music which led to the Beatles, the Vampires, Grateful Dead, The Monkeys, The Demons, etc, etc.

These streams of philosophy have dictated the belief and lifestyle of millions for the worse. Influence is a big factor. Whether a person will go to Heaven or Hell is determined by what he or she believes.

Thank God for Paul, Peter, James, John, Spurgeon, Wesley, Moody, Sunday, Jones, Rice, Roloff, Green, Hyles and all the others who have left their impact upon our generation. They still live in the hearts of millions.

As the Bible puts it, 'he being dead yet speaketh.' Solomon in his wisdom said, *"For as he thinketh in his heart, so is he"* (Proverbs 23:7).

Our actions and destiny will be determined by our exposure to these different philosophies.

APRIL 3
The Awesome Throne of God

When Isaiah saw the vision of the throne of God, he fell down and cried, "Woe is me." It is a good thing that we will be in our glorified bodies when we see God on His throne.

When Paul talked of an out-of-the-body experience, (II Cor. 12:2), he could not find words or terms to explain what he had seen and experienced. He later quoted Isaiah and said, *"Eye hath not seen, nor ear heard, neither have entered into the heart of man, the things which God hath prepared for them that love him"* (1 Cor. 2:9).

John later wrote of seeing God's throne and described Him as like a jasper or a sardine stone, glistening and glowing in brilliance.

Ezekiel described Him as a sapphire (Ezekiel 10:1), and Daniel saw it as a fiery flame (Daniel 7:9). A beautiful emerald rainbow circled the throne. Lightning flashed and thunder roared. The river of life flowed from the throne (Rev. 22:1) and into the crystal sea.

Twenty-four other thrones surrounded God's throne, and each seated an elder, who was dressed in white raiment, and had crowns of pure gold on their heads. Seven burning lamps shined brightly and represented the seven spirits of God. Four living creatures cried out continually, Holy, Holy, Holy, Lord God Almighty.

The tree of life bore twelve kinds of fruit each month, and the leaves on the tree gave healing to the nations. The millions of saints from all ages were there and multitudes of angels also.

What an awesome sight and experience this is going to be! However, as Jesus explained to Nicodemus, *"Except a man be born again, he cannot see the kingdom of God."*

APRIL 4
Here Am I

Moses was alone far out on the back side of a desert taking care of his father-in-law's sheep. It was so quiet you could hear a pin drop.

Suddenly God came on the scene in a fire in a bush. He spoke to Moses telling him that He was the God of his fathers, Abraham, Isaac, and Jacob. Moses answered, "Here am I."

When I pastored near Ft. Knox in Kentucky, the young recruits were sent there from all over the country. They would be assembled on the parade ground and a drill sergeant with a Smokey bear hat on would bark out orders to, "Forward march, right face, halt," and so on.

About that time a major would come onto the field and call out, "Sergeant!" That soldier would snap to attention, salute the major, and say, "Yes, Sir," meaning, "I don't know what you're going to ask me to do, but yes, I will do it." This what Moses is saying; I am ready to obey orders without question.

If a person is in the business world, it would be like a person laying a legal-size piece of paper on the desk, blank on both sides, and ask us to sign our name to the right bottom corner of the page.

I would prefer that the paper be filled with information: what are the details, working conditions, salary level, and such. After reading the contract several times, sharing it with my wife, asking my kids what they thought of it, and contacting some of my pastor friends for advice, I would be willing to sign the paper. By this time God would have chosen someone else.

He wants me to sign the blank page, no questions asked. Then He will reveal His plan.

APRIL 5
The Old Coin

The coin was old, but it was pure gold. It had been minted as a fifty dollar piece way back. The owner picked it up for a fraction of its value. It had been hidden away for a long time. He knew the longer he kept it the more it would increase, and he planned to sell it someday and add it to his retirement package.

In a mission conference he was attending, a dedicated young missionary whose wife had died during the birth of their child, presented his burden for a group of people in a small village in Ghana, Africa. Several hundred people had been saved and were meeting under a tree.

His heart was touched; when the offering was taken, the only money he had was the coin. He explained to the missionary that he knew it was not much in light of the great need, but maybe every little bit would help.

The missionary, Steve Volante, took the coin to a coin dealer for appraisal and could hardly believe his ears when the dealer offered him one hundred and fifty thousand dollars for it. His mind went back to the account of the widow's mite. She gave her all to the Lord.

Millions of people have been inspired and many millions have been given to the work of the Lord because of her sacrifice. This is a story similar to that of the little lad with five loaves and two fishes that fed five thousand men, plus women and children.

The old adage says it well, "It's not what you would do if a million became your lot, but what you will do with the dollar and a quarter you've got."

APRIL 6
Getting Out of the Pit

The story is told of a man who fell into a very deep pit. There was no way for him to climb out of the pit. He made every effort to jump or climb out. He had no rope or anything that he could use. There was no way he would be able to get himself out without some outside help.

A man came along and threw down a ladder. There were ten steps on the ladder. He started to climb up, but each one of the rungs is one of the ten commandments. The rule is that the man cannot put his foot on any commandment that he has broken. Suddenly Jesus jumps down into the pit, tells the man to climb onto His back. He then climbs out stepping on every one of the steps that He did not break.

Jesus said, *"I am the way, the truth and the life: no man cometh to the Father, but by me"* (John 14:6).

Beginning with Adam every person on earth has broken God's laws. *"There is none righteous, no, not one"* (Rom. 3:10), *"There is not a just man on the earth, that doeth good and sinneth not"* (Ecc. 7:20).

Jesus explained in the Sermon on the Mount that if a person hates someone he is guilty of murder, and to lust is to commit adultery. He is saying that the inward thought is just the same as the outward act.

James adds to that, *"For whosoever shall keep the whole law, and yet offend in one point, he is guilty of all"* (James 2:10). There is no way a person can go to Heaven on his own.

APRIL 7
The Price of a Miracle

Sally was eight years old when she heard Mommy and Daddy talking about her little brother, Georgi. He was very sick. Only a very expensive surgery could help him and that was out of the question. She heard Daddy say, "Only a miracle can save him." Sally went to her bedroom and got her piggybank. She shook all the change out and counted it.

Grasping her coins in her hand, she made her way to the corner drug store. She waited patiently, the pharmacist was busy talking to another man. She cleared her throat. That did no good. Finally she took a quarter from the hanky and banged it on the counter. That did it!

"And what do you want?" the pharmacist asked.

"My brother is sick and is going to die and I want to buy a miracle. My Daddy says only a miracle can save him. How much does a miracle cost?"

"We don't sell miracles here," said the druggist.

The well-dressed man stooped down and asked, "What kind of a miracle does your brother need?"

"I just know he's really sick and Mommy says he needs a miracle. How much does one cost?"

"How much do you have?" asked the man.

"A dollar and eleven cents," Sally answered.

"Well, what a coincidence," smiled the man. "A dollar and eleven cents...the exact price of a miracle. Take me to where you live."

That man was Dr. Carlton Armstrong, renowned surgeon, specializing in Georgi's malady. The operation was completed, without charge, and soon Georgi was home and doing well.

"That surgery," Mommy whispered. "It's like a miracle. I wonder how much it would have cost?"

Sally smiled. She knew exactly how much a miracle cost...one dollar and eleven cents.

APRIL 8
Big Mistake

Oksana Kostento, a Russian tour guide, rode with 52 children on the bus to the airport for a once-in-a-lifetime vacation to Barcelona, Spain. Once there she discovered they were at the wrong airport. The correct one was two hours away. After rearranging flight schedules they boarded another flight. Three hours into this flight, they collided with another plane 31,000 feet over Germany. Everybody in both planes were killed.

What a terrible mistake, affecting hundreds of people. The Bible records literally dozens of mistakes that are still affecting people hundreds of years later.

Think about the mistake of Adam and Eve in the Garden of Eden; the people who laughed at Noah's warnings—Lot when he pitched his tent toward Sodom—Esau when he sold his birthright for a mess of pottage—Achan when he saw, coveted and took the gold at Jericho—Jonah running away from God's plan—David not controlling his lust—Peter's cursing and denying the Lord—Judas betraying the Lord for 30 pieces of silver—Ananias and Sapphira's lying to God—the prodigal son forsaking his father and home—the five foolish virgins neglecting to get oil for their lamps—King Agrippa's almost being persuaded—and Felix's waiting for a more convenient season that never came.

These are some of many fatal mistakes recorded in the Bible. People are still making similar mistakes and paying an awful price for doing so.

In 1 Corinthians 10 Paul tells of the terrible consequences the children of Israel experienced because of their rebellion and disobedience; then he says, *"Now all these things happened unto them for ensamples: and they are written for our admonition"* (v.11).

What a terrible mistake not to heed the examples God has given us.

APRIL 9
That Young Hypocrite

All of us have heard the old expression, "That old hypocrite." I want to tell you about "that young hypocrite." He was eleven years old. His name was Charlie Click. Charles is a preacher now and pastor of a fine church. Charles says, "I went forward in a revival meeting at our church to get saved. A deacon prayed for me and then said, "Get up son, you're all right now."

"I knew I was not all right," said Charlie. "I had not prayed, repented, or anything else." What a terrible thing it would have been if Charles had died during that time.

Jesus said, *"And ye begin to stand without, and to knock at the door, saying, Lord, Lord, open unto us; and he shall answer and say unto you, I know you not whence ye are"* (Luke 13:25).

A year later while standing on the creek bank watching a baptismal service, the Holy Spirit began to work again in his heart. He became deeply convicted of his sin. At that moment, Charlie bowed and prayed, "Oh, dear Lord, please come into my heart and save my soul."

"For a whole year, I was a hypocrite," declared Bro. Click. "But now that's all changed." Now as a pastor of a soul-winning Baptist church, he sees the importance of dealing thoroughly with all who come to the altar.

There are many folks sitting in the pews these days who have been through the same type of experience in the past and have not ever bothered to correct the matter like Charlie. Wouldn't it be great if a lot of people would take courage from Charlie's story and make things right with the Lord?

APRIL 10
Spiritual Vertigo

We have a number of pilots at our Franklin Road Baptist Church. When they get together, the subject sooner or later leads to vertigo.

Vertigo is defined as disorientation. While flying in clouds or a dense fog, visibility is zero. A pilot may not be able to tell whether he is flying upside down, sideways, or even up or down. If he is well-trained, he will turn to his instruments and believe what they tell him regardless of how he feels or what he might think about his situation.

His temptation to go by his feelings instead of the instruments has cost many a pilot his life. God has given us the truth about life, death, and eternity in the Bible. The conditions around us are many times confusing, frustrating, and uncertain. It is easy to become disoriented and bewildered.

Sometimes we experience "spiritual vertigo." Many are swayed by the experiences of life. Then there is exposure to some who tell us that this is the way it happened to them. They had a certain feeling, or saw a certain vision; and we are tempted to believe that this is the way we can know God's plan for us. Logic and reason will lead to disaster. The way to be safe is to turn to the instrument of the Word of God and believe what He says about every circumstance and experience of life.

As David puts it, *"Blessed is the man who walketh not in the counsel of the ungodly, not standeth in the way of sinners, nor sitteth in the seat of the scornful, But his delight is in the law of the Lord; and in His law doth he meditate day and night"* (Psa. 1:1-2).

APRIL 11
God and a Sandstorm

Sennacherib, the king of Assyria, brought a great army against Israel boasting that God had not been able to prevent him from conquering their neighbors and that He would not be able to keep him from doing the same to them. That very night a lone angel came on the scene and slew 185,000 of his soldiers (2 Kings 19:35).

In our day we wonder if God would intervene and help us when we fight against heathen nations. During the invasion of Iraq by United States forces the worst sandstorm in one hundred years brought our forces to a sudden halt. A drenching rain came the next day and made a quagmire that made it impossible to move forward. The news media was predicting doom and gloom. After the weather cleared, the marine unit involved looked out and saw thousands of land mines that would have decimated our tanks and our soldiers uncovered by the wind and washed off by the rain. They would have all been killed and the battle lost.

One person once asked George Washington if he thought God was on his side. His reply is reported to be, "It is not that God should be on our side, but that we be on His."

"Jesus Christ the same yesterday, and to day, and forever" (Hebrews 13:8). Isaiah the prophet said, *"With him is an arm of flesh; but with us is the LORD our God to help us, and to fight our battles"* (2 Chron. 32:8).

These principles not only work for nations but for churches, homes, and individual lives. *"The LORD saveth not with sword and spear: for the battle is the LORD's, and he will give you into our hands"* (1 Samuel 17:47).

APRIL 12
Do Nice Guys End Up Last?

Nice guys end up last; or do they really? Is it really possible for a humble and quiet-spirited individual to be leader of the pack?

Jesus said, "The meek shall inherit the earth." This is another paradox; it doesn't seem right but it works. Our Bible says that Moses was the meekest man on earth and yet God used him to stand up to the strongest man alive in his day, the Pharaoh of Egypt.

He was able to deliver 3 to 3 ½ million Israelites out of bondage and maintain his position of leadership for over 40 years. Jesus, Himself, the very creator of the universe and Saviour of the world said, "I am meek and lowly in heart."

Meekness has been defined as "the spirit in which we accept God's dealing with us and the way we respond to mistreatment and justice without retaliation." Meekness is really a submission and trust in the Lord, allowing Him to work His power through our weakness.

Peter speaks of this as being a quality of great price. *"But let it be the hidden man of the heart, in that which is not corruptible, even the ornament of a meek and quiet spirit, which is in the sight of God of great price"* (1 Peter 3:4).

We are talking here about a willingness to be governed. We are to submit to the higher powers. *"Submit yourselves therefore to God. Resist the devil, and he will flee from you"* (James 4:7).

Believers submit themselves to God, wives submit to husbands, children submit to parents, younger submit to the elders, and Christians are told to submit to one another in the Lord. The nice guys are going to end up way out in front.

APRIL 13
Getting Old and Loving It

For many years I've dreaded getting old. I saw people with all the ailments and problems that old age brings and wished for some way to avoid all of it. Since dying young seemed to be the only alternative, I finally decided I would accept it and move on.

As I approach my 86th birthday I am really excited about the whole matter. I have discovered that getting old is an outside thing. Someone said, "You can be 80 years young or 40 years old." Staying young is an inner thing.

Paul wrote, *"For which cause we faint not; but though our outward man perish, yet the inward man is renewed day by day"* (2 Cor. 4:16).

According to my Bible, I'm going to get a glorified body, live a thousand years on the earth in the millennium, and have access to the new Jerusalem.

During that time there will be no pain, no sorrow, no death, no problems with sight or hearing, no heart or gall bladder problems, and a hundred other things I will not have to be concerned about. As one line in an old gospel song says, "Won't it be wonderful there."

Every year I get a little closer, and it is more exciting than Christmas coming. Paul the apostle spoke of, "having a desire to be with Christ which is far better." He also said "to die is gain." Then again, "But as it is written, Eye hath not seen, nor ear heard, neither have entered into the heart of man, the things which God hath prepared for them that love him." The older we get, the closer we are to all those beautiful blessings, so let the years roll on.

APRIL 14
Lincoln Shot

On this day in 1865, John Wilkes Booth, an actor and Confederate sympathizer, fatally shot President Abraham Lincoln at Ford's Theater in Washington, D.C., five days after Confederate General Robert E. Lee surrendered his army at Appomattox Court House, ending the Civil War.

Booth initially plotted to capture Lincoln and take him to Richmond, the Confederate capital. However, the day of the planned kidnapping, the president failed to appear at the spot where Booth and his six fellow conspirators lay in wait. Two weeks later, Richmond fell to Union forces.

In April, with Confederate armies near collapse, Booth hatched a plan to save the Confederacy. Learning that Lincoln was to attend a performance at Ford's Theater on April 14, Booth masterminded the assassination of Lincoln, Vice President Andrew Johnson, and Secretary of State William H. Seward.

By murdering the president and two of his successors, Booth hoped to throw the government into disarray. On April 14, conspirator Lewis

Powell burst into Secretary of State Seward's home, seriously wounding him and three others, while George Atzerodt, assigned to Vice President Johnson, lost his nerve and fled.

Meanwhile, Booth entered Lincoln's private theater box and shot the president in the back of his head. Booth leapt to the stage and shouted, "The South is avenged!" Although Booth broke his leg he managed to escape on horseback. The president was carried to a house opposite Ford's Theater.

The next morning, Lincoln, age 56, died—the first U.S. president to be assassinated. Booth was finally cornered in a barn near Bowling Green, Virginia, and died from a possibly self-inflicted bullet. Of eight charged with the conspiracy, four were hanged and four were jailed. Lincoln, the 16th U.S. President, was buried on May 4, 1865, in Springfield, Illinois.

APRIL 15
The Woman Was Really a Man

A preacher friend of mine in another state went into a restaurant to eat breakfast. Before sitting down he threw his coat over the back of the booth. It hit the person sitting at the next booth. He quickly apologized saying, "I am terribly sorry madam." The "woman" turned around and "he" wasn't a "Madam" at all but a long-haired gentleman. My preacher brother again graciously asked his pardon. "I didn't mean to embarrass you or be unkind," he said.

The preacher introduced himself and suggested that since they were both having breakfast alone he might join him. As they sat across from each other in the booth, they talked about church and heaven and then dying and then about getting saved.

My friend took him through several verses on sin, judgment, the death of Christ on the cross, then to the verse, *"For whosoever shall call upon the name of the Lord shall be saved"* (Romans 10:13).

In just a few moments the young man with tears streaming down his cheeks opened his heart and received Christ. The next day while my preacher friend was working in his room a knock came at the door. A clean-cut, freshly shaven young man stood at the door.

"I wanted to come by and tell you what I have done," he said.

"Who are you and what did you do?" He asked the young fellow.

"Don't you remember me?" He asked. "I had breakfast with you yesterday!" It was the same fellow. He had gone to the barber shop for a shave and a haircut.

The Bible says *"Therefore if any man be in Christ, he is a new creature: old things are passed away; behold, all things are become new"* (2 Cor. 5:17).

APRIL 16
Measuring Your Faith

". . .According to your faith be it unto you" (Matthew 9:29).

These words were spoken by Jesus to two blind men. They were rewarded by their faith because their eyes were opened. Dr. Vance Havner points out that Jesus did not say, according to your "fate" or according to your "fortune"; nor did He say, according to your "fame," "friends," or "feelings," but He did say, *"According to your faith."* (Matthew 9:29). There are five different kinds of faith affecting our lives.

1. NATURAL FAITH. This is faith in a bank where money will be safe, faith in a mailbox that our letter will be delivered, or faith in an employer that we will be paid at the end of the week.

2. INTELLECTUAL FAITH. A woman baking a cake following a recipe is exercising intellectual faith. She believes a cake will result from pouring in certain ingredients.

3. HISTORICAL FAITH. We believe Napoleon actually lived. We believe George Washington was the first President of the United States and that Abraham Lincoln gave the Gettysburg Address. That's historical faith.

4. SAVING FAITH. This is Bible faith that God will keep His promise and save us by grace, through faith.

5. VICTORIOUS FAITH. This is the faith of a child of God that helps him to exercise prayer and obedience in the Christian life, believing that God will give certain rewards and benefits because He has promised to do so.

We read in the Scriptures, *"And this is the victory that overcometh the world, even our faith"* (1 John 5:4). In this message we are not discussing natural faith, intellectual faith, historical faith or saving faith; but let us consider victorious faith that helps the Christian to do things for God.

APRIL 17
Saved in the Barn

I was out visiting several years ago and stopped by a home, where the lady of the house was a regular attendee at our church. I inquired about the husband.

"He's out in the barn," the lady told me. I asked if she thought he would mind if I visited with him there. She thought he would not mind at all. I went to the barn and found him working with his cows. I told him I had come to help him get ready to meet God.

He seemed interested and listened patiently to my presentation of the gospel. I asked him if he would be willing to receive Christ as his personal Saviour. "You mean, here in the barn?" he asked.

"Jesus was born in a barn," I reminded him, "and you can be born again in a barn." He had never thought of that. His expression immediately changed. He liked the idea.

"All right; I'll do it," he said, as he removed his hat and bowed his head to pray.

Some are saved at the altar of a church, but I have heard stories of men and women who invited Christ to save them in their cars, in hospitals, in jail cells, in factories, in foxholes, and in dozens of other places. I have seen men get saved under a tree and in a Walmart parking lot. Paul was saved on the Damascus road and the Ethiopian eunuch on a chariot along the way home.

The Apostle Peter wrote that God *"is longsuffering to us-ward, not willing that any should perish, but that all should come to repentance"* (2 Peter 3:9).

The Lord doesn't care where a person is. He is willing to save a person regardless of where he is.

APRIL 18
Gratitude

Once a man became dissatisfied with his property and decided to sell it. He ran an ad describing it. Reading the real estate ads the next day, he saw a description of a place he thought was just what he was looking for. When inquiring, he discovered it was his own property.

Someone wrote the words in a song "Count your blessings. Name them one by one, and it will surprise you what the Lord has done." Paul tells us how to keep from becoming dissatisfied in 1 Thes. 5:18, *"In every thing give thanks: for this is the will of God in Christ Jesus concerning you."* The psalmist not only said Bless the Lord O my soul, but also asked in Psalms 116:12, *"What shall I render unto the LORD [for] all his benefits toward me?"*

I made a list of one hundred and twenty-five bad things that never happened to me, and when I begin to feel sorry for myself I read through the list and find myself praising God.

Alexander Whyte, the Scottish preacher, always began his prayers with an expression of gratitude. One cold, miserable day his people wondered what he would say. He prayed, "We thank Thee, O Lord, that it is not always like this." Longfellow said, "After all, the best thing to do when it's raining is let it rain."

In Russell Conwell's famous "Acres of Diamonds," he tells of the man who heard of a place where people were finding large diamonds and becoming rich. He sold his small farm and went in search of fortune. After a long empty pursuit, he became disheartened and flung himself off a cliff and committed suicide. A fortune of diamonds was discovered in the stream that flowed through his property back home.

APRIL 19
Turned Aside

God came down to visit Moses. He chose to appear in a burning bush. Imagine the Omnipotent, Omnipresent, Omniscient creator of the universe confining Himself to a bush on the backside of a desert. That would be like reducing all the fire in the world to one match head, or boiling all the rain since Noah to one rain drop, or all the snow that ever fell from the sky into one snowflake, or all the iron into one nail, or all the copper into one penny, or all the silver into one dime. That would be something like Jesus being, *"the fullness of the Godhead bodily"* (Col. 2:9).

The bush burned and burned but it did not burn up. God never burns up. He is eternal. When a person catches on fire for God, they will not burn out either. Getting stirred or revived will not burn up one's energy, or his time or his money. We will have more of all of these if we allow God to burn in us.

When Moses saw the bush burning, he said, *"I will now turn aside and see this great sight, why the bush is not burnt."* He was standing between the flock of sheep and the bush. One is his secular job and the other his spiritual responsibility. He decided to give priority to the spiritual.

Jesus said, *"Seek ye first the kingdom of God, and His righteousness; and all these things shall be added to you"* (Matthew 6:33).

I submit that if Moses had been busy with the secular area of life he never would have heard the call of God to go to Egypt and rescue God's people. He would have missed his life's calling. **It's time to turn aside.**

APRIL 20
Victory over Depression

In spite of the fact that the Bible says *"Thanks be unto God, which giveth us the victory through our Lord Jesus Christ"* (I Cor. 15:57) and *"In all these things we are more than conquerors through Him that loved us"* (Romans 8:37), there is much doubt, discouragement, and depression even among Christians.

These things cause people to do some very strange things.

1. Some people begin to think wrong thoughts such as John when in prison began to doubt and sent friends to ask Jesus if He were really the Messiah or should they look for another. Then Mary and Martha sadly told Jesus that if He had come a little earlier, their brother would not have died.

2. Other folks do wrong things, like Moses who smote the rock in the wilderness rather than speak to it.

3. Then still other people say wrong things like Job who stated, *"Let the day perish wherein I was born, and the night in which it was said, There is a man child conceived"* (Job 3:3).

4. Then there are some who pray wrong prayers like Elijah who prayed for God to take his life.

5. In another case people saw wrong things like the ten spies in Canaan who saw giants in the land and saw themselves as grasshoppers.

6. Others go to wrong places like Jonah fleeing to Tarsus and Elijah hiding under a juniper tree.

7. Finally, there are some who develop a wrong spirit like the children of Israel murmuring, grumbling, and complaining to Moses.

We would all do well to hear these words from the Bible, *"Now thanks be unto God, which always causeth us to triumph in Christ"* (2 Cor. 2:14).

APRIL 21
Use Your Key

Jessie Pointdexter had a big heart. When I called and asked if he could cut my hair, the answer was always the same, "Come on over." In five minutes I would be there getting trimmed. They always insisted I join them for lunch and I would agree. When I tried to pay for the lunch, the haircut, and the big basket of produce from the garden, and several jars of things Shirley had been canning, they always said, "You know you don't owe us anything. If you had not won us to the Lord, we would not be going to Heaven. We'll never get you paid," they added. I usually left with tear-filled eyes because of the love they had for me.

One Sunday night Jessie walked up and put a key in my hand. I said, "Thank you; now, what does this key open?" He explained that it opened a new double-wide trailer home he had built at Lake Cumberland.

He added, "The freezer inside is filled with venison and trout." He also explained that there was a beautiful fiberglass bass boat with the key under the seat. "I want you to take advantage of all this any time you can," he added.

I only took advantage of these good things two nights in ten years, but it was there for me all that time. I remembered that it is like that with our relationship with God.

We have the key to some wonderful benefits and never take advantage of them. James 4:2 says, *"Ye have not, because ye ask not."* God wants to open the windows of Heaven and pour out blessings upon His children, but they will not use their key and do His will.

APRIL 22
Saved or Lost

In the *Titanic* display at Gatlinburg, Tennessee, it is noted that when the passengers made reservations for the maiden voyage, they were placed in five or six different categories. Some were listed first class, others second class, still others third class, then crew, etc.

The ship, built in Ireland by the White Star Lines, was four days into the journey on April 14, 1912, with 2,223 souls onboard. The lifeboat capacity was only 1,178.

When the *Titanic* hit the iceberg and began to sink, the awful reality of the crisis was realized. 1517 perished in the shocking tragedy. On a desk back in the shipping office lay two pieces of paper. On one were the words, "Jane Doe found; saved." The other contained the words, "John Doe found; lost." As reports came in from rescue crews, names were listed on the sheets according to their fate.

Our society still puts people into categories. Some are classified as male and female, rich, others poor, citizens and non-citizens, some famous, others unknown.

The Bible divides mankind into the latter classes. Everyone is either saved or lost. In one place it says 'Come ye blessed of the Father' then in another, 'Depart from me, I never knew you.'

In I John 5:12 we find the words, *"He that hath the Son hath life; but he that hath not the Son of God hath not life."* Also, John 3:18 adds, *"He that believeth on him is not condemned: but he that believeth not is condemned already, because he hath not believed in the name of the only begotten Son of God."*

Jesus said, *"Rejoice, because your names are written in Heaven"* (Luke 10:20). The Bible also says, *"Whosoever was not found written in the book of life was cast into the lake of fire"* (Rev. 20:15).

APRIL 23
Benefits of Death

The Bible teaches us that there is great benefit in death for a believer. Obviously I am not referring to physical death. There are seven types of death given in the Bible that will bring benefit and blessing.

First, there is death to sin. *"Likewise reckon ye also yourselves to be dead indeed unto sin, but alive unto God through Jesus Christ our Lord"* (Romans 6:11).

Second, death to self. Paul gave us a great truth when he said, *"I am crucified with Christ: nevertheless I live; yet not I, but Christ liveth in me: and the life which I now live in the flesh I live by the faith of the Son of God, who loved me, and gave himself for me"* (Galatians 2:20).

Third, we are dead to the flesh. *"And they that are Christ's have crucified the flesh with the affections and lusts"* (Galatians 5:24).

Fourth, we are to be dead to the world. *"But God forbid that I should glory, save in the cross of our Lord Jesus Christ, by whom the world is crucified unto me, and I unto the world"* (Galatians 6:14).

Fifth, we are dead to the law. *"Blotting out the handwriting of ordinances (law) that was against us, which was contrary to us, and took it out of the way, nailing it to his cross"* (Colossians 2:14).

Sixth, we are dead to Satan. *"Forasmuch then as the children are partakers of flesh and blood, he also himself likewise took part of the same; that through death he might destroy him that had the power of death, that is, the devil"* (Hebrews 2:14).

Seventh, we are dead to principalities and powers. *"And having spoiled principalities and powers, he made a shew of them openly, triumphing over them in it"* (Colossians 2:15).

APRIL 24
True Riches

"There is that maketh himself rich, yet hath nothing: there is that maketh himself poor, yet hath great riches" (Proverbs 13:7).

A rich landowner named Carl often rode around his vast estate so he could congratulate himself on his great wealth. One day while riding around his estate on his favorite horse, he saw Hans, an old tenant farmer. Hans was sitting under a tree when Carl rode by. He asked Hans what he was doing.

Hans said, "I was just thanking God for my food."

Carl protested, "If that is all I had to eat, I wouldn't feel like giving thanks."

Hans replied, "God has given me everything I need, and I am thankful for it." The old farmer added, "It is strange you should come by today because I had a dream last night. In my dream a voice told me, 'The richest man in the valley will die tonight.' I don't know what it means, but I thought I ought to tell you."

Carl snorted, "Dreams are nonsense," and he galloped away, but he could not forget Hans' words: 'The richest man in the valley will die tonight.'

He was obviously the richest man in the valley, so he invited his doctor to his house that evening. Carl told the doctor what Hans had said. After a thorough examination, the doctor told the wealthy landowner, "There is no way you are going to die tonight."

Nevertheless, for assurance, the doctor stayed with Carl, and they played cards through the night. The doctor left the next morning and Carl apologized for becoming so upset over the old man's dream.

At about nine o'clock, a messenger arrived at Carl's door. "What is it?" Carl demanded.

The messenger explained, "It's about old Hans. He died last night in his sleep."

APRIL 25
Three Lives of Man

Does a cat have nine lives? Some really believe they do. Others think this is a silly notion. Since my philosophy is based on the teaching of the Bible, I dismiss the whole notion, quickly.

In this regard, cats are just like men, *"It is appointed unto man once to die"* (Hebrews 9:27). That settles it for me.

On the other hand, I believe that man can have three lives.

One life, the physical, extends from birth to death and is pictured as the dash between the two dates on one's tombstone. The Bible calls this man the "natural man" (1 Cor. 2:14).

Believers, however, are given, "eternal life" as a gift of God. Jesus said, *"I give unto them eternal life; and they shall never perish"* (John 10:28). This begins with the "new birth" spoken of by our Lord in the conversion with Nicodemus in John chapter three.

A third life is available for the believer, but it must be pursued. This life is called, 'abundant life.' Jesus told of this when He said, *"I am come that they might have life, and that they might have it more abundantly"* (John 10:10b). This abundant life is one of fullness, joy, and peace.

Years ago a bumper sticker was quite common. It said, "I've found it." Many never do. The unbeliever only has one life; while the believer has two, and can have three lives, if he or she chooses.

Instead of "joy," why not "joy unspeakable"? Instead of "peace", why not, "peace that passeth all understanding"? Instead of getting a prayer answered once in a while, why not get, "exceeding, abundantly, above all you ask or think"?

Why not add abundant life to the two lives you now have?

APRIL 26
The Preacher Really Hit Him

Have you ever felt that the preacher was talking right to you in his sermon? That's exactly the way Garvey Osborne felt the night he went to church with me.

Garvey was a bad drinker. His life was a wreck. I took an interest in him when he came to work with me at an automobile plant. He said that he would like to get things fixed up with the Lord but just had never gotten around to it. After quite a bit of persuasion, he agreed to go with me to a tent revival meeting.

"If that preacher talks to me tonight, I'll go forward and get saved," he told me. The sermon was directly to him. The preacher couldn't have been more direct. Every word was fired in his direction.

When the invitation was extended, I asked him if he thought the Lord had been speaking to him.

"No sir, not me," he insisted, "he wasn't talking to me."

Just a few moments later, he glanced over at me with tears swelling up in his eyes. He asked, "Will you go down there with me?"

Of course, I was delighted to go with him, and a few moments later, we were on our knees together. He invited Christ into his heart and received a full pardon for his sins.

That was over forty years ago. I received a call from his granddaughter who was saved as a result of his influence on her. She told me, "I wanted you to know that Grandpa died recently with Jesus in his heart and a bundle of tracts in his pocket."

The Lord talks to a lot of people who do not listen, but thank God for those who do.

APRIL 27
He Was Crazy

Sometime after the days of the eight-track player, the forty-five RPM, and the LP record, but before the CD, DVD, or the MP3 player, I listened to a sermon on a cassette tape by an old preacher by the name of R.R. Brown on the "Maniac of Gadara."

On a Holy Land trip a couple of years ago, I visited Gadara on the coast of the Sea of Galilee and tried to imagine this poor crazy man running around in the graveyard, naked, cutting and bruising himself as he stumbled and fell against the grave markers.

Dr. Brown described the wild-looking man as a poor creature with a fearful look on his face; long, stringy hair, dirty and bruised body; darting from behind one tombstone to another. Then he said that the poor fellow had not received Christ as his Saviour, but he was crazy. Then he asked, "What's your excuse?"

He went on to declare that the man had not been baptized, did not go to Sunday school, was not regular in church attendance, did not read his Bible, did not have a prayer life, was not a tither, and did not attempt to win anybody to the Lord, did not dress appropriately, did not treat his neighbor well, was a lousy father to his children, and was a very poor husband to his wife; then after each of these thoughts, he would drive home his point, "But he was crazy! What's your excuse?"

The sermon hit hard against a lot of people who are wildly running around in the spiritual dead world, bruising and damaging themselves with drug habits, alcohol, sex problems and such, and ignoring the Bible and church. At least this crazy man had an excuse.

APRIL 28
Saved Twice

Years ago I heard about a young boy knocking on doors giving out tracts. With one tract left, he rang a doorbell several times, then knocked a couple more times. Starting to leave, he felt impressed to try again.

He rang the bell, and the door slowly opened. Standing in the doorway was a very sad looking elderly lady. She softly asked, "What can I do for you, son?"

With radiant eyes and a smile the little boy said, "Ma'am, I'm sorry if I disturbed you, but I just want to tell you that "JESUS REALLY DOES LOVE YOU," and I came to give you my very last gospel tract. It will tell you all about Jesus and His great love."

Sunday morning in church the Pastor asked, "Does anyone want to say anything?" An elderly lady stood.

"No one here knows me. Before last Sunday I was not a Christian. My husband passed on, leaving me all alone. Last Sunday I came to where

I no longer wanted to live. I took a rope and went into the attic of my home. I fastened the rope to a rafter in the roof, then stood on the chair and fastened the rope around my neck. Standing on that chair, I heard my doorbell ring. I thought, "I'll wait a minute, and whoever it is will go away." The ringing continued so I loosened the rope and went to answer the door. There on my front porch was the most radiant little boy. He smiled, and said "Ma'am, I just came to tell you that JESUS REALLY DOES LOVE YOU." Then he gave me this gospel tract. I read it, and I have received Christ. My soul has been saved as well as my life."

APRIL 29
Change Me Over

While making hospital rounds, I walked into a room with five patients, introduced myself, and explained that I would like to pray for them. One lady mentioned that she lived near our church, so I invited her to visit us sometime.

"Oh no, I'll not be there," she blurted out. "I'm a Quaker," she declared, "and we don't go to other churches."

I tried to be friendly and explained that we would still like for her to come. She flatly told me again, "Don't count on it."

The lady in the next bed was very nervous and started crying. She asked if I would pray for her and tell her how she could be right with the Lord.

With the other ladies listening in, I explained the simple plan of salvation and she committed herself to Christ. She immediately relaxed and thanked me for taking time to help her.

The next day I went back, and the woman who said she would not be coming to my church remarked, "I'm glad you came back. I want you to 'change me over.'"

"Do what to you?" I asked.

"You know, do for me what you did for her," pointing to the woman who had been saved the day before. "Make a Baptist out of me," she said.

I explained that being a Baptist would not do any more than being a Quaker and that she needed to become a Christian. She was sweetly converted.

On my way home I wondered what had changed her. Obviously the other women in that room had gone to bat for me. Some Baptist had lied to her or cheated her out of some money and built up a barrier. When that was torn down, the door was open and the gospel got through.

APRIL 30
Seeing the Invisible

Elisha's servant could not see the great heavenly host that was protecting them from the Syrian army; he became scared in his soul.

Elisha saw the angelic crowd watching over them and was completely relaxed. The prophet then prayed that the servant's eyes be opened. They were and then he too saw the angelic band (2 Kings 6:8-17).

Jesus gave parables that were easy for His disciples to understand, while the scribes and Pharisees missed it completely. *"Therefore speak I to them in parables: because they seeing see not; and hearing they hear not, neither do they understand"* (Matthew 13:13).

Paul wrote, *"But the natural man receiveth not the things of the Spirit of God: for they are foolishness unto him: neither can he know them, because they are spiritually discerned"* (1 Cor. 2:14).

We believers see things that others don't see; We hear things that others don't hear; and we feel things that others don't feel. The world's philosophy is "seeing is believing." The Christian philosophy is just the opposite. We say, "believing is seeing." The songwriter tells us of a land that is fairer than day and "by faith we can see it afar."

Hebrews 11:1 speaks of "the evidence of things not seen." At the same time, it also speaks of Moses being encouraged by 'seeing Him that is invisible.'

We see God in a number of ways, but it is always by faith. God's kingdom is invisible. Jesus told Nicodemus unless he was born again he could not see the kingdom of God. He said *"Lo, I am with you always"* (Matthew 28:20). Eternal values are invisible. Paul also tells of things that are not seen that are eternal (2 Cor. 4:18).

MAY 1
100% of Your Prayers Answered

After preaching to a large congregation in Florida, I was approached by a man who asked a question that set me back. I had preached that evening that, although it was not very likely, it was possible to get 100 percent of our prayers answered.

My text was John 15:7, *"If ye abide in me, and my words abide in you, ye shall ask what ye will, and it shall be done unto you."* I then gave a number of illustrations from my own life. I told how God sent a piano player just minutes after we prayed for one. In another case, a man offered me the use of a bulldozer just minutes after we prayed for a bulldozer. I added the account of how I prayed three days for suits to wear to college classes, and two days later the Lord gave me three suits. While sitting at the table praying for food, someone knocked at the door and gave us food.

The gentleman with the question asked me if I had prayed for my wife to be healed of the cancer that took her life five years before. He was very sincere, telling me of the death of his own wife. I assured him that I did. Of course the unspoken question was hanging there.

"Why did God not heal her?"

I shared with him that both my wife and I sensed that He was going to take her home. She told me that she had an assurance that this was her ministry. We both accepted that it was God's will. We claimed 2 Cor. 4:1, *"Therefore seeing we have this ministry, as we have received mercy, we faint not."*

The Lord allowed us to want what He wanted.

MAY 2
Believe, Then Act on It

Something spooked Napoleon's horse. It bolted and ran away. A private in Napoleon's army gave chase, caught the horse, and returned it to the emperor. Napoleon turned to the private and said, "Thank you, Captain."

The newly promoted soldier went straight to the quartermaster for his new uniform and captain's bars on his shoulders. He made his way to the officer's quarters and began to share in all the privileges and benefits of an officer. He believed the emperor. One word made the difference.

Our Bible is filled with stories of people who believed the words of

Jesus. The blind saw. The dead were raised. A cripple walked. A deaf man heard. A leper was cleansed. All this because Jesus spoke the word.

Someone said, "He said it, I believe it, and that settles it." That's good. Someone else said, "He said it; and it doesn't matter whether you believe it or not, that still settles it." That's right too.

One of the names given to Christians in the Bible is "believers." Our Bible says, *"Believe on the Lord Jesus Christ, and thou shalt be saved and thy house"* (Acts 16:31). By believing, we can go to heaven when we die. *"By grace are ye saved, through faith..."* (or believing) (Ephesians 2:8).

A man brought his demon-possessed son to Jesus. It was a last resort. He had tried everything else. Jesus said to him, *"If thou canst believe, all things are possible to him that believeth"* (Mark 9:23).

Maybe somebody has a mountain that needs moving. We either believe that He has saved us because we are trusting Him to get us into Heaven or we don't. That one word makes the difference. My Bible says I'm saved. I believe it; that's settled.

MAY 3
Can I Take Joe's Place?

Joe, the governor's most trusted assistant, died in his sleep one night. The governor had depended on Joe for advice on every subject, from pending bills to wardrobe decisions. In addition, Joe had been his closest friend. So, it was understandable that the governor didn't take kindly to the droves of ambitious office-seekers who wanted Joe's job.

"They don't even have the decency to wait until the man is buried," the governor muttered. At the funeral, one eager beaver made his way to the governor's side.

"Governor," the man said, "is there a chance that I could take Joe's place?"

"Certainly," the governor replied. "But you'd better hurry. I think the undertaker is almost finished."

I'm sure we can all look around us and find a number of people of whom we have said, "I would like to take his/her place." But I dare say that you have never made that statement of someone who had died, or was about to die. Why would anyone want to trade places with someone like that?

It is for that reason that God's love for us is so difficult to comprehend, for that is exactly what Jesus did for us.

"He was wounded for our transgressions, he was bruised for our iniquities: The chastisement of our peace was upon him; and with his stripes we are healed. All we like sheep have gone astray; we have turned every one to his own way; and the LORD hath laid on him the iniquity of us all" (Isaiah 53:5-6).

Paul the apostle said it this way: *"But God commendeth his love toward us, in that, while we were yet sinners, Christ died for us"* (Romans 5:8).

May our lives be forever lived in gratitude to the One who "took our place."

MAY 4
Omni Caring

In my prayers each morning, it has become my habit to thank God for His omnipresence, His omniscience, His omnipotence, plus His mercy, love, grace, eternality, immutability, justice, truth, and His holiness. I like to remind myself that God is total and complete in all these areas.

In a book I was reading, the author used the term, "Omni Caring." It got my attention. God is aware and has a personal interest in everything that comes our way. Our Bible says, *"Are not two sparrows sold for a farthing? and one of them shall not fall on the ground without your Father. But the very hairs of your head are all numbered"* (Matthew 10:29-30). He keeps pretty close tabs on His own.

The word "omni" means "all" or "total." He cares more than a mother cares for her baby, and more than a man cares for his new car. We're talking about complete coverage here. He is interested in all our bruises, scrapes, events, situations, and circumstances, frustrations, and heartaches.

David wrote, *"His going forth is from the end of the heaven, and his circuit unto the ends of it: and there is nothing hid from the heat (x-ray) thereof"* (Psalm 19:6). He sees all, hears all, knows all, and He cares about all of it.

Ezra wrote, *"For the eyes of the LORD run to and fro throughout the whole earth, to shew himself strong in the behalf of them whose heart is perfect toward him"* (2 Chron. 16:9).

He is concerned about our relationship with Him. He wants everybody saved. He is concerned about our spiritual level. All His blessings depend upon how close we are to Him. He is concerned about our discernment level. The more we understand God, the more we will praise Him.

MAY 5
A Certain Man

Jesus gave a parable of a certain man who had two sons. One became a prodigal. The other worked and helped his father on the farm but was offended and became childish because of the attention given to his wayward brother.

Who were these boys? What were their names? What was the father's name? Who was the girl that was married at Cana of Galilee? How old was she? Who did she marry? What was the nobleman's man's son's name in John chapter four, and the impotent man's son in chapter five? How old were they?

These people were types of individuals. What we do know teaches us principles, and the principles are the important part of the story.

In every miracle and parable, it is not the where and what in the account but Who made it happen. If Jesus had not been there, we would not know about the wedding, the nobleman, the impotent man, the blind man in John chapter nine, or Lazarus, or any other of the miracles and parables. He is the point of the story.

Now, we need to ask ourselves, who are we, where do we live, and what do we do for a livelihood? How much education do we have and how many degrees are listed after our names?

With all due respects, who cares, and what difference does it make? This is not about us. When a person sees the truth of Galatians 2:20, *"I am crucified with Christ: nevertheless I live; yet not I, but Christ who liveth in me: and the life which I now live in the flesh I live by the faith of the Son of God, who loved me, and gave himself for me."*

Our light is to shine that they might see Christ in us.

MAY 6
Meditation

The value of finding a quiet, secluded place to meet with God cannot be overemphasized.

Paul wrote from his prison cell encouraging his fellow-believers to think and give their attention to things that were true, honest, just, pure, lovely, of good report, virtuous, and filled with praise (Phil.4:8).

Joshua wrote of meditating day and night that we might observe to do all that was written in the Bible that our way might prosper.

David wrote in Psalm 1 advising us to meditate in the law day and night and promised that those who do will prosper (Psalm 1:2).

Paul added, *"Meditate upon these things… that thy profiting may appear to all"* (I Timothy 4:15).

A young evangelist spoke to our elementary chapel on the word, meditation. He asked the children to get an imaginary sponge the shape and size of a basketball. He then asked them to squeeze the sponge and make it the size of a softball, then again to make it the size of a baseball, and finally the size of a golf ball.

"Now," he said, "I want you to get a two-gallon bucket of water." One little boy raised his hand to ask, "Where am I supposed to get this bucket of water?"

"The same place you got the sponge," the speaker replied. He then asked the boys and girls to put the sponge into the bucket and turn it loose. He explained that the sponge would drink up about a gallon of the water. He then pointed out that our brain is like the sponge.

It looks like a sponge and acts like one. When we absorb Biblical principles, we subconsciously become more scriptural. The more scriptural we are the more spiritual we will be. It really pays to soak, saturate, and absorb.

MAY 7
Dividing Up Men

After Adam and Eve sinned in the garden of Eden, all men were put into one category. The Bible declares, *"For there is no difference: for all have sinned, and come short of the glory of God"* (Romans 3:22b-23). Here God sees mankind as sinners.

From the human viewpoint, people are divided into two categories: male and female, adult and child, rich and poor, good and bad, big and little, saved and lost, etc. Jesus spoke of the broad way and the narrow way.

After Jesus died on the cross and was resurrected, the Bible labels people in three different ways. We are either the natural man (1 Cor. 2:14), the spiritual man, (1 Cor. 2:15) or the carnal man (1 Cor. 3:1).

Later the Apostle Paul divides us again into four categories. He speaks of the gold, silver, wood, and earthen vessels, vessels of honor and vessels of dishonor (2 Timothy 2:20).

The gold describes committed Christians who are all out for the Lord.

The silver are humanized Christians who have been neutralized by their humanistic exposure and secularism.

The wood people are Christianized humanists. They have been taught morals and ethics and are decent law-abiding citizens that make good neighbors, but they are lost and will never see heaven.

The earthen crowd are committed humanists who do not believe in the God, of the Bible. They have no time for church. They campaign for the rights of homosexuals, women to have abortions, mother earth people, snail darters, and the spotted owl, etc.

We would all do well to examine ourselves to see what category we fall into. Jesus spoke of the time when the Lord will put the sheep on one side and the goats on the other in the judgment.

MAY 8
Christian or Humanist

Solomon was the wisest and wealthiest of all men. On one occasion he said, *"There is a way that seemeth right unto a man, but the end thereof are the ways of death"* (Proverbs 14:12). The only problem with Solomon's statement is that he doesn't tell us what or where the way that leads to death is. We seem to be left to figure it out for ourselves. However, we know that the Bible does not leave us hanging. There is always an answer to every question and a solution to every problem that is mentioned in the Word of God.

Jesus explained in the famous Sermon on the Mount that there was a broad way that leads to destruction and many there be that go therein, and then he spoke of a narrow way that leads to eternal life and said that few there be that find it.

Neither Solomon nor Jesus are talking about a highway, or a road, or a path, or even an alley. They are talking about a way of thinking or a philosophy. One of these ways is man's way. That is human or humanistic. Humanism says, "I think," "I believe," "This is my opinion," "This is the way I look at that."

We call that ego-centric philosophy. I want my way, I am going to do my thing. This, of course, is the broad way that Jesus spoke of in the

Sermon on the Mount. This way leads to eternal death.

Jesus also spoke of the narrow way and that is "Christo" centric philosophy. What does the Bible say about it? What will the Lord have me to do? Does it agree with the Word of God? Every person is a Christian or a humanist.

MAY 9
Spiritual Hypothalamus

The most important organ in the human body is the size of a small prune and lies on the underside of the brain. It is actually a small switchboard that gives balance and equilibrium to every function of the body and is called a hypothalamus. This master gland alerts and controls hunger, thirst, body temperature, blood sugar, emotions, water supply and several dozen other body functions.

In like manner the Spirit of God who lives in the body of a believer uses the Bible to help us with balance in our faith and practice. Jesus spoke of both "hearing" and "doing." James wrote about "faith" and "works." The psalmist urges us not to be like the horse or the mule. The horse is impulsive and jumpy, and the mule is stubborn. The priest wore bells and a pomegranates all the way around the hem of his robe. One of these is to be seen and the other heard. David prayed that the Lord would neither make him rich and allow him to get self-sufficient, or poor that he might be tempted to steal. He was praying for balance.

People have a tendency to major on minors or minor on majors. We believe in baptism but not baptismal regeneration. We are to pray but not move to a cave and act like a monk never doing anything else. We teach the sovereignty of God but not hyper-Calvinism. We believe in the second coming of Christ but not date setting.

We are to be holy, but not holier than thou; disciplined, but not demanding; meek but not weak; discerning but not critical; self-reliant, but not self-sufficient.

Paul touched on this when he said, *"Let your moderation [balance] be known unto all men"* (Phil. 4:5).

MAY 10
Why I Love Mom

Mom and Dad were watching TV. Mom said, "I think I'll go to bed." She went to the kitchen to make sandwiches for tomorrow's lunches, took meat out of the freezer for tomorrow's supper, checked the cereal box levels, filled the sugar container, put spoons and bowls on the table and filled the coffee pot for the next morning.

She then put some clothes in the dryer, put a load into the wash, ironed a shirt, and secured a loose button. She picked up the game pieces left on the table and put away the telephone book.

She watered the plants and emptied a wastebasket. She yawned and headed for the bedroom. She stopped by the desk, wrote a note to the teacher, counted out some cash for the field trip, and pulled a textbook out from under the chair. She signed a birthday card, addressed and stamped the envelope and wrote a quick note for the grocery store. She put both near her purse.

Mom then washed her face, put on her night solution and age- fighting moisturizer, brushed her teeth, and filed her nails.

Dad called out, "I thought you were going to bed."

"I'm on my way," she said. She put water into the dog's dish and put the cat outside, then made sure the doors were locked. She looked in on the kids, hung up a shirt, and threw some dirty socks in the hamper.

In her own room, she set the alarm, laid out clothing for the next day, and straightened up the shoe rack. She added three things to her 6 most important things-to-do list. She said her prayers.

About that time, Dad turned off the TV and announced, "I'm going to bed." And he did...without another thought.

MAY 11
Biblical Church or Social Club

In my travels I find many church congregations that have drifted from the Biblical plan of rescuing the perishing and the discipling of new converts, and settled into a club atmosphere.

Recently a friend told me that he had been asked to serve on a pulpit committee to help in the search for a pastor for his church. He told the committee that he did not know much about selecting a new pastor, but he believed they needed to make up their mind whether they wanted a pastor who would lead their church in a soul-winning and discipling program or settle for a religious club.

The deacons and pulpit committee located their man and gave an enthusiastic recommendation to the congregation. He was a solid fundamental, a soul-winner, an excellent preacher, and a good man of God. The congregation voted him down. They wanted a club.

I fear that they wrote Ichabod over the ministry of their church. Personally I believe that the Holy Spirit packs up and moves out when this happens, leaving a church without the Lord's help in their program.

Dr. Walter Hughes told our people in a sermon he preached in our church, "God didn't call me to cuddle the saints, but to collar sinners."

To concentrate on reaching without teaching or the opposite of teaching without reaching brings unbalance and disobedience to the Lord's command.

The great commission still says, *"Go ye therefore, and teach all nations, baptizing them in the name of the Father, and of the Son, and of the Holy Ghost: Teaching them to observe all things whatsoever I have commanded you: and, lo, I am with you alway, even unto the end of the world"* (Matthew 28:19-20).

MAY 12
By Faith

It was a privilege to attend the morning service of our own church recently. We are out on the road continually. Dr. Mike Norris, our pastor, had selected the theme "By Faith" as the slogan for the year. A big banner on the wall pictures a shield of faith from Ephesians chapter six and the words, *"Without faith it is impossible to please Him"* (Hebrews 11:6). The bulletin also had this same slogan printed in large letters.

Great truths came to mind as I thought on this. We trust what Jesus did, not what we do to get us to Heaven.

First, faith saves. *"For by grace are ye saved through faith; and that not of yourselves: it is the gift of God"* (Ephesians 2:8).

Second, faith sees. The writer of Hebrews spoke of seeing Him who is invisible (Hebrews 11:27). Nicodemus was told by Jesus that unless he was born again, he would not be able to see the kingdom of God (John 3:3). The song says it well, "There's a land that is fairer than day, and by faith we can see it afar."

Third, faith serves. Believing that people are blinded by the god of this world, we travel, preach, teach, drive buses, give, knock on doors, and more to further the cause of Christ and please the Lord.

Finally faith sends. Why would anyone quit a good paying job, sell their house, attend years of Bible college to prepare for the Lord's work?

We believe God has called us and by faith we respond. Paul wrote, *"But as it is written, Eye hath not seen, nor ear heard, neither have entered into the heart of man, the things which God hath prepared for them that love him"* (1 Cor. 2:9).

MAY 13
Dictaphone Man Saved

My Dictaphone had heard me give the Bible plan of salvation many times, yet it still has never responded to accept Christ as its Saviour.

With George the Dictaphone repairman…. well now, that's an entirely different story. George was working on the Dictaphone in my office when he heard me ask my secretary to bring me my file on "Heaven."

"Heaven," he commented. "Wouldn't it be great to know for sure you were going there when you die?"

"Yes," I assured him, "that would be great, and according to the Bible you can know that for sure." A look of interest came on George's face. "Has anyone ever taken the Bible and shown you how you can know for sure that you are going to heaven?" I asked.

"No," he answered, "No one has ever done that for me."

With his permission, I opened my Bible and explained the good news that God really loves us, that Christ died for us sinners, and that He is willing to give us the gift of eternal life. Then I read Romans 10:9, *"That if thou shalt confess with thy mouth the Lord Jesus, and shalt believe in thine heart that God hath raised him from the dead, thou shalt be saved."* George acknowledged his sin and realized that he was lost and bound for an eternal hell. He readily grasped the account of the death, the burial, and the resurrection of Christ.

When I offered to pray and asked him to pray and invite the Lord into his heart, he eagerly did so. I prayed first, and then he invited Christ into his heart. Another soul was born into the family of God. This time, a Dictaphone repairman.

MAY 14
Eleven Miracles

"When thou walkest through the fire, thou shalt not be burned; neither shall the flame kindle upon thee" (Isaiah 43:2).

In Elmer Bendiner's book *The Fall of Fortress,* he describes one bombing run over the German city of Kassel:

Our B-17 was barraged by Nazi antiaircraft guns. That was not unusual, but on this particular occasion our gas tanks were hit. Later, as I reflected on the miracle of a twenty-millimeter shell piercing the fuel tank without touching off an explosion, our pilot, Bohn Fawkes, told me it was not quite that simple.

On the morning following the raid, Bohn had asked our crew chief for that shell as a souvenir of unbelievable luck. The crew chief told Bohn that not just one shell but eleven had been found in the gas tanks—eleven unexploded shells where only one was sufficient to blast us out of the sky.

It was as if the sea had been parted for us. Bohn was told that the shells had been sent to be defused. The armorers told him that intelligence had picked them up. They could not say why at the time, but Bohn eventually sought out the answer.

Apparently when the armorers opened each of those shells, they found no explosive charge. They were clean as a whistle and just as harmless.

Empty? Not all of them. One contained a carefully rolled piece of paper. On it was a note in Czech. The intelligence people scoured our base for a man who could read Czech.

Eventually, they found one to decipher the note. It set us marveling. Translated, the note read: "This is all we can do for you now."

"The angel of the LORD encampeth round about them that fear him, and delivereth them" (Psalm 34:7).

MAY 15
They Would Not Let Me In

I was scheduled to speak at a conference in San Paulo, Brazil. There were to be about two hundred missionaries in the day meetings and fifteen hundred at night.

I flew to San Paulo. The young woman at immigration looked through my passport several times, then smiled and said in broken English, "Visa, Visa." I handed her my Visa card. "No, No," she said. I told her that I did not have a visa and you do not need a Visa to come to Brazil.

"Oh, you do now," she said. They had changed the law. They confiscated my luggage, and passport, and put me under house arrest.

I knew of a Christian lawyer in the city, I called him and he contacted the American embassy for me. The ambassador called to tell me that he was in touch with Washington as well as the powers that be in Brazil.

Nothing could be worked out. I did not get to speak in the conference, nor was I able to get any of my twelve hundred dollars back. I had planned well, got a substitute for my pulpit, paid for my ticket, and I was as sincere as one could be, but they would not let me in.

When I got back home, I told our folks about the experience and told them that some of them would get right to the gate of Heaven and would not be able to go in because they were not really saved.

Two of our teachers came to the altar weeping and confessing that they did not really have the matter settled. Both of them got their visas that morning.

The Bible says, whosoever's name is not written in the book of life will be cast into the lake of fire.

MAY 16
Strength to Make a Difference

"Thine, O LORD, is the greatness, and the power, and the glory, and the victory, and the majesty" (1Chron. 29:11).

How do we explain the life and ministry of D.L. Moody, Charles Finney, Jonathan Edwards, Kevin Wynn, Rick Martin, Lee Roberson, Jack Hyles, and a number of other men and their miracle ministries?

Our Bible teaches that God is the most powerful force in the universe. He spoke and billions of galaxies with billions of stars in each one came into existence. The same Bible teaches that God incarnated that same power into a human body. *"The Word was made flesh, and dwelt among us"* (John 1:14).

Jesus said, *"All power is given unto me in heaven and in earth"* (Matthew 28:18). Isaiah called Jesus "Immanuel" or "God with us" (Isaiah 7:14). God then arranged to make that same power available to believers.

The body of the believer is the temple of God who dwells in us (1 Cor. 6:19). Paul wrote to the believers at the Colossian church, "Christ in you, the hope of glory."

Through the ages men and angels have tried to channel and harness that power for their own personal benefit. Satan tried. (Isaiah 14:14).

When Simon tried to buy this power for his life, Peter told him, *"Thou art in the gall of bitterness, and in the bond of iniquity"* (Acts 8:23).

Now, God wants to have the liberty to work through believers to accomplish great and mighty things.

In order for this to happen, I must draw nigh to God (James 4:8). I must present myself as a living sacrifice (Romans 12:1). I must yield myself as an instrument of righteousness (Romans 6:13).

This will lead to personal victory, personal influence, and change the atmosphere around me.

MAY 17
Pressing toward the Mark

We do not believe that sinless perfection is possible in the flesh, but that still should be our goal.

Pressing and striving to reach the level of spirituality spoken of by Jesus when He said, *"I do always the things that please him"* (John 8:29) was undoubtedly what the Apostle Paul was making reference to when he said, *"I press toward the mark, for he prize of the high calling of God in Christ Jesus"* (Phil. 3:14).

We are predestined to be conformed to the image of his Son (Romans 8:29) and will eventually reach that goal. While struggling with our Adamic nature we will experience a lot of failure; but if we are to be pleasing to the Lord, when we fall, we must get up, brush ourselves off, forget those things which are behind (Phil. 3:13), and set out to win next time.

The golfer must be trying to get a hole in one or at least an eagle. The bowler may have a split or even a gutter ball but he must be trying for a strike next time. The baseball player must not be satisfied unless he gets a home run.

Peter quotes the Lord saying, *"Be ye holy;* (perfect) *for I am holy"* (1 Peter 1:16). The writer of Hebrews admonishes us with the words, *"Let us go on unto perfection"* (Hebrews 6:1).

Comparing ourselves with others and excusing ourselves with the "Nobody's perfect" attitude will cause us to come short of what God wants for us, and what the Bible says is available to us.

Maybe our aim is not high enough. Someone has said, "If we aim at nothing, we will hit it every time." The mark is perfection, and if at first we don't succeed, try, try again.

MAY 18
See God through the Telescope

David wrote *"The heavens declare the glory of God"* in (Psalm 19:1). The inconceivable size of the universe and its amazing predictability tells us that God is behind it all.

Our sun is 93,000,000 miles from the earth. It is 866,000 miles in diameter or forty times that of earth. Betelgeuse is 215,000,000 miles in diameter and 248 times the size of our sun. Arcturus is 25,600 times the volume of the sun. Antares has a diameter of 400,000,000 or more than four times the distance of the sun from the earth.

Epsilon's diameter is ten times that of Betelgeuse or 2,150,000,000 miles. Light travels at the speed of 186,000 miles per second. If it were possible for a bullet to travel around the earth at the speed of light, the person who fired the gun would get hit 7½ times before he could jump out of the way.

Our galaxy is so huge that it would take 100,000 years for light to travel from one edge of our galaxy to the other. Our galaxy has over 100 billion stars (suns), and some scientists estimate that there are over 500 billion to a trillion galaxies similar to our Milky Way.

The Lord said to Abraham, *"Look now toward heaven, and tell the stars, if thou be able to number them"* (Genesis 15:5). Jeremiah said, *"As the hosts of heaven cannot be numbered, neither can the sand of the sea be measured"* (Jeremiah 33:22). Isaiah said, *"It is he that sitteth upon the circle of the earth,... [and] that stretcheth out the heavens as a curtain. Lift up your eyes on high, and behold who hath created these things, that bringeth out their host by number; he calleth them all by names, by the greatness of his might for that he is strong in power; not one faileth"* (Isaiah 40:22-26).

MAY 19
See God Through the Microscope

David not only spoke of the heavens declaring the glory of God, but he also talked of the firmament showing His handiwork (Psalm 19:1). Some see God in the vastness of creation while others are impressed with the infinite smallness of the other worlds that can be seen through a microscope.

Most matter is made up of tiny building blocks called molecules. If all the molecules in a teaspoon full of water were grains of sand, we could build a highway six lanes wide from New York City to San Francisco.

Molecules are made of even smaller units called atoms. An atom is five thousandths of one millionth of an inch. Atoms consist of protons, electrons, and neutrons. The electrons are whirling around the neutrons millions of times per second.

Inside these are dozens of particles made up of infinite universes called peons. Inside these are even smaller universes called positrons, then down inside these are neutrinos, then mesons, then antiparticles, and subatomic worlds.

Scientists have been able to detect little infinitesimal planetary systems inside these infinite units fifteen levels down. They use terms such as one thousandth of a millionth of a millionth of an atom. All these little universes have design, order, and predictability.

God put this all into motion when He created the earth and set into motion all the laws that keep it all together and in motion.

Paul explained, *"For by him were all things created, that are in heaven, and that are in earth, visible and invisible, whether they be thrones, or dominions, or principalities, or powers: all things were created by him, and for him"* (Col. 1:16).

MAY 20
See God Through the Stethoscope

A study of the unique and miraculous functions of the various parts of the human body will cause any honest person to say with David, *"I will praise thee; for I am fearfully and wonderfully made: marvelous are thy works; and that my soul knoweth right well"* (Psalm 139:14).

Dr. Peter Steincrohn says it well: "Our body is the world's most incredible piece of machinery." It manufactures, improves, and repairs itself. It is an intricate assembly of thousands of mechanisms working together in synchronized obedience to direction. Our body contains trillions of living cells.

Each cell contains a DNA count that would take 100 volumes of 500 pages each to describe. These same cells have 46 chromosomes, except for the reproduction cells that have only 23. The male sperm with 23 chromosomes joins the female egg with 23 and a new life begins.

Each cell also contains from 3,000 to 30,000 genes that are called "seeds of inheritance." These genes determine the color of our eyes, hair, height, weight, etc.

Our eyes are really television cameras constantly recording everything we see in color and sending it to the brain for storage.

Our ear drums are miniature grand pianos. The sounds we hear vibrate off the strings and send them to our brain for interpretation and storage in the memory.

Our heart is the most efficient pump in the world.

Our liver performs over 500 different functions.

A study of our lungs, and the 30,000 miles of telephone wires called nerves, thousands of miles of plumbing called blood vessels, the many yards of living skin that acts as an air conditioning system, and then the human mind are just a few of the miracle-working parts of the body.

It is believed that the 10 billion brain cells can contain more information than the nine billion volumes in the Library of Congress.

It surely would take more faith to believe that this all came about through an evolutionary process than the Biblical statement, *"So God created man in his own image"* (Genesis 1:27).

MAY 21
See God Through the Periscope

Who made the oceans? Who shut up the sea with doors? David wrote, *"The sea is his and he made it:"* (Psalm 95:5). We also read in Job where God asks *"who shut up the seas when they brake forth...?"* (Job 38:1,4,8)

Where did all the water come from? Three fourths of the earth is covered with water. If it were all leveled out, the earth would be 1½ miles under water. Although the ocean averages 2 miles in depth, the land above the water averages ½ mile in height.

In a cubic mile of sea water there is $93,000,000 worth of gold and $8,500,000 in silver, plus 7 tons of uranium and 5 grams of radium.

A cubic mile of sea water, according to the Dow chemical company, contains at least five billion dollars-worth of chemicals.

Imagine the value of the fish, crabs, oysters, and the lobsters put there by God for the good of mankind. Surely someone planned the currents and tides that help maintain heat and cold.

To keep the fish alive and the water healthy, the Lord has set three cycles into motion.

First the food cycle with more plankton growing than grain on the land surface of the world.

Then the oxygen cycle providing necessary oxygen for the thousands of varieties of sea life. Plankton takes in carbon dioxide and gives off oxygen.

Third is the phosphate cycle. Fish get their calcium for bones from the plankton, and when the fish die, they drift to the bottom where the phosphate is absorbed back into the soil to feed the plankton again. *"Oh Lord, how manifold are thy works!"* (Psa. 104:24).

MAY 22
See God in the Deep

The Psalmist said, *"These see the works of the Lord, and his wonders in the deep."* (Psalm 107:24)

The vast world of the depths of the sea is as strange as another planet. It is a world of total darkness, eternal cold, and enormous pressure.

Charles Thompson remarked, "It is almost as hard to imagine life existing in these conditions as in fire. Some of the fish in these deep sea valleys have telescope eyes set on long stalks. Others are equipped with headlights like a car, and they have the ability to turn them off and on at will. One species have little lanterns hanging below their eyes. The electric eel is equipped with a generating apparatus that produces electric current up to 500 volts several times each minute.

Those who view these undersea gardens through glass bottom boats look upon a fairyland of sea flowers, unbelievable coral formations, and strange fish that one would not believe if he did not see for himself.

A study of the seahorse with its head of a stallion, tail of a monkey, power of a chameleon to change color, eyes that pivot independently as it scans the surface with one and the action in the water beneath it with the other, and kangaroo-like pouch for little ones will cause one to believe that somebody put that together.

The male seahorse carries between 300 and 600 eggs in the pouch until they are born. The thousand kinds of fish in the sea and every type of marine life is especially adapted to its own environment and to the place in the scheme of things the Creator assigned to it.

"Bless the LORD, all his works in all places of his dominion" (Psalm 103:22).

MAY 23
See God Through the Gyroscope

Ships and planes are equipped with gyroscopes for balance. In the natural world God has instituted the principle of balance into creation.

Dr. Fred Meldau stated, "The perfect balance and universal interdependence of all life on earth witness to the superintendence of a master mind."

Checks and counterchecks keep things in balance. Bats and birds keep insects in check. Large fish eat small fish by the hundreds. Hawks keep down the mice population. If all the offspring of a single pair of house flies lived to mature and reproduce, the earth would be blanketed beneath a layer of flies 50 feet deep in six months. The Lord has worked that problem out by giving the toad an appetite for flies. One toad will eat 30 flies an hour. A giant frog was observed snapping up mosquitoes, fifty per minute. A swallow will devour as many as 2,000 mosquitoes per

117

day. Field mice have six or seven litters a year and average ten mice per litter. Fortunately for us, mice have a lot of enemies such as foxes, coyotes, badgers, skunks, weasels, wildcats, hawks, owls, lizards, ravens, snakes, and barn cats. A barn owl has been called "a living mouse trap."

A codfish will release 4,000,000 eggs in a season, an oyster 1,000,000, and a sunfish 300,000,000. All kinds of fish and sea creatures eat these eggs by the hundreds or the ocean would fill up within a short time.

Animals as well as human beings breathe in oxygen and exhale carbon dioxide, while green plants take in carbon dioxide and give off oxygen. David said *"Be ye not as the horse, or as the mule"* (Psalm 32:9). The mule is stubborn while the horse is jumpy and quick. There must be balance in our action as well as our reaction.

MAY 24
See God Through Your Eyes

Next to the brain, the eye is the most wonderful of all God's gifts to His creatures.

All of the more than 38,000 vertebrate animals known to zoologists, 4,000 mammals, 14,000 birds, 4,000 reptiles, 2,000 amphibians, and 14,000 fish are born with functional camera-type eyes. Even the invertebrates including spiders, crabs, centipedes, and millipedes all have eyes.

Hawks and eagles can see the slightest movement in the grass far below where they are soaring in the air. The big eyes of the owl are designed to see at night.

One type of water beetle has eyes that can see above the water and below the water at the same time. The alligator can be completely hidden in the river except for two small eyes protruding out to observe everything going on.

Camels have built-in wind glasses to keep out the blowing sand. Snakes have no eyelids but they have a permanent shield covering. The compound eye of the dragonfly has 30,000 facets to enable it to catch insects on the wing. Grasshoppers have two separate eyes each with thousands of lenses and three smaller ones totaling five. Crayfish and lobsters have eyes on stalks. The pupil of the human eye adjusts to darkness and light. Starfish have an eye in the end of each of its five points. The eye of the pigmy shrew is the size of the head of a pin, but it is identical and functions the same way the grapefruit-sized eye of the great blue whale. The kingfisher has a double set of eyes. They catch insects in the air, then dive into the sea and catch fish.

Anyone not blinded by the god of this world will be able to see the handiwork of God in the marvel of the eye.

MAY 25
See God in the Singing of the Birds

"And God created...every winged fowl after his kind: and God saw that it was good" (Genesis 1:21).

Every bird has a song, and each has its own place in the orchestra. One mockingbird was observed imitating 32 different species of songbirds over a ten-minute period. Who fashioned the throat of this one bird so that it might produce over one hundred types of other bird sounds?

There are 10,000 different species of birds, each with its own distinct sound and characteristics. The law of regularity and variety in creation is applied here. All of them are birds but no two are alike.

John Burroughs tells us that the bobolink expresses hilarity; the sparrow's song, faith; the bluebirds, love; the catbird, pride; the flycatcher, self-conscientiousness; the hermit thrush, serenity; and the robin, a military call. The house wren bubbles with emotion.

Dr. Lee Roberson preached a sermon entitled, "A Thousand Preachers for Every Sinner." He pointed out that every cemetery, every salvage yard, sunrise, and sunset, and even a blade of grass has a message from God.

This is especially true of the bird and his song. *"He that hath an ear, let him hear what the Spirit saith unto the churches"* (Rev. 2:11).

One author wrote, "The cardinal with its clear vibrant whistling has all the free spirit of a comely boy on his way to the swimming hole."

That may be the reason why I was so excited when I looked out our kitchen window at the tree in my back yard and counted 24 beautiful cardinals perched near our feeder. What a way to start a day and a year!

Even the caged canary has a cheerful song.

MAY 26
Bible Invitations

How wonderful it is to see a picture of Jesus with outstretched hands inviting people to come to Him in time of need. Our Bible is filled with invitations from the Lord.

To Noah He said, *"Come thou and all thy house into the ark"* (Genesis 7:1).

Moses invited his father-in-law to *"Come thou with us and we will do thee good."* (Numbers 10:29)

Isaiah said, *"Come now and let us reason together"* (Isaiah 1:18). Then again, *"Ho, every one that thirsteth, come ye to the waters, and he that hath no money; come ye, buy, and eat"* (Isaiah 55:1).

On one occasion Jesus told of a King who said, *"all things are ready: come unto the marriage"* (Matthew 22:4). To the sinner the Lord says come for redemption: *"Come; for all things are now ready"* (Luke 14:17). The debt has been paid. All the details have been cared for.

To the sinning saint He says, come for restoration: *"Come, and let us return unto the LORD: for he hath torn, and he will heal us; he hath smitten, and he will bind us up"* (Hosea 6:1). Like the prodigal son, the father is waiting with the robe and ring.

To the suffering saint He says, come for rest. *"Come unto me, all ye that labour and are heavy laden, and I will give you rest"* (Matthew 11:28). It is not a matter of working and bearing heavy burdens, but according to His mercy and grace are we able to enter into rest.

To the Saviour, we extend an invitation to return. *"Even so, come, Lord Jesus"* (Rev. 22:20). This is the answer to every question and the solution to all our problems. As one pastor used to say on his radio program, "Perhaps today."

MAY 27
Fake Flowers

An evangelist friend of mine tells of visiting in a home in Phoenix where a lady had been given a beautiful house plant by friends. She was careful each morning to set it in the sink and allow water to drip on to it for a few minutes. She had carefully nursed the plant for ten years.

One morning she put it in the sink, started the dripping, and got busy about other things. When she remembered she rushed to the sink to find the flower in the pot, but all the soil had washed away. She picked up the plant carefully and realized that it was an artificial flower. It looked so real she had watered it for ten years.

Churches are full of fake, hypocritical people who look like Christians, act like Christians, and go through all the motions. They have everybody fooled, even themselves, but not God. Someday they too will be found out.

Jesus spoke of this kind when He said, *"Howbeit in vain do they worship me, teaching for doctrines the commandments of men. For laying aside the commandment of God, ye hold the tradition of men, as the washing of pots and cups: and many other such like things ye do"* (Mark 7:7-8).

He also said, *"Not every one that saith unto me, Lord, Lord, shall enter into the kingdom of heaven; but he that doeth the will of my Father which is in heaven. Many will say to me in that day, Lord, Lord, have we not prophesied in thy name? and in thy name have cast out devils? and in thy name done many wonderful works? And then will I profess unto them, I never knew you: depart from me, ye that work iniquity"* (Matthew 7:21-23).

MAY 28
A Friend of the King

In four thousand years of history Zabud was mentioned just one time. We do not know if he was married, if he fathered any children, where he was born, or how long he lived. All we know is that, "he was the king's friend." The king was Solomon, the wisest, wealthiest and most successful man in the world. He is a type of Christ and Zabud was his very close friend.

To describe the characteristics of this man, we must use words like counselor, confidant, or comrade. To describe his qualities, words such as dependable, trustworthy, companion, loyal, defender, good, virtuous, moral, righteous, and advocate do not do him justice.

We must incorporate other descriptive phrases like one who encourages, one that supports, one that helps out in time of need, one who is there sometimes just to listen, one who loves me when I am unlovable, or the person who introduced me to Jesus.

One word sums up it all: **friend.**

Solomon may have had him in mind when he wrote, *"A man that hath friends must show himself friendly: and there is a friend that sticketh closer than a brother"* (Proverbs 18:24).

It is written that God and Moses conversed face to face as friends. (Exodus 33:11) Three times we are told that Abraham was a friend of God (2 Chronicles 20:7) (Isaiah 41:8) (James 2:23).

John wrote of Jesus, *"Greater love hath no man than this, that a man lay down his life for his friends"* (John 15:13). Jesus said, *"Ye are my friends, if ye do whatsoever I command you"* (John 15:14).

It would do us well to heed the words of Solomon, *"He that loveth pureness of heart, for the grace of his lips the king shall be his friend"* (Proverbs 22:11).

MAY 29
Holy Ground

When God appeared to Moses in the burning bush on the back side of a desert, He told him to take off his shoes because it was holy ground. I think when we read this account we have a tendency to think, what does this have to do with me in my time and my place? That was over four thousand years ago and thousands of miles away.

Paul tells us in 1 Corinthians 10:6, 11 that the things that happened to folks in the Old Testament was for our ensamples and our examples. This as well as all the stories, experiences, and happenings in the lives of Bible characters are recorded for our benefit.

He also wrote that, *"All scripture is given by inspiration of God, and is profitable for doctrine, reproof, for correction, for instruction in righteousness: that the man of God may be perfect, throughly furnished unto all good works."* (2 Tim. 3:16)

The times when God appeared to Abraham on Mount Moriah, to Jacob at Bethel, to Samuel in his bed chamber, to Saul on the road to Damascus, to Martha in her living room, were just as much holy ground as when He appeared in the bush.

Now, when we meet together in our church services, God is there too. Jesus said, *"For where two or three are gathered together in my name, there am I in the midst of them"* (Matthew 18:20). I am persuaded that none of these places were any more holy ground than a church service where more than two or three are gathered.

We ought to be able to feel His presence and hear Him speak to us in His still, small voice. A church service is a time to meet with God and never be the same.

MAY 30
Delivered from the Tribulation

Paul the Apostle explains that believers will be "caught up" together with other believers to be with the Lord and that we should comfort one another with his words (1 Thess. 4:17). We call that the "rapture."

He then tells us that a terrible time will follow that event called the tribulation period. He goes to great lengths to assure believers that they will escape the horror of that time. He writes, *"For God hath not appointed us to wrath, but to obtain salvation by our Lord Jesus Christ"* (1 Thess. 5:9).

At one time during that period, one third of the world's population will be killed. Later one fourth of the remaining population will die. John writing from the Isle of Patmos tells us, *"Because thou hast kept the word of my patience, I also will keep thee from the hour of temptation, which shall come upon all the world, to try them that dwell upon the earth"* (Rev. 3:10).

The tribulation period is referred to as "Jacob's Trouble." Jeremiah prophesied, *"Alas! for that day is great, so that none is like it: it is even the time of Jacob's trouble; but he shall be saved out of it"* (Jeremiah 30:7). Then Isaiah looked into the future several thousand years before and said, *"Come, my people, enter thou into thy chambers, and shut thy doors about thee: hide thyself as it were for a little moment, until the indignation be overpast"* (Isaiah 26:20).

It is during this seven-year period that the Antichrist will gain control of the earth and declare himself to be God. The world will see the fulfillment of humanism, secularism, and atheism. Then God will set up His kingdom and show the result of total obedience to His will.

MAY 31
Regarding Iniquity

The Psalmist gave clear warning that, *"If I regard iniquity in my heart, the Lord will not hear me"* (Psalms 66:18). Isaiah added, *"The Lord's hand is not shortened, that it cannot save; neither his ear heavy, that it cannot hear: But your iniquities have separated between you and your God, and your sins have hid his face* *from you, that he will not hear"* (Isaiah 59:1b-2). If God does not hear, then we do not get the things that we ask him for.

The word "regard" means to harbor or hold in place. When David saw Bathsheba without her clothes on, that was not a sin, but he allowed what he saw to affect his thinking causing him to lust and harbor what he saw in his heart and that led to the sin of adultery and then murder.

There was nothing wrong with Aachen seeing the gold, silver, and beautiful garments; but he coveted, he took, then he lied and died.

In both cases there was harboring and regarding. We cannot control what we see. Things appear suddenly on television screens and billboards. It is almost impossible not to hear vile talk and wickedness. It is everywhere. We cannot even prevent bad thoughts. Our thoughts are influenced from our exposure to the philosophies of Charles Darwin, Karl Marx, Plato, Aristotle, Socrates, John Dewey, and other secular humanists and atheists.

Then we cannot prevent wrong feelings. We are plagued with a fallen nature from our father Adam. What can we do then about these things? As Barney on the Andy Griffith show said, "Nip it in the bud." Martin Luther told his preacher boys, "You will not be able to keep the birds from flying over your head, but you can keep them from building a nest in your hair."

"Commit thy way unto the Lord:...and he shall bring it to pass" (Psalm 37:5).

JUNE 1
Infinite Versus Finite

"Eye hath not seen, nor ear heard, neither have entered into the heart of man, the things which God hath prepared for them that love him" (1 Cor. 2:9).

How do we grasp words like unlimited, almighty, exhaustless, never-ending, omnipotent, omniscient, and omnipresent? These words are inconceivable to our human mind. We are talking about the "unthinkable."

Paul told of going to heaven and seeing things not lawful for him to talk about. Even for one who spoke seventeen languages, there were not enough words or phrases in his vocabulary to describe the "indescribable" things he saw.

We read that the love of God is "measureless." The Bible speaks of the breadth, length, depth, and height of God's love that "passeth knowledge." Then we read of a peace that "passeth understanding," or unimaginable peace. What about "joy unspeakable" and "full of glory"?

We are promised "inconceivable" answers to prayer. He promises "to do exceeding, abundant, above all that we ask or think." (Ephesians 2:10) That would be "unlimited wealth." Paul uses the term, "unsearchable riches in Christ Jesus." The Lord promises to open up the windows of heaven and pour out "unlimited blessings" upon us that we will not be able to receive.

When Jacob asked God what His name was, God asked, "Why do you ask my name?" He was saying the world would not contain the books that would have to be written for Him to tell Jacob His name.

Isaiah touched on this and said, "His name shall be called 'wonderful,' 'counselor,' 'mighty God,' 'prince of peace,' 'everlasting father.' " In our glorified bodies we will know as we are known, and we will be able to see, hear, feel and know it all.

JUNE 2
Cry In The Night

Paul Myers sat down in the wharf pilings along the San Diego waterfront and shivered in the cold. He reflected on his life, his Christian mother, his success in business, and his beautiful family.

His family and money had vanished because of his sinful life, and he had wandered all that night in a drunken stupor. Though a young man, Paul Myers was at the "end of the line."

The clanging of a ship's bell and the cry of a ship's watch startled him, "Eight bells and all's well!" The time was 4:00 a.m. on a Sunday morning, and soon families would be going to church. Paul Meyer was filled with a desire to hear the preaching of God's Word, so he made his way to a church.

That morning he found no welcome among the well-dressed members, and no one even spoke to him. The sermon did not mention the Saviour who could rescue a bitter and broken man. The answer he needed was not found in the formal service that morning.

Meyers went back to his cheap hotel, a desolate man. Noticing a Gideon Bible, he began to read, and God's Word touched his heart. Paul Meyers was saved and his life was changed. The Lord allowed Meyer the second chance he so wanted. From destitution he became a thriving evangelist and used his talent to begin a radio program.

Dr. Russell Dennis remembers hearing on the radio the fog horn, the clanking bell, and the voice ring out, "Eight bells…and all's well!" as the Haven of Rest radio program began. Known as "First Mate Bob", Paul Myers took the words he had heard on a desolate morning, and used them to share the love of Christ to millions for 37 years.

JUNE 3
She Quit Her Beer

On a flight from California, a woman sat down in the seat beside me, buckled her seat belt, and remarked, "Boy, I sure hate to go home."

"Where's home?" I asked.

"Arab, Alabama," she stated.

"Why would you hate to go home?" I enquired further.

"Because," she blurted out, "I've been in California burying my husband; and now I have to go home to an empty house. It's going to be weird," she continued, "I don't know how I'm going to handle it."

"It doesn't have to be that way," I told her. When she asked why, I explained that I had buried my wife, and Mary had buried her husband, and when we got home from the funerals it was not strange and awful.

When I explained that we both had Jesus in our hearts and that He was right there with us; and His presence gave us comfort and helped us in a tremendous way.

"Maybe that's what I need," she said. The stewardess interrupted us to ask if we wanted a beverage. I asked for a Coke, Mary asked for Sprite, and she ordered a beer. As I began to explain how to get Jesus into her life, she asked for another beer, and before I got around to helping her pray, she ordered a third one.

I was about to get discouraged; but I thought if she gets about half drunk, it will be easier for her. I gave her the gospel and offered to pray with her. She prayed a simple prayer and with tears running down her cheeks, she said, "Amen," then stated, "Maybe I ought not to be drinking this beer."

Praise the Lord I believe she got in.

JUNE 4
Not As Tough As We Thought

In one of the large cities of South Carolina, Richard Brown had retired from his twenty years in the military, and now he was Chief of Police. He not only looked and sounded tough, he was tough. The crooks in that town stayed clear of Richard, if they could.

Several of the men in the church where I was preaching had attempted to win him to Christ, but that just didn't fit into his life style or macho image. Now, he was lying flat on his back in a hospital bed and facing surgery for cancer in one of his glands. One of his friends called and asked me to visit him and try to win him to the Lord.

I spent some time in prayer about the matter and drove to the hospital and approached his room with some apprehension. To my complete surprise, he was receptive and very responsive. His shell and toughness was gone. In fact big tears welled up in his eyes when I told him I was concerned about him and wanted to be sure he was saved.

He listened intently as I led him through the verses that explained that he was a sinner, that he was on his way to hell, that Jesus died on the cross to pay for his sin, and that if he would turn the whole matter over to Christ and invite Him into his heart, he would be saved. He did just that.

The outer shell had been laid aside and a tender and caring man readily opened his heart and received Christ as his personal Saviour. The grip of his handshake as I was leaving told me he was really serious in his decision. He wasn't as tough as we thought.

JUNE 5
Sometimes Dead Men Live

Glen Tomlinson was having a drug problem. He was also mending from back surgery and had not gone back to work yet.

He decided to take a vacation trip to Florida and that helped him to see that the grass was not any greener on the other side. He headed back home to Louisville, Kentucky. Now that he was back home with his live-in girlfriend, things had gone from bad to worse.

They were both feeling guilty about living in sin. That's when some of our bus workers stopped by and told them that things could be better for them. After chatting with them for a while about the peace they could have if they would get things right with the Lord, they promised to come to church. And they did. Our bus captain was happy to see them ready for the ride to church the next morning.

They and were back again on Sunday night. The gospel message did it's work. They were both saved and both of them followed the Lord in baptism.

When Glen called long distance to let his mother know about his decision to trust in the Lord, she sobbed out, "Glen, this can't be; you're supposed to be dead!" He assured her that he was very much alive.

While in Florida, Glen had been mugged. His wallet was taken. In a later robbery attempt, the mugger was shot and killed by a policeman. When the police found Glen's identification, they called his mother.

The dead had come back to life in more ways than one. Jesus said, *"I am the resurrection and the life: he that believeth in me, though he were dead, yet shall he live"* (John 11:25).

JUNE 6
Seniors and Prisoner Swap

Let's consider putting our senior citizens in jail, and the criminals in a nursing home. This way the seniors would have access to showers, hobbies, and walks; they would receive unlimited free prescriptions, dental and medical treatment, wheelchairs etc; and they would receive money instead of paying it out.

They would have constant video monitoring, so they could be helped instantly if they fell or needed assistance. Bedding would be washed twice a week, and all clothing would be ironed and returned to them.

A guard would check on them every 20 minutes, and bring their meals and snacks to their cell. They would have family visits in a suite built for that purpose.

They would have access to a library, weight room, spiritual counseling, pool, and education. Simple clothing, shoes, slippers, P.J.'s and legal aid would be free on request.

Private, secure rooms would be available for all, with an outdoor exercise yard and gardens. Each senior could have a P.C., a T.V., radio, and daily phone calls.

There would be a board of directors to hear complaints, and the guards would have a code of conduct that would be strictly adhered to.

The "criminals" would get cold food, be left all alone, and unsupervised. Their lights turned off at 8 p.m., showers once a week, live in a tiny room, and pay $5000.00 per month, and have no hope of ever getting out. Justice for all.

When the Bible with its spiritual wisdom is ruled out and is replaced with secular humanistic thinking in our society, the inmates begin to run the asylum. It will be wonderful when the Lord sets up His Millennial kingdom on earth and shows mankind how things could have been in any one of the other six dispensations.

JUNE 7
Policeman's Grandmother

While driving into our small town, I noticed a policeman pulling in behind me with his blue light flashing. I knew I had not violated any law and wondered what this was all about. He got out of his squad car and walked slowly up to my car and politely introduced himself to me. I was ready to show him my driver's license.

"Good morning, Reverend," he smiled and said, "my grandmother is over at the local hospital. I wonder if you would go over there and win her to the Lord Jesus for me." At that time I had a radio broadcast and told conversion stories each day. Undoubtedly that policeman had heard some of these stories and thought maybe I could help his grandmother.

"I certainly will," I answered. I drove straight to the hospital and found his grandmother. She was a typical white-haired lady with a beautiful smile.

I explained that her grandson had told me about her being in the hospital and that he was concerned about her. I then explained the simple story of the gospel. She was very receptive. In just a few moments, she put her faith and trust in the Saviour. I was glad that officer knew that I was a soul winner.

I thought to myself, "What a wonderful thing it would be if everybody in town knew that I was a soul-winner. It would be great to be called on to go win someone's loved one to Christ."

The Bible says in Daniel 12:3, *"[those] that be wise shall shine as the brightness of the firmament; and they that turn many to righteousness as the stars for ever and* ever" In Proverbs 11:30, the Bible says *"the fruit of the righteous is a tree of life, and he that winneth souls is wise"*.

JUNE 8
What If Everyone Tithed

In James E. Carter's book on stewardship, he tells of a small town Baptist church of many years past which had an amazing experience along the line of what happens when everyone tithes.

The day came when their long-time church treasurer resigned. The church then asked the local grain elevator manager to take the position. He agreed under two conditions: First, no treasurer's report would be given until the end of the first year, and, second that no questions be asked about finances during that year.

Since most of them did business with him and knew that he was a highly trusted man, they agreed and he assumed the job. At the end of his first year as church treasurer, he gave his report: The church indebtedness of $228,000 had been paid in full. The minister's salary had been increased by 8%. The missionary giving had been increased by 200%. There were no outstanding bills, and there was a cash balance of $11,252!

Immediately the shocked congregation asked, "How did you do it? Where did the money come from?" He quietly answered: "Most of you bring your grain to my elevator. Throughout the year I simply, without your knowledge, withheld ten percent on your behalf and gave it to the church in your name. You didn't even miss it! Do you see what we could do for the Lord if we were all willing to give at least the tithe to God?"

And so the new treasurer had made his point. It would be well for all Christians to realize that God's law of sowing and reaping is involved in the Bible plan of tithing and giving offerings. *"For whatsoever a man soweth, that shall he also reap"* (Galatians 6:7).

JUNE 9
Lessons from a Blowout

While traveling at seventy miles per hour on I-24 through Chattanooga, Tennessee, we were startled by a loud noise that sounded like a gun shot.

The car started to vibrate, so I quickly maneuvered between two tractor trailers and pulled over on the shoulder to check out the blowout of one of my rear tires.

We could easily have been killed in the heavy traffic. I thought of the surprise of the incident. There are so many of them in life, including death. Just a few weeks ago three of my friends, who were only forty five-years old dropped over dead of heart attacks.

Enoch and Elijah were the only two exceptions. Then there was the suddenness of it all. It happened so quick. So many go out to meet God without a lot of notice. In most cases there is no time to prepare.

Then it was a very scary thing. We could easily have been crushed between the big trucks. Just today the news told of twenty-nine people being killed in a truck and bus crash in India. I was glad that our situation was so easily resolved.

I simply called AAA, and in thirty minutes a man came, changed the tire, accepted the tract and five-dollar tip that I gave him, and we were on our way home.

Because I was prepared both spiritually and otherwise, it was no big deal. The prophet Amos warns, *"Prepare to meet thy God"* (Amos 4:12).

Preparing for death as well for unseen circumstances is a mark of wisdom. Even Boy Scouts are taught a motto, "Be prepared." Solomon warned, *"Thou knowest not what a day may bring forth"* (Proverbs 27:1). Felix never found the convenient season he was hoping for.

JUNE 10
A Child's Question

Once a child was ready to be born. So he asked, "Lord, they tell me you are sending me to earth tomorrow; but how am I going to live there being so small and helpless?"

"I chose an angel for you. She will be waiting for you and will take care of you."

"But tell me, Here in Heaven, I don't do anything else but sing and smile; that's enough for me to be happy."

"Your angel will sing for you and will also smile for you. And you will feel your angel's love and be happy."

"And how am I going to be able to understand when people talk to me, if I don't understand the language that they talk?"

"Your angel will tell you the most beautiful and sweet words that you will ever hear; and with much patience and care, your angel will teach you how to speak."

"And what am I going to do when I want to talk to you?"

"Your angel will place your hands together and will teach you how to pray."

"I've heard that on earth there are bad men. Who will protect me?"

"Your angel will protect you even if it means risking her life."

"But I will always be sad because I will not see you anymore."

"Your angel will always talk to you about me and will teach you the way for you to come back to me."

At that moment voices from earth could already be heard, and the child, in a hurry asked softly, "Oh God, if I am about to leave now, please tell me my angel's name."

"You will call your angel: Mommy."

Just a note to encourage you to let your mom know how much you appreciate her.

JUNE 11
It Was A Dream

I pulled into the parking lot of a restaurant. I was the only one parked in my area. I was driving a borrowed vehicle. When I came out, a fellow was sitting in the car next to mine.

My vehicle had smashed into the side of the other car and had a lot of damage. The driver approached and asked about insurance and identity. He had called the police. In a moment a lawyer showed up. I wasn't sure whether the ministry that owned the car was insured.

I was scheduled to be in a meeting shortly. The frustration began to build. I could tell that my blood pressure was getting above a safe level. How could bad things like this happen to a good fellow like me?

Then, suddenly I woke up; I was dreaming! What a relief, to awake and find everything was fine. As I began to thank the Lord that none of this had happened, a beautiful thought came to me.

One day soon, I will awake and be in the presence of the Lord and have my glorified body. I thought of the song: "Just think of stepping on shore and finding it Heaven."

I'll be able to leave behind glasses, false teeth, hearing aids, razors, toothbrushes, and such. I'll be happy to kiss my blood pressure medication goodbye, and dump out all those bottles of vitamins.

I won't need my books, and I will know as I am known or have perfect understanding of all things. *"Eye hath not seen, nor ear heard, neither have entered into the heart of man, the things which God hath prepared for them that love him"* (1 Cor. 2:9).

JUNE 12
Exception to the Rule

It is rare when a person in his seventy or eighties gets saved. When one is saved at ninety-three, most will agree, that is a miracle.

Mable Kline was educated and healthy, had taught school most of her life, and was now living in a retirement home in Kansas.

When she fell and broke her hip, she wanted to die. Mable told her grandson Chris that she did not believe in God or the Bible. Chris took me to see her.

I sat down on her bed and said, "Mable, Chris tells me that you are an unbeliever." She said, "That's right."

I told her that I was going to read her a verse from the Bible. I read, *"But the fearful, and unbelieving, and the abominable, and murderers, and whoremongers, and sorcerers, and idolaters, and all liars, shall have their part in the lake which burneth with fire and brimstone: which is the second death."* (Rev. 21:8).

I explained to her that she was listed right along with a horrible bunch of people and that all of them were going to be cast into the lake of fire and she was in bad trouble. I told her I was going to pray for her and asked if that would be allright with her. She said it would.

I prayed, then asked her to follow me in prayer. After every phrase of the prayer she said, "yes, yes, yes." She never would say anything but, "yes."

A few days later she told Chris that she wanted to join his church. Chris told her, she must have her faith in Jesus first. She said, "I do have my faith in Jesus, and I believe." She died just a few days later.

JUNE 13
No Way You Can Live It!

A preacher friend recently told of his teenage daughter who caused everybody to be late for school and work, because her hair refused to cooperate and then she slipped and fell, and got a run in her hose, and sent her books flying in five different directions.

When she finally did get in the car, she said to her preacher Daddy, "I don't care what you preach, I don't care what you think, I don't care what the Bible says, there is no way you can live the Christian life." Her Dad smiled and lovingly answered, "You are exactly right! There is no way you can do it!" He continued, "But, you can let Christ live His life through you."

Many times I have made the statement to my congregations, "God is not at all interested in what you or I will go out and do for Him today. He is interested in what we will allow Him to do through us. Since He knows all things and understands everything about everyone and about everything, He can do a much better job than we can."

This is the difference between the natural and the supernatural. Paul explained, *"I am crucified with Christ: nevertheless I live; yet not I, but Christ liveth in me"* (Galatians 2:20). He also said, *"Christ in you, the hope of glory"* (Colossians 1:27). He has. He can. And he will live his life through us if we give it to him and let him be in control. Why not *"present your bodies a living sacrifice, holy, acceptable unto God, which is your reasonable service"* (Romans 12:1). John explains it this way, *"He must increase, but I must decrease"* (John 3:30).

JUNE 14
Where Is Zebedee?

Where is Zebedee? We wouldn't know who Zebedee is or anything about him if it weren't for his sons James and John Zebedee, and Mrs. Zebedee who pleaded for Jesus to allow her two boys to sit on the right and left side of His throne.

James Zebedee became the pastor of the church at Jerusalem and was the first martyr. John Zebedee was chosen to write 50 chapters of the Bible.

These two fellows were insiders with Jesus. They were on the Mount of Transfiguration with Him, they were in the fishing boat, they were in the Garden of Gethsemane, and they were both at Calvary.

John was at the grave of the Lord, and I am sure they are both in heaven with the Lord right now, but where was Zebedee? He was too busy mending his nets! When his sons left their nets and followed Jesus, he stayed and kept the business open.

There is nothing wrong with mending nets. There is nothing wrong with owning a boat. There is nothing wrong with going fishing, or a dozen other similar things; but these things kept Zebedee from meeting Jesus. Zebedee never got to see Jesus work miracles.

He never got to hear Him preach. He missed out on the Mount of Transfiguration experience and the raising of Jarius's daughter. He was not there when Jesus hung on the cross. He never looked into the empty tomb. He missed all that because he was too busy mending his nets.

Where is Zebedee? He just might be suffering in torment at this very moment because he was too occupied with his nets. He might be saying, "I wish I had given Him more."

I hope you won't let that happen to you!

JUNE 15
You Can Go to Heaven When You Die

What must one do to be saved?

What a question that is! Men and women have been asking that question for thousands of years and hundreds of answers have been given in reply.

Some say you must keep the ten commandments, live right, do the best you can, join the church, be baptized, do unto others as you would have them do unto you, pay your honest debts, treat your neighbor right, and dozens of other well-meaning things.

When the hardened jail-keeper at Philippi asked his prisoners, Paul and Silas, how to be saved, they gave a very simple answer. *"Believe on the Lord Jesus Christ, and thou shalt be saved"* (Acts 16:31).

They did not suggest that he stop doing bad things, start doing good things, be baptized, or join some church. They simply asked the jail keeper to put the matter into the hands of the Lord Jesus and trust Him to take care of it for him.

The jailer did just that and was saved there on the spot! His family also put their trust in the Lord, and they too were saved then and there. *"For by grace are ye saved through faith; and that not of yourselves: it is the gift of God: Not of works, lest any man should boast"* (Ephesians 2:8-9).

How important it is to keep the matter very simple and not add a whole lot of things to what the Bible teaches. It is not what I think, or what you think, or what someone else thinks, it is what the Bible says that will settle this matter for us.

John warns us in the book of Revelation that it is a serious matter to add to or take away from what the Bible says (Rev. 22:18-19).

JUNE 16
The Tumbleweed

Dr. Kenny McComas tells of a weed in South America that compares to the tumbleweed in the prairie lands of North America.

When the ground becomes too dry to support life it loosens its roots and frees itself to roll wherever the wind may take it. If it finds a little moisture, it hesitates there and puts down its roots and absorbs what it can. When that spot becomes dry, it pulls up its roots and rolls on. Most of its lifetime is spent searching for water and it seldom comes upon an area that will give permanent satisfaction.

The dry surface of the world system is like that. People go from experience to experience, job to job, from one mate to another trying to find happiness. Many try alcohol, drugs, sex, pleasure and such, but never seem to find it. Paul speaks of being carried about by every wind of doctrine. The various religions of the world and humanistic philosophies of self-seeking people never provide peace and satisfaction.

Paul also said, *"I have learned, in whatsoever state I am, therewith to be content"* (Phil. 4:11). Paul tried searching in the office of the Pharisee, in the political pursuit, and in striving for financial success, but to no avail.

He found what he was looking for in Christ. His values were changed, and he put down his roots in a Biblical relationship with the Lord. He gives some unique advice to those who are searching and seeking. *"Be careful* (anxious) *for nothing; but in every thing by prayer and supplication with thanksgiving let your requests be made known unto God. And the peace of God, which passeth all understanding, shall keep your hearts and minds through Christ Jesus"* (Phil. 4:6).

JUNE 17
He Quit Making Moonshine

Jessie Poindexter went fishing in Kentucky. His kinsfolk all live in that area. He got to thinking about the need to do some different kind of fishing while he was there so he reeled in his line, loaded his gear into the pickup, and headed off toward his uncle's house.

His uncle, now 87 years old, still worked with his mule and milked his cows. They did small talk for a while. Uncle Joe confessed to Jessie, "I just can't seem to turn out near as much work as I used to."

He got a new mule and just in case the mule decided to throw him off, he took him behind some trees and got on him. The new mule worked as good as the old one he'd worn out. Finally, Jessie got him in his pickup and asked him if he was going to heaven when he died.

"Oh, I quit 'makin' moonshine a long time ago," declared Uncle Joe. "I don't even drink the stuff anymore," he said, "and I got all my debts paid, too. Don't see no reason why I wouldn't."

He confessed that he didn't know anything about "getting saved" or being "born again." He couldn't remember any time when he had "accepted Christ as his Saviour."

Jessie took his Bible and slowly, deliberately explained how to settle things with God and get his sin covered and get Jesus in his heart. The old man invited Jesus into his heart.

He told Jessie, "I've really wanted to do that for a long time."

He's been in heaven for a long time now. There must be a lot more folks out there who would like to do that, too.

JUNE 18
It's the Fruit

During a recent election we kept hearing the brazen statement, "It's the economy, stupid." At our house, we taught the children not to call people stupid, dummy, and etc.

That phrase however drives home their point. In the book of Proverbs, Solomon said, *"The fruit of the righteous is a tree of life; and he that winneth souls is wise"* (Proverbs 11:30). The accent of this pointed proverb is that it is the fruit, dear friend. That is the main business.

The root of the tree is also vital and very important but who cares about the root? We say, "Out of sight, out of mind." We could care less about the trunk of the tree. Then what about the branch, or the limbs, or the leaves, or the blossoms, or the sap in the tree, or the bark on the tree? We have no mention of the bees that pollinate the blossoms, or the sunshine and the rain that is absolutely necessary to getting fruit.

All these parts of the tree and nature are essential and vital to producing fruit, but none of these are the main business. It's the fruit we are interested in.

It is not the buildings, the pews, the music, the offerings, the attendance, the sports program, the deacons, the ushers, the Sunday School, the teachers, the buses, the radio program, the bulletins, the choir, or any other of the many things we are involved in around the church that the Lord is the most interested in. It is the precious souls of men that Jesus died for. He died for sinners, not buildings or programs. Let's keep the main thing the main thing. It's the fruit, dear friend. Let's go get them.

JUNE 19
Confidence in My Dad

A group of botanists went on an expedition in the Alps. They were searching for new varieties of flowers. One day one of these scientists, looking through his binoculars spotted a rare species of flower growing at the bottom of a deep ravine far below. To reach this flower, someone would have to be lowered down into that ravine.

There was a local youth who was tagging along out of curiosity seeing what these scientists were up to. The scientists asked the boy if he would be willing to help them. He was small, light, and could easily be lowered down to take some samples of that special flower. He was told that they would wrap a rope around him and all these men would have a hold of the rope and lower him down to the bottom of ravine to get the flowers. They tried to assure him not to worry and that he would be safe. The boy was excited but was very apprehensive.

He looked over the edge and thought, "Man, that is really pretty far down there." He was kind of scared to do what they asked and said, "If you'll wait, I'll be right back," and ran off leaving all the men standing there with cameras in hand.

When he returned, he had an older man with him. Approaching the head botanist, he said I am ready to go over the edge now, but this man MUST hold the rope.

The botanist looked at him and said, "Who is he?" "He is my dad." That boy had confidence in his dad to hold that rope. He knew his dad would never ever let it go. He didn't have confidence in the other men, but his dad was his dad!

JUNE 20
Priority in Praying

"I exhort therefore, that, first of all, supplications, prayers, intercessions, and giving of thanks, be made for all men" (I Timothy 2:1).

After a serious and solemn plea, *"I exhort therefore,"* Paul gives a strong word on the priority of the need, *"first of all."* He then pinpoints the focus of our energy in prayer, *"for Kings and for all that are in authority."* He next stresses the point of the matter, *"that we may lead a quiet and peaceable life;"* then he shows us the personal result of this; *"godliness and honesty."*

After his personal challenge on the importance of bathing every situation in prayer that will please God, the Apostle lays down some basics.

He emphasizes that God has first, a universal plan of salvation. He wants *"all men to be saved and to come unto the knowledge of the truth"* (v4) since Jesus is the Truth and the only way of salvation (John 14:6). He wants all men to come to Christ.

Second, he mentions the unscriptural philosophy of pluralism. Japan has thousands of gods, and India, millions. He makes it clear, *"There is one God, and one mediator between God and men, the man Christ Jesus"* (v5).

Third, he reveals the price of this salvation. He points them to Jesus, *"who gave himself a ransom for all"* (v6). He adds that untold people are to be told.

The story of Jesus is *"to be testified in due time"* (v6). Paul gets personal in the matter by preaching the unconditional personal responsibility of believers. He states, *"Whereunto I am ordained a preacher, and an apostle, …. a teacher"* (v7).

He concludes by repeating the universal priority of prayer, *"I will therefore that men pray every where, lifting up holy hands, without wrath and doubting"* (v8).

JUNE 21
Proving the Point

Our Bible divides the history of mankind into seven periods that we call dispensations. They start with Innocence in the garden of Eden, then Conscience with Adam and Eve after the fall, next Human government with Noah, after that Promise with Abraham, then Law with Moses, then our own period of Grace through Jesus Christ, and finally the Millennium when Christ rules over the earth with a rod of iron.

Paul speaks of our period in Ephesians 1:10 (see also 3:2), *"That in the dispensation of the fullness of times he might gather together in one all things in Christ, both which are in heaven, and which are on earth."* Each of these periods end with a judgment period except the last one. Each judgment seems to be worse than the one before. The awful tribulation of seven years of horror and terror will follow the period of grace.

The Lord seems to be saying, "This is what the teachings of humanism and secularism lead to." The end result of the philosophy of Plato, Aristotle, Socrates, Karl Marx, Charles Darwin, John Dewey, Sigmund Freud, John Maynard Keynes, Julius Wellhausen and Soren Kierkegaard is self-centered living, me-first attitude, immorality, robbery, and killing. This seven years will be hell on earth.

After the Lord proves His point, He is going to come in great power with the angels and saints and arrest the devil and put him in the bottomless pit for a thousand years. He will then set up His kingdom on earth and He will show all people who ever existed on the earth how things could have been during any of the other six periods of time. There will be peace on earth and good will toward all men.

It will be heaven on earth.

JUNE 22
Don't Gamble and Lose It All

A Christian attorney told the story of a case assigned to him by his law firm when he was a fledging lawyer.

A plane had crashed and 80 people were killed. The attorney was to pursue a settlement for the families of the deceased with the airlines. Attorneys for the airline after much haggling and negotiations had offered

250 million dollars—a 3 million dollar settlement for each victim of the crash.

The attorney felt it was the best deal they would get. He suggested they take it and settle before going into court. They hesitated; he begged and then pleaded with them.

Some suggested they might get five million or even ten million. He agreed that was a possibility, but they needed to realize also that they might lose and not get anything. They turned down his advice; they wanted more.

After a long and grueling battle in court, the jury stayed in session a while. Finally, they returned, and the room grew silent. The judge took the paper slip, read it, then announced the verdict.

"Nothing."

That's right "Nothing."

They decided the airline was not at fault and the people got exactly nothing. They had a sure thing, but they gambled and lost everything.

King Agrippa heard Paul the Apostle give the gospel and stated, almost you persuade me to be a Christian. Agrippa has now been in hell for over two thousand years. We preach, plead, and beg sinners to accept the special deal that God has offered.

Free eternal salvation simply by repentance and faith and yet many people take their chances and hope to do better. It is a sad mistake to gamble with one's soul.

JUNE 23
Lunch-Box Evangelism

In one episode from the comic strip "Peanuts," Lucy comes up to Linus, and tells him that she has "converted" someone in her class to her way of thinking religiously. Knowing his sister, Linus couldn't believe it.

"How did you do it?" he asked.

Lucy explained, "I told him everything I believe and asked him if he believed it, too. When he didn't see it my way, I just hit him over the head with my lunch box until he believed it!"

We've all seen some instances of "lunch-box evangelism". It's not very effective. Unfortunately, there are times that the way we talk and the way we act make it difficult for us to share our faith with those around us.

Listen to these words of advice Peter gives to Christian women who

141

are married to non-Christian husbands: *"Likewise, ye wives, be in subjection to your own husbands; that, if any obey not the word, they also may without the word be won by the conversation of the wives; While they behold your chaste conversation coupled with fear"* (1 Peter 3:1-2).

Peter isn't saying that we shouldn't talk to people about the Christian life, but he is saying that it is essential for others to see us actually living that life before we try to speak to others about their need.

Paul touches on this too, *"Ye are our epistle written in our hearts, known and read of all men"* (2 Cor. 3:2). The old adage, "what you say with your actions speaks so loud, I can't hear a word you're saying with your mouth."

Know someone who needs to hear the gospel message? Put your lunch box away and be careful of the example that you set around them.

JUNE 24
Eliminating Enemies

Boston Red Sox third baseman Wade Boggs used to hate going to Yankee Stadium because of a fan. The guy had a box seat close to the field, and he would torment Boggs by shouting obscenities and insults.

One day before the game, Boggs was warming up, the "fan" began his typical routine, yelling "Boggs, you stink." Boggs decided he'd had enough. He walked directly over to the man who was in the stands with his friends. Wade took a new baseball out of his pocket, autographed it, tossed it to the man, and went back to the field.

The man never yelled at Boggs again; in fact, he became one of Wades' biggest fans at Yankee Stadium. Other players have been known to deal with antagonistic fans by returning obscenities, or spitting on them, or even, on occasion, punching them in the nose. Boggs dealt with his tormentor by befriending him.

We may find ourselves in Wade's shoes someday. Our natural inclination is to fight back, but there is a better way to eliminate enemies once and for all. Abraham Lincoln made this observation: "I destroy my enemy when I make him my friend."

Also on this subject, the apostle Paul said, *"Recompense to no man evil for evil. Provide things honest in the sight of all men. If it be possible, as much as lieth in you, live peaceably with all men"* (Romans 12:17-18). *"...Why do ye not rather take wrong,"* (1 Cor. 6:7).

Tossing an autographed baseball to the loud mouths you have to deal with may or may not repair a rift, but it will accomplish two things: One, it will knock holes in the case they have built against you. Two, you will have done your part toward to establishing terms of peace.

JUNE 25
Hearing Those Voices Again

The lady was hysterical. She was hearing those strange voices again. They had put her in the mental hospital the last time that happened. She had been hearing those voices since her new baby came.

"I have been thinking about killing myself," she confessed.

"And where would you go if you did that?" I asked. "To heaven or to hell?" She hadn't given any thought to that. "You need someone to come here and stay with you and help you with this." I suggested.

"Who would do that?" She asked.

Of course I was talking about the Lord Jesus Christ. She was so desperate and listened intently to every word I spoke. I don't know voices she was hearing, but I do know that they were real to her. I am sure that they were not of the Lord so I carefully explained her problem of original sin.

"Would you go to heaven if you died right now?" I asked."

"I'm afraid not," she replied.

"Would you like to know for sure that you are going to heaven?" I questioned further.

"Yes. Yes, I would," she quietly answered. I explained the entire plan of salvation to her and led her to pray the sinner's prayer. A big smile broke across her face as she said, "I feel better all ready."

Her little eight-year-old daughter who had been listening to every word kept looking at me with big hungry eyes. I asked her, "Honey do you want Jesus to come into your heart too?" She shook her head up and down to say yes so we prayed again.

"Greater is he that is in you, than he that is in the world" (I John 4:4).

JUNE 26
A Living Sacrifice

"Verily, verily, I say unto you, Except a corn of wheat fall into the ground and die, it abideth alone: but if it die, it bringeth forth much fruit" (John 12:24).

The following is the petition that missionary Adoniram Judson made to Ann Hasseltine's father asking for her hand in marriage, knowing that missionary life in India in that day could likely be a death sentence.

"I have now to ask, whether you can consent to part with your daughter early next spring, to see her no more in this world; whether you can consent to her departure, and her subjection to the hardships and sufferings of missionary life; whether you can consent to her exposure to the dangers of the ocean, to the fatal influence of the southern climate of India; to every kind of want and distress; to degradation, insult, persecution, and perhaps a violent death.

"Can you consent to all this, for the sake of Him who left his heavenly home, and died for her and for you; for the sake of perishing, immortal souls; for the sake of Zion, and the glory of God? Can you consent to all this, in hope of soon meeting your daughter in the world of glory, with the crown of righteousness, brightened with the acclamations of praise which shall redound to her Saviour from heathens saved, through her means, from eternal woe and despair?"

—(Courtney Anderson, *To the Golden Shore*)

Ann's father let her make the decision, and she said yes. She did not see her parents again in this world, and she did suffer great hardships. She did die young, but she did it for the sake of the Saviour and lost souls. What a wonderful example and challenge.

—Copied from David Cloud

JUNE 27
What Does God Look Like?

A kindergarten teacher was observing her classroom of children while they drew pictures. She would occasionally walk around to see each child's artwork.

144

As she got to one little girl who was working diligently, she asked, "What is your picture going to be?"

The little girl replied, "I'm drawing a picture of God."

The teacher paused and said, "But no one knows what God looks like."

Without missing a beat, or looking up from her drawing the girl replied, "They will when I get through."

Our Bible does say, *"God is a Spirit: and they that worship him must worship him in spirit and in truth"* (John 4:24). It also says, *"Now unto the King eternal, immortal, invisible, the only wise God, be honour and glory forever and ever. Amen"* (1 Timothy 1:17).

God has revealed Himself to us in the person of His Son Jesus Christ. When one of the disciples asked Jesus to show Him what God looked like, He said, "Have I been with you all this time and you still don't know me?"

When Jesus comes into our heart at salvation we begin to manifest His traits and characteristics in our attitude and habit patterns. Other people are able to see God in us.

Our attitude, expressions, habits, patterns, and our language, ought to reveal God in us. Jesus said, *"Let your light so shine before men, that they may see your good works, and glorify your Father which is in heaven"* (Matthew 5:16).

Paul adds to this when he said, *"As ye have therefore received Christ Jesus the Lord, so walk ye in him"* (Colossians 2:6). That just may be the only hope someone has of heaven.

JUNE 28
A Big Conversion

Jim weighed 400 plus pounds, was six feet, two inches tall, and was still growing. I had always heard that the bigger they are the harder they fall. I thought to myself, if that applies to spiritual matters, this could be a real conversion experience. A church member had told me about big Jim.

"I believe he's just about ready to be saved," his friend told me. When I arrived at his house, I found him eating a big bowl of ice cream. It was easy to see that he was heading for four hundred fifty pounds, and it would not take long.

I came right to the point with Jim about my reason for coming to see him. I asked if I might show him some verses from the Bible about how to go to heaven.

145

"Why yes, that would be fine," he said as he continued to eat his ice cream. I began by sharing the problem of original sin.

"Do you realize that you are a sinner?" I asked him.

"Oh yes, I know that," he replied. As I continued, he suddenly stopped eating and began to listen. When I suggested that we pray and ask the Lord to save him, he started to pray.

He said, "Lord, I know that I am a big sinner. I know too that Christ died for me. Here and now, I accept Christ as my Saviour."

Jim came to church and took his stand for Christ and was baptized. Later he gained more weight. I was glad I baptized him when he was smaller.

He became a steady consistent believer and walked with the Lord until the Lord called him home in the early 1990's. His was truly a big conversion.

JUNE 29
He Met Christ in the Parking Lot

I'm not really sure why I stopped to talk with him, but I'm sure glad I did. He was just standing there by his car on the Walmart parking lot. He was waiting for his wife to finish shopping.

He was a friendly guy, and we talked about a lot of things. It was then I asked him that question. "Do you plan to go to heaven when your life is over?" I asked him.

"I've thought a lot about that," he answered. He listened intently as I read several verses from the Bible. We prayed together, and he invited Christ to come into his heart and take over his life.

"Is it all settled?" I asked.

"Yes sir," was his answer. He really seemed to have an assurance. Just then his wife came out of the store and they got into their car and drove away. My wife also came out of the store and we got in our car and also drove away. I shared the unique experience with my wife and we rejoiced over a newborn soul.

Eight days later a call came from his wife. "I just wanted to thank you preacher for helping my husband make his peace with God," she said. "Thank you too, for the letter you wrote to him to help him get off on the right foot," she continued. "He never got to read your letter, though. He died on Wednesday and we buried him on Friday," she informed me. "You know," she said softly, "I think the Lord arranged that whole thing on the parking lot. You will never know what it means to me to know that he is now in heaven."

JUNE 30
Go on South

A single drop of water sprung up from the damp soil in Minnesota. That drop merged with another, then another. Soon it began to trickle downward to where it was joined by a number of other trickles and it then became a clear sparkling stream. It continued heading south and joined stream after stream and turned into a creek, then a river, all the time going south.

As it flowed and rippled along, birds came to drink, then deer, and duck and geese landed on its waters to swim and catch the fish that were now enjoying the blessing of the cold, fresh current.

The happy, sparkling river provided moisture for plants and flowers all along its route. It was going somewhere and being a blessing as it went. When people began to throw trash and dump their waste into the fresh, clean water, and some chemical plants dumped pollutants waste in, still the river kept going. People even pushed old cars over the bank; then even when they built a dam across from bank to bank, the river filled the area full and finally flowed over the top and helped folks by turning turbines and creating electricity and all the while still going south.

After flowing through Illinois, Kentucky, Missouri and Louisiana, the mighty Mississippi River reached the Gulf of Mexico. All the hindrances and barriers had been a heavy burden, but determination and persistence won out as it always does.

The Apostle Paul pressed toward the mark of the high calling of God in Christ Jesus. He admonished others to *"Be ye steadfast, unmovable, always abounding in the work of the Lord, forasmuch as you know you labor is not in vain in the Lord."* (1 Cor. 15:58) Don't ever quit; keep on going south.

JULY 1
A Blind Man Who Sees

Manus Castle is legally blind, but he has a deep spiritual discernment that enables him to see what many others do not see.

Manus and his pastor friend Horace Jacobs were eating together in a local restaurant. After the waitress brought their food they quietly bowed their heads and asked a blessing over the meal. A lady at a nearby table had been attracted to them because she had noticed his blindness. She watched courteously as they prayed.

When they rose to leave she motioned for them to come by her table. She expressed to them how impressed she was with their boldness to pray in public. She then began to tell a story of depression and burden. She told of a great desire for help to get right with the Lord.

They used a copy of the New Testament and carefully led her through some verses dealing with the real cause of her defeat and then how to be saved.

Just as the woman at the well, or the Roman centurion, the Ethiopian eunuch, and the Philippian jailer, she came to Christ and a brand new life.

How important it is to be consistent in small things like asking for God's blessing on our meals in public. Not only is God looking but we never know who else is looking or listening.

The Bible says, *"Ye are our epistle written in our hearts, known and read of all men: Forasmuch as ye are manifestly declared to be the epistle of Christ ministered by us, written not with ink, but with the Spirit of the living God"* (2 Cor. 3:2-3). As Paul said, *"Therefore, my beloved brethren, be ye steadfast, unmoveable, always abounding in the work of the Lord"* (1 Cor. 15:58).

JULY 2
A Brief Testimony

Praise the Lord for an assembly line worker willing to witness on the job. Ernie Habecker shared the gospel to me and others day after day on the job at the General Motors plant in Wilmington, Delaware until I received Christ as my Saviour. He followed up my decision with encouragement and counsel to give my all to the Lord.

I soon became aware that the Lord wanted me to give myself to His service. That led me to quit my job, sell my newly built home, and go to Bible college, and prepare for the ministry. My goals, motives, ambitions, outlook, purpose, and direction were completely re-directed by these decisions. The exposure to soul winning, bus ministry, and evangelistic preaching gave me direction for my future ministry.

My first church consisting of thirty five people began to grow. I grew as the church grew. After several years of a twenty-four-seven approach, we had sixteen buses, a Christian school, a daily radio ministry, a printing ministry, a great mission program, a monthly church publication, and an attendance of over a thousand per Sunday.

The Lord called scores of young people into full-time service and sent them away to Bible college to prepare for the ministry. After more than sixty years that work still has the hand of God upon it.

The Lord has been very real and personal through the years and proven Himself in hundreds of times and ways. My three pastorates have had the touch of God upon them, and my opportunities to travel to every state and fifty-three foreign countries preaching the Word of God has brought fulfillment unspeakable. I look forward to all that the future holds.

Witnessing at work pays dividends.

JULY 3
The Pledge Of Allegiance

The time was 1923.

An old sage called the children together and said, "Boys and girls, I have been listening to you recite the Pledge of Allegiance and it appears that it has become monotonous to you. If I may, I would like to recite the Pledge and give you a definition of the words.

"I—meaning me, a committee of one

"Pledge—dedicate all of my worldly goods to give

"Allegiance—my love

"To the Flag—our standard, Old Glory

"Of the United—that means that we have all come together

"States—communities that have united into 48 great states. 48 individual communities with pride and dignity and purpose, with imaginary boundaries, yet united to a common cause

"Of America and to the Republic—a government is the people and it's from the people to the leaders, not from the leaders to the people

"For which it stands! One nation—meaning, so blessed by God

"Indivisible—incapable of being divided

"With Liberty—which is freedom

"And Justice—the principle of dealing fairly with others

"For all—which means, friend, it's as much your country as it is mine.

Since I was a boy, two states have been added, and two words have been added to the Pledge of Allegiance—"under God." Wouldn't it be a pity if someone said, 'That's a prayer' and that should be eliminated from schools, too?'

What a man of wisdom, Red Skelton. He must have had a vision of what would happen 20-30 years in the future.

This should be posted on the walls of every school in America, every Congressional office, the Supreme Court, and the homes of all our school children.

—by Red Skelton

JULY 4
The Price Of Freedom

On this special day when we remember those who shed their blood and sacrificed their lives to assure us of the freedoms we enjoy and the suffering and pain we have been spared, I am reminded of an account shared with us by Dr. Russell Dennis, president of Heritage Baptist University and originally published in Three Leaves Press by Debbie Applegate.

On February 5, 1860, Dr. Henry Ward Beecher stood before his Brooklyn congregation with a dramatic plea. Next to him, stood a nine year old mulatto slave girl who was destined for the slave market.

The request that day was for a love offering from the congregation to purchase the freedom for this girl…a kind of reverse slave auction.

Dr. Beecher led his large congregation in giving. He had long promoted freedom, encouraging his sister, Harriett Beecher Stowe, as she wrote *Uncle Tom's Cabin* eight years before. The congregation went wild with emotion, and gave over $1,000 worth of cash and jewelry.

After the gifts were received, the preacher reached down into the pile, and pulled out a gold, ruby star ring. Rev. Beecher placed it on the child's finger and lovingly said, "Now remember that this is your freedom-ring."

America's famed genre painter of that age, Eastman Johnson, captured the sacredness of the emblem in his painting "The Freedom Ring."

The Bible tells us that we were slaves to sin, and we were helpless to pay. But Jesus Christ made that payment with his life's blood, and the Bible records His words: *"If the Son therefore shall make you free, ye shall be free indeed"* (John 8:36). *"For the law of the Spirit of life in Christ Jesus hath made me free from the law of sin and death"* (Romans 8:2).

JULY 5
Keeping America Free

"Righteousness exalteth a nation: but sin is a reproach to any people"
(Proverbs 14:34).

Our land is important, but our Lord must be more important. The first commandment must be a first priority.

The great wall of China is one of the wonders of the world. Built of stone and bricks, it was begun in 221 B.C. and snakes itself 2,000 miles across the northern borders of China.

The walls are twenty-five feet wide at the base, twenty-five feet high, and have thirty foot towers every two hundred to three hundred yards.

When it was completed, the people settled down behind it with a sense of safety and security. The walls were too high for an enemy to scale and they were too strong to be battered down.

But in the first few years after the walls were completed, they were breached three times by the enemy. Was it because the enemy was able to scale the walls? No, they were too high for that. Was it because some foe battered them down? No, they were too thick for that. It happened because three times the enemy bribed a gatekeeper.

In like manner the great Roman empire fell from within.

Clarence Flynn wrote:
> "I know three things must always be,
> To keep the nation strong and free.
> One is a hearthstone bright and dear,
> With busy, happy loved ones near;

One is a ready heart and hand,
To love and serve and keep the land;
And one is a worn and beaten way,
To where the people go to pray.
As long as these are kept alive,
The nation and people can survive.
God keep them always everywhere,
The home, the flag, and the place of prayer."

JULY 6
God Saves All Kinds

Testimony time was always special in our church. One by one the people would stand and give God praise for saving their souls and changing their lives. One man had been a "hit man" for the Mafia and now was faithful worker in our church. Another had been the "town drunk" and now he was a godly family man and the treasurer of the church. Still another told how he had been saved in jail.

None of us ever ceased to be amazed at Jake's testimony, nor did we ever get tired of hearing it. Jake stood to tell how grateful he was to God for delivering him from the life of a drunkard.

He spoke of how sorry he was for the abuse he had caused his wife and kids. He told us that even his cat knew he was saved, because when he came home on a drunk he used to kick it off the porch. Now he stopped to pet her.

He also told of the "bootleg joints" around town where he spent most of his time and all his money. Everyone would say "Praise the Lord."

Then one of our most refined ladies stood. She said, "All of us know about Jake and the "bootleg joints", but not many of you know that I operated one of those joints. I sold Jake liquor many times. I praise the Lord that He saved me too." All of us were shocked. Nobody even dreamed that she had been a real bad sinner, too.

The Lord not only saves the down and out, but He also saves the up and out. *"Therefore if any man be in Christ, he is a new creature: old things are past away; behold all things are become new"* (2 Cor. 5:17).

JULY 7
Prodigal In Key Of F

Feeling footloose and frisky, a featherbrained fellow forced his father to fork over his farthings.

Fast he flew to foreign fields and frittered his family's fortune, feasting fabulously with floozies and faithless friends. Flooded with flattery he financed a full-fledged fling of "funny foam" and fast food. Fleeced by his fellows in folly, facing famine, and feeling faintly fuzzy, he found himself a feed-flinger in a filthy foreign farmyard.

Feeling frail and fairly famished, he fain would have filled his frame with foraged food from the fodder fragments.

"Fooey," he figured, "my father's flunkies fare far fancier," the frazzled fugitive fumed feverishly, facing the facts. Finally, frustrated from failure and filled with foreboding (but following his feelings) he fled from the filthy foreign farmyard.

Faraway, the father focused on the familiar form and flew to him and fondly flung his forearms around the fugitive.

Falling at his father's feet, the fugitive forlornly floundered, "Father, I have flunked and forfeited family favor."

Finally, the faithful Father, forestalling further flinching, flagged the flunkies to fetch the finest fatling and fix a feast.

The frugal first-born felt it was fitting to feel "favored" for his faithfulness and fidelity to family, father, and farm. In foolhardy fashion, he faulted the father for failing to furnish a fatling and feast for his friends. Frowning and finding fault, he fumed, but fussing was futile. His flaw was in his feeling about the fairness of the festival for the found fugitive. The farsighted father figured, "Such fidelity is fine, but what forbids fervent festivity for the fugitive that is found? Unfurl the flags and finery, let fun and frolic freely flow. Former failure is forgotten, folly is forsaken. Forgiveness forms the foundation for future fortune."

JULY 8
The Blessing Of Trouble

Have you discovered the blessing of trouble?

Jesus taught his followers a very wonderful but very strange truth. He said, *"Blessed are they that mourn: for they shall be comforted"* (Matthew 5:4). This is one of the many paradox statements in the Bible. He is saying, we are happy to be sad or fortunate to be unfortunate.

Does joy really come out of sorrow or blessings out of trouble? He also said, *"Blessed are ye, when men shall revile you, and persecute you, and shall say all manner of evil against you falsely, for my sake. Rejoice, and be exceeding glad: for great is your reward in heaven: for so persecuted they the prophets which were before you"* (Matthew 5:11-12).

I know a man whose tractor turned over, fell on his leg and broke it. From his hospital bed he told me how thankful he was because somebody came by and led him to Christ. He will get to go to Heaven now because of his trouble.

Paul the apostle said, *"For our light affliction, which is but for a moment, worketh for us a far more exceeding and eternal weight of glory"* (2 Cor. 4:17). Jesus was right, they that mourn shall be comforted.

One of our men stood in a testimony meeting at church and said, "Praise the Lord somebody stole my car this week." We were all dumbfounded. He continued, by telling us that he talked to the cop who came to take the report about his soul and won him to the Lord.

Job testified, *"Before I was afflicted I went astray: but now have I kept thy word"* (Psalm 119:67).

JULY 9
Paul Broke A Commandment

In making a call on one of the back roads near our church, I found that my visit came at a bad time. Supper was almost ready, and the three boys were glued to their favorite TV show. It seemed that they could care less about salvation, church, or going to Heaven; and I knew the sooner I left, the better it would suit everybody.

After offering prayer, I said good-bye and left. But the man followed me out the door and down the driveway to my car. I said good-bye three or four more times, but he kept following me.

Finally he said, "I need to talk to you, Preacher." He looked back toward the house and up and down the road and then whispered to me, "I broke a commandment."

"You did!"

"I am afraid I did." He was so serious.

"Do you want to tell me about it?"

"I've got to tell somebody," he volunteered. He told me a messy, wicked story. Sure enough, he had broken one of the commandments all right.

"I've got bad news for you, Paul," I said.

"That's what I was afraid of."

I quoted James 2:10 and explained that he was now guilty of breaking all the law.

"Oh, no!" he exclaimed.

"There is worse news than that," I reminded him.

"There is?" he asked.

"Yes. You must go to Hell now because the wages of sin is death."

"That's terrible!"

"But there is good news, Paul," I quickly reminded him. With that I gave him the Gospel and urged him to trust Christ. He did so and then said, "Come on back in here and tell my wife and three boys about this." All four of them accepted Christ. Then the whole family came Sunday and were baptized.

JULY 10
Slipping Through The Cracks

Tina was going into the hospital for surgery. Her feet were crooked and she walked funny, but her big smile and girlish charm soon made one forget that. Her mother wanted me to talk with her about baptism.

"When were you saved, Tina?" I asked.

"Oh, Jesus has been in my heart since I was born," she replied. Her answer made me realize that she did not actually understand what being saved was really all about.

I'm afraid that her church, her former pastor, her Sunday school teacher, and her parents had been made to believe that good people go to Heaven. The Bible is clear that, "it is not by works of righteousness."

I explained to her about her inherited sin, about heaven, about hell, and the death, burial, and resurrection of Christ, and then about praying the sinner's prayer.

"Would you want to pray that prayer right now and ask Jesus to come into your heart and become your Saviour?" I asked.

"Yes I would, I would like to do that right now," Tina quickly answered. She did pray and she did get Jesus in her heart. Her surgery went well and she also came to church and awkwardly walked forward to make a profession of her faith in Christ and be baptized.

I was glad I did not let her slip through the cracks because she thought she had it settled. I thought about what Jesus said to His disciples, *"Bring in hither the poor, and the maimed, and the halt* (lame)*, and the blind"* (Luke 14:21).

Tina was one of the lame Jesus was referring to. It would really be sad for a person to be crippled in this life and then miss heaven, too.

JULY 11
Our Abundant God

Jesus indicated that there was a difference between "life" and "abundant life" (John 10:10). "Life" here refers to everlasting life and the gift of salvation (John 3:16). The other has reference to maturity and fulfillment.

One might be content with having the joy of the Lord which is our strength (Nehemiah 8:10) another might not be content until they have gained *"joy unspeakable and full of glory"* (I Peter 1:8).

What a blessing to have peace, but how much better to have, *"peace which passeth all understanding"* (Phil. 4:7) and *"perfect peace"* spoken of by the prophet Isaiah (Isaiah 26:3).

What a blessing it is to get a prayer answered, but how much more exciting it is to get, *"exceeding abundantly above all we ask or think"* (Ephesians 3:20). It is nice to have our needs met, but how much more blessed it is to have the windows of Heaven opened and have so many blessings poured out on us that we are not able to receive them (Malachi 3:10).

When the Lord used Elisha to help the widow He not only filled up the meal barrel and the cruse of oil, but He arranged it so that the barrel did not run out, nor did the cruse of oil, as long as the need was there (1 Kings 17:16).

And let us not forget the account of the thousands of people who were fed in the miracle of the loaves and the fishes, and when it was all over, all of them were filled and fully satisfied, and there were twelve baskets full, left over (John 6:5-13).

Some say "the sky is the limit," but we believers know that God is the limit, and God has no limit. He is the "Almighty" God.

JULY 12
Getting Born Again, Too

Mrs. Jones had just prayed and invited Christ to come into her heart and save her. She was delighted with the whole experience and told me that she had wanted to do that for a long time, but didn't know how.

When I asked her if she were really saved and believed that she would go to heaven if she died, she quickly stated, "Yes, I'm saved and I believe I'll go to heaven when I die. This is wonderful," she said, "Now could I ask you one more thing."

"Sure," I answered, "what is your question?"

"Can I get born again, too?" she inquired. She wanted to be sure she had it all.

What a joy to take a Bible and explain to her that the new birth was included in what she had already done. She accepted my explanation without question and went away rejoicing.

Jesus explained to Nicodemus that until he was born again he would not be able to see, or understand the things of God. Paul feared that Satan would cause people to miss the simplicity of the gospel.

Now, the rest of her questions were not that easy. She wanted to know what to do about her live-in boyfriend. Then there was the problem of a son on drugs, a daughter with psychological problems, another daughter with an illegitimate child who also had a live-in boyfriend. Then too, there was the problem of the two live-in boyfriends not getting along with each other.

These problems will not be easy to solve, but she went home to get started to untangle the web that sin had been spinning around her family. With Christ in the picture things should take a turn for the better.

JULY 13
The Ant And The Grasshopper Fable

The ant works hard in the stifling heat all summer long, building his house and gathering supplies for the winter. The grasshopper thinks he's a fool and laughs and dances and plays the summer away. Come winter, the ant is warm and well fed. The grasshopper has no food or shelter so he dies out in the cold.

Modern American Version:

Come winter, the shivering grasshopper calls a press conference and demands to know why the ant should be allowed to be well fed while others are starving.

CBS, NBC and ABC show up to provide pictures of the shivering grasshopper next to video of the ant in his comfortable home.

Kermit the Frog appears on Oprah with the grasshopper, and everybody cries when he sings "It's not easy being green."

Hillary Clinton make a special guest appearance on the CBS Evening News to tell a concerned panel that they will do everything they can for the grasshopper who has been denied the prosperity he deserves by those who benefited unfairly during the Reagan summers.

Hillary gets her old law firm to represent the grasshopper in a defamation suit against the ant, and the case is tried before a panel of federal hearing officers that Obama appointed from a list of single-parent welfare moms.

The ant loses the case. The story ends as we see the grasshopper finishing up the last bits of the ant's food in the government house he's in, which just happens to be the ant's old house. The ant has disappeared in the snow.

And on the TV, which the grasshopper bought by selling most of the ant's food, they are showing Obama standing before a wildly applauding group of Democrats announcing that a new era of "fairness" has dawned in America.

JULY 14
No Bibles In Jonestown

We were all amazed and shocked when reports of the mass suicides came in from Jonestown. The media reported that over 900 people had died from drinking cyanide-laced Kool-Aid. The investigation revealed that Jim Jones had led them in suicide drills and prepared them for this unbelievable deed.

Before this clan migrated from California to the small country of Guyana, Jones had convinced his followers to sell all their possessions and pool them together in his organization. To escape the laws of California and the problems of relatives of clan members who were attempting to retrieve their loved ones from his control, he bought the large tract of land in the jungle of Guyana and relocated his followers there.

When Leo Ryan, a California congressman showed up with a camera crew to investigate the many complaints from family members, shooting broke out resulting in the death of Congressman Ryan, a reporter, cameraman, and two others. This was followed by the mass suicide.

Jones had been influenced by a number of cult leaders such as "Father Divine" and "Daddy Grace". He studied Gandhi and Buddha. He claimed to be the reincarnation of Gandhi, Buddha, Jesus, and Lenin. He renounced the Bible saying the "letter killeth," calling the Bible a "paper idol."

One part of the report given by the army major in charge of the gruesome investigation was either overlooked or ignored by the media. He said, "There were no Bibles in Jonestown."

People who depart from the Bible become their own god. When men usurp the authority of God and do it their own way, things like this results. Solomon said, "Where there is no vision (Biblical revelation), the people perish." That was certainly true in this case.

JULY 15
A Mayor Is Saved

Recently a letter came from a small town in the Ukraine. The mayor of the town of 3500 was so pleased that one of our couples had been bringing food, clothing, and toys to a local orphanages and providing special programs for the local village school, that she invited them to have lunch with her.

Just as our missionary couple sat down to eat, the mayor, Valentina, stood up and said, "I want to repent." They led her to Christ as her subordinates looked on.

Later Vilkah, their young interpreter spoke up saying, "I want to repent, too." He was also saved then and there. All this took place just after the wall came down and people in several Eastern European countries were experiencing a small window of freedom.

The dormant seed of the gospel had been planted in the hearts of the old people before the communist takeover. Many had secret desires to find out about being saved.

On a trip with thirty-five other Christian workers to the Ukraine, we had over thirty-four hundred decisions for Christ in two weeks.

God is no respecter of persons. He will save a Russian bureaucrat just as quickly as He will a Sunday school child.

As Paul stated, *"For I am not ashamed of the gospel of Christ: for it is the power of God unto salvation to everyone that believeth; to the Jew first, and also to the Greek"* (Romans 1:16). And of course that includes the former communist Ukrainian.

Jesus said, *"Let your light so shine before men, that they may see your good works, and glorify your Father which is in heaven"* (Matthew 5:16).

Mayor Valentina had seen the good works and love for the children by our missionaries.

JULY 16
Alaska Crash

As Paul Harvey would have said, "Now the rest of the story..."

Alaska Airlines flight 261, flying from Washington State to Alaska developed engine trouble and crashed into the Pacific Ocean killing all on board. An airline pilot involved in the investigation of the crash related that he listened to the cockpit voice recorder from the downed plane and reported that for the last 9 minutes of the flight, the wife of the pastor from Monroe, Washington, can be heard sharing the Gospel with the passengers over the airplane's intercom system. The pastor and his wife were returning from a mission trip.

Just before the final dive into the ocean, she can be heard leading the sinners prayer for salvation! The pilot also told investigators that the flight data recorder from the plane indicates that there is no good explanation for the plane remaining in the air for those final 9 minutes. But it did remain in the air until the pastor's wife finished sharing the Gospel and presumably lead many to Christ in those final moments.

Who knows when a believer will be confronted with an emergency situation, such as this troubled plane, an automobile accident, a sinking boat, or a dying patient in a hospital? I have always been glad that I learned the boy scout motto at twelve years of age, "Be Prepared."

On the other hand it might be that our opportunity to, "rescue the perishing, care for the dying, snatch them in pity from sin and the grave," will come in a restaurant, at a gas station, or on an elevator.

"They that sow in tears shall reap in joy. He that goeth forth and weepeth, bearing precious seed, shall doubtless come again with rejoicing, bringing his sheaves with him" (Psalms 126:5-6).

JULY 17
Laboring And Heavy Laden

"Come unto me, all ye that labour and are heavy laden, and I will give you rest" (Matthew 11:28).

We usually look upon this verse as a promise of comfort to those who carry heavy physical, social, financial, emotional or family burdens.

Those may be the applications of the verse but the interpretation seems to be something entirely different. Those who are laboring are those who are trying to get into to heaven by doing good works.

There are still multitudes of folk who hope to gain salvation by attending church, praying, reading the Bible, giving money, and by treating others as they would want to be treated.

The Bible clearly states, *"For by grace are ye saved through faith; and that not of yourselves: it is the gift of God: Not of works, lest any man should boast"* (Eph. 2:8-9). And, *"Not by works of righteousness which we have done, but according to his mercy he saved us, by the washing of regeneration, and renewing of the Holy Ghost"* (Titus 3:5).

We cannot labor our way into heaven. As Jesus told Nicodemus *"ye must be born again"* (John 3:7) all the labor is done. Jesus paid it all. It is now

161

a matter of believing or trusting Jesus to take care of this for us. *"Believe on the Lord Jesus Christ and thou shall be saved"* (Acts 16:31).

Those who are heavy laden are those who are loaded down with guilt. We are guilty because of original sin. *"For as by one man's disobedience many were made sinners"* (Rom. 5:19).

Like Pilgrim in the story of Pilgrim's Progress, our heavy load is laid down at the cross and we enter into peace by faith. Jesus promised, *"I will give you rest."* It is a gift to be received.

JULY 18
Saved Or Really Saved

We've all heard someone ask, when a soul winner reports that they won someone or a number of people to Christ, "Yeah, but how many of them really got saved?"

Dr. Curtis Hutson used to say, "I can't find anything in the Bible about a difference between 'getting saved', and 'really getting saved.'

When I went to the maternity ward to visit Juanita Brown at the birth of her first baby, I reminded her of the importance of being sure to give attention to the spiritual need of her little boy and make sure he would go to heaven at the end of his life on earth.

I knew she would really care for the physical needs of food, clothing, education, etc. but I pointed out that all these were temporal and that the eternal soul of the little boy the Lord had given her was the really important part of him.

When I inquired about where she stood on this matter, she confessed that she did not have this really settled herself. I took a few moments and pointed out that she needed to get this really settled so she would have the Lord's help in getting her children saved. I gave her a simple presentation of the gospel. She responded to the simple story of Jesus being born of a virgin, living a sinless life, dying on the cross for her sin, then rising from the grave. She accepted Christ, and later came to church and was baptized.

I hired her to be our church secretary and outside of a few times when she took off to have a couple more babies, she worked continually for four different pastors. She retired recently after fifty years of faithful service. I think that she really got saved.

JULY 19
Hail From Heaven

A doctor and his wife, became convicted by the Lord to give up their comfortable life style and go as missionaries to an isolated area of Africa. A plague struck and the natives were taken with high fevers. Many of them were dying. The doctor tried everything, but could not find a cure.

Their son came down with the dreaded plague and began to burn with the fever. They tried everything, but to no avail. The doctor and his wife got on their knees beside their boy, and prayed, knowing if God did not intervene their boy would die.

The temperature in the village was over one hundred degrees, and the boy's temperature went up to one hundred and six. The doctor said if he just had some ice to pack the boy in, he believed they could get the fever down and prevent death. They were at least one hundred miles from a place that would have ice but he knew that it would melt before they could get back to their village. It was a hopeless situation.

He told the Lord about the need for ice and asked Him for help. The doctor said, "After I prayed, a breeze began to blow. The sky clouded up. Thunder sounded and lightning flashed. Soon there was a heavy downpour of rain, then it happened. It began to hail. Hail stones fell out of the sky the size of baseballs. This continued until there was a foot of ice everywhere."

The doctor packed his boy in ice and instructed the natives to do the same. Not one died after that. God had worked an unmistakable miracle. *"Call unto me, and I will answer thee, and shew thee great and mighty things, which thou knowest not"* (Jeremiah 33:3).

JULY 20
Man With A Red Lantern

In his life story Dr. Art Wilson, a respected Christian leader from the Mid-West, tells of driving late at night through a terrible rain storm to get to his next speaking engagement.

The road was narrow and the blinding rain made it almost impossible to see the road. After a while Dr. Wilson said he thought he saw a little red light up ahead. As he came over a hill he saw it again and then again.

The blinding rain made it almost impossible to tell what it was. As he approached the spot a sudden flash of lightening lit up the area and there stood a man in the road with a lantern. Dr. Wilson became angry thinking the man wanted him to help pull his car out of the ditch and he needed to get on to his meeting. He was sure to get wet and muddy.

He rolled down the window to see what the man wanted. The man explained that the heavy rain had washed away the bridge up ahead. Had he continued, he would have surely lost his life.

"To think," he said, "I was angry at the man who was trying to save me."

A lot of folks have that same reaction when the preacher tries to warn them of the consciences of sin. Please don't get mad at the man with the red lantern!

The Bible tells the man of God to *"preach the Word; be instant in season, out of season; reprove, rebuke, exhort with all longsuffering and doctrine"* (2 Tim 4:2).

Wise indeed is the man who heeds. *"Now we exhort you, brethren, warn them that are unruly, comfort the feebleminded, support the weak, be patient toward all men"* (1 Thes. 5:14).

JULY 21
Meeting God

Do you plan to see God someday? Jesus said in the famous Sermon on the Mount, *"Blessed are the pure in heart: for they shall see God."*

This surely will be one of the most awesome experiences that any of us have ever had. John said, *"No man hath seen God at any time; the only begotten Son, which is in the bosom of the Father, he hath declared him."*

In the Old Testament several people did see God, but in angelic form and it truly was an awesome experience. Every time God appeared in angelic form, the first words that proceeded out of His mouth were, "fear not."

Daniel fell down in awe. At the time of the birth of Christ, Zechariah and Elizabeth as well as Joseph and Mary along with the shepherds in the field, all saw an angel. Every one of them were frightened and stricken with awe.

What does it mean to be "pure in heart"? These are the ones who will see God. Possibly it means to be made pure by being washed in the blood of Jesus Christ. That, of course, refers to being saved.

Also, it might mean to be pure in motive and intent which would lead to pure lives and clean bodies. The dictionary says that pure means to be single minded or unmixed with any other. That would mean allowing my interest and goals to be totally centered around my relationship to God as Jesus said, *"Seek ye first the kingdom of God, and his righteousness; and all these things shall be added unto you"* (Matthew 6:33).

Believers will be in glorified bodies when they see God and will be equipped to relate to Him. Seeing God is an experience that we really should be looking forward to.

JULY 22
World's Biggest Ear

One can read in the history of Greece about the Ear of Dionysius. This cruel king constructed a huge tunnel two hundred and fifty feet long and eighty feet high between the palace and his prison. The tunnel was an exact duplicate of the human ear and made a perfect 'whispering gallery'. Dionysius spent much of his time setting in his chair of ease in his parlor listening to the whispering of the prisoners as they plotted and planned their escape and his overthrow. He would then order those men out for hearing and expose their deeds and send them to their judgment.

Modern electronic bugs have replaced that huge devicebut none can match the all hearing ear as well as the all seeing eye of our mighty God.

The Bible tells of God hearing the murmurings of the children of Israel in the wilderness journeys (Exodus 16:7). We read in Psalm 34:15 that His eyes are open to their righteousness and His ears are open unto their cries. Peter wrote that His ears are open to their prayers (1 Pet. 3:12).

Then John gave witness to this when he recorded the words, *"And this is the confidence that we have in him, that, if we ask any thing according to his will, he heareth us"* (1 John 5:14).

How solemn we ought to be before Almighty God who hears all that we say and who even knows the thoughts and intents of hearts. How it must bless the heart of God for His children to send our words of praise and prayer to the waiting ear of our Lord. *"Neither his ear heavy, that it cannot hear"* (Isa. 59:1).

It would do us well to remember also that He knows all and never forgets.

JULY 23
You Can Get Prayers Answered

Dr. John R. Rice wrote in his classic book on prayer, "God delights to hear and answer prayer."

The Lord has warehouses full of unclaimed benefits waiting for His children to ask for them. James reminds us that, *"ye ask, and receive not, because ye ask amiss"* (James 4:3).

If I am to get all my prayers answered, there are some things I must get settled.

First, *"If ye abide in me, and my words abide in you, ye shall ask what ye will, and it shall be done unto you"* (John 15:7). The word, 'abide' is what an unborn baby is doing in the mother's womb. The mother is nourishing, caring, loving, and protecting it.

Second, sin must be put away. David wrote, *"If I regard iniquity in my heart, the Lord will not hear me"* (Psalm 66:18). Of course if He does not hear me I do not get my prayer answered.

Third, I must be obedient to the Lord. The Bible says, *"Whatsoever we ask, we receive of Him, because we keep His commandments, and do those things that are pleasing in His sight"* (1 John 3:22).

Fourth, we must pray in faith. Jesus said, *"And all things, whatsoever ye shall ask in prayer, believing, ye shall receive"* (Matthew 21:22).

Fifth, we must pray in the Spirit. Paul explained, *"the Spirit also helpeth our infirmities:... and maketh intercession for us with groanings which cannot be uttered"* (Romans 8:26).

Finally, we must be earnest in our praying. James tells us, *"The effectual fervent prayer of a righteous man availeth much"* (James 5:16).

Prayer is a very effective and wonderful tool. How foolish we are not to practice prayer and see great and mighty things which we know not.

JULY 24
Worthless Bird Dogs

It is natural for dogs to chase birds, so they have to be retrained to point instead of chase.

A frisky puppy may be equipped with all the necessary tools, big feet, long legs, and a sense of direction, but if he doesn't learn to point the birds, he will be worthless as a bird dog.

After some good training the dog will pick up the scent and take off in the direction of the bird. As he gets close, he suddenly freezes and points the bird with his nose and leaves his tail sticking straight out behind him waiting for his master's command.

A good Christian must learn to 'wait upon the Lord'. Isaiah the prophet wrote, *"They that wait upon the Lord shall renew their strength; they shall mount up with wings as eagles"* (Isaiah 40:31).

There are three areas that the Bible warns believers to beware. They are the world, the flesh, and the devil.

John the beloved, cautions us concerning the world. He said, *"Love not the world, neither the things that are in the world. If any man love the world, the love of the Father is not in him"* (1 John 2:15).

Paul the apostle tells us his secret of keeping focused on the Lord. He said, *"But I keep under my body, and bring it into subjection: lest that by any means, when I have preached to others, I myself should be a castaway"* (1 Corinthians 9:27).

Then James tell us that the Devil like a roaring lion is seeking to destroy us. He advises us to *"resist the devil, and he will flee from you"* (James 4:7). In all three of these areas we must stop, focus, and wait on the Lord.

JULY 25
He Would Not Move His Letter

Johnny Lucas had been attending our church for almost three months. Everybody who talked with him told me that he was going to move his church letter to our church and become a member. I watched every Sunday to see if he was going to respond to the invitation. Finally, I decided to visit in his home and discuss the matter with him.

On my first visit he told me his membership was in Phoenix, Arizona, and that he intended to transfer it to our church. I thought it was settled, but two or three more Sunday's went by and he still did not make the move.

On my second visit, I told him I would be glad to write and request that they transfer his letter of confirmation to our church. That's when he looked at me and quietly said, "Pastor my problem is that I am not saved." Of course that changed everything.

"Johnny," I said "we can take care of that right now." With my Bible I explained the good news of the gospel to him and he readily invited

Christ to become his Saviour. The next Sunday he walked down the aisle, made a profession of his faith in Christ and was baptized, to everybody's amazement.

There are many well-meaning folks sitting in churches who know in their heart that the matter is not settled but because they have gone through the motions of a profession and baptism, they are too embarrassed to make the move.

What a terrible thing it must be for a person to feel the pressure of conviction every time an invitation is given in church. What a relief to make the move and settle the matter once and for all.

JULY 26
Out Of God's Will

A missionary couple finished deputation and took their two children to the field of God's leading.

The wife was unhappy. She constantly complained and cried. She voiced her fear that the children would be victims of wild animals in the area. Day after day she drained on the victory of her missionary husband. She pleaded with him to give it up and take her home.

Finally he gave in, resigned from the mission and moved his family back to New Jersey. He got a job and moved the family into a trailer. Everything went well for several months until one afternoon when the children were playing under the trailer, one of them came running into the trailer screaming. Snakes had bitten both of their little boys. A call to the father brought him quickly home and a race for the hospital. It was too late. Both boys died from the poisonous snake bites. The thing she feared most out in the jungle happened to them here in the safety of their home.

It has been said, "It is safer in the jungles of Africa in the will of God than at home in America out of God's will." The word of God recorded by Isaiah the prophet would be good to consider at a time like this. *"Fear thou not; for I am with thee: be not dismayed; for I am thy God: I will strengthen thee; yea, I will help thee; yea, I will uphold thee with the right hand of my righteousness"* (Isaiah 41:10).

The accounts of Daniel in the lion's den, the three Hebrew boys cast into the fiery furnace, and dozens more like these are included in the Bible to build our faith that we might trust God.

JULY 27
An Unspeakable Gift

The story is told of a blind girl who hated herself because she was blind. She hated everyone and everything except her loving boyfriend. He was always there for her.

She told him, "If I could only see the world, I would marry you."

One day, someone donated a pair of eyes to her. The surgery was performed and the transplant was successful. When the bandages came off, she was able to see everything, including her boyfriend.

He asked her, "Now that you can see the world, will you marry me?"

The girl looked at her boyfriend and saw that he was blind. The sight of his closed eyelids shocked her. She hadn't expected that. The thought of looking at them the rest of her life led her to refuse to marry him.

Her boyfriend left in tears and days later had a note sent to her saying, "Take good care of your eyes, my dear, for before they were yours, they were mine."

Even though Jesus did more than give His eyes, thousands of people reject Him and refuse to allow Him to become their Saviour.

They live on enjoying the benefits of what He did for them. He willingly shed His blood, suffered the shame and reproach of the mob and the pain of the crucifixion when He could have called for ten thousand angels to destroy the world and set Him free. He endured the cross to give us the gift of eternal life.

The apostle Paul calls it the, "unspeakable gift." The Bible clearly teaches that the privilege of going to Heaven when we die is the gift of God and does not come by our own works or behavior (Ephesians 2:8-9).

James calls salvation the perfect gift, and that it comes down from an unchangeable God.

JULY 28
Almost As Bad As Job

Next time I start feeling sorry for myself, I am going to remember Diane O'Dell. Diane was three years old when she was stricken with polio. She spent the next fifty-eight years in an iron lung.

On May 29, 2008 there was a power failure at her house. The family had prepared for such a happening and made an attempt to start a generator. They could not get it started and Diane died. She was 61 years old. Talk about everything going wrong.

Even Job did not have to endure his troubles that long. From the time I was saved at a General Motors assembly plant in Wilmington, Delaware, during my Bible college training, as I pastored my three churches for a period of more than forty years, and while I was serving the Lord in evangelism and traveling in mission work to forty-three countries over a period of eighteen years, Diane was lying in that iron lung struggling for every breath.

What a contrast in my fifty eight years and hers. I have never even seen an iron lung. I've never been a victim of a tornado, a hurricane, an earthquake, a flood, a fire, or an armed robbery. I've never had a heart attack, cancer, a brain tumor, or even an ulcer.

I've never experienced a plane crash, a shipwreck, and auto accident, or a train wreck. None of my family have committed suicide, been raped, murdered, killed by a wild animal or killed by a roadside bomb.

I've not had to lay in a casket, been hung, electrocuted, burned at the stake, or even jailed. I have been spared from divorce, drug addiction, or alcoholism. I want to cry out with David, *"Oh that men might praise the Lord for His goodness, for His wonderful works to the children of men!"* (Psalm 107:8).

JULY 29
Raising Pigeons

The Apostle John was believed to be Pastor of the church of Ephesus. Tradition says that he raised pigeons. On one occasion one of his members came by on his way home with his bow and some arrows.

The hunter chided the old preacher when he saw him giving attention to one of his pigeons. John remarked that he noticed that his bow string was loosened. The hunter explained that when not hunting he kept his bow string loosened so that when it was tightened it would do much better.

With that John remarked that he used the same remedy for his mind. After relaxing it for a while it works much better. That is one reason we take off and go to church and fellowship with other believers. It gets us ready for Monday morning.

In the beginning God set this principle into motion by resting Himself on the Sabbath then declaring the seventh day a day of rest. He then stated that the land should be given rest. This principle was given as a commandment of the Lord. The captivity of Israel of 490 years in Egypt and the 70 years of captivity in Babylon was a direct result of ignoring this basic command of the Lord. It has been proven over and over and many illustrations have been given of even animals and machinery lasting longer and serving better when this practice was observed.

The results show in the spiritual, physical, mental, emotional, financial, domestic, and the social areas of our lives. Isaiah the prophet declared that if the people would let the day of rest be a delight and honor the Lord He would cause them to ride upon the high places of the earth, and feed them with the heritage of Jacob (Isaiah 58:14).

JULY 30
My First Sin

In the first grade I sat in the seat just behind Billy Baldwin. Billy had a little red car with black rubber wheels. It fell off his desk and was lying under my desk. I picked it up and put it into my pocket. I had never had a little car like this one and I wanted it bad.

When Billy couldn't find his car he started crying and told the teacher. She asked all of us to help find it. We looked everywhere. She said it has to be here and we will look until we find it.

I began to panic. I felt so guilty. I knew I was about to be found out. There was a small hole in my pocket, so I pushed the car into that hole until it made the hole big enough for the car to slide through. It rolled down my pant leg and onto the floor.

I picked it up and said, "Here it is! I found it under my desk!" I'm sure she knew I had it, but she did not expose me. The kids never knew the truth, but I did. I knew that I was a thief and a sinner of the worst kind.

Later I would understand about my sinful nature that I had inherited from my father and grandfather, all the way back to our first father Adam. *"Wherefore, as by one man sin entered into the world, and death by sin"* (Romans 5:12). I would also learn that, *"For the wages of sin is death"* (Romans 6:23). I would also learn that, *"God commendeth His love toward us, in that, while we were yet sinners, Christ died for us"* (Romans 5:8). Then I accepted Christ and was saved.

171

JULY 31
Secular Versus Spiritual Mindset

The human mind can be divided into three types, the scientific, the secular, and the spiritual. When God created Adam, he was blessed with a built in computer. It was filled with several yotabytes of information. He knew everything that God knew, except for evil.

He knew the names of all the animals, plants, birds, and himself. He knew that he was created by God and that God made the sun, moon, and the stars, and that they did not come into existence by evolution. Now, when you and I were born, our minds were empty.

We did not know who we were, what we were, where we were, or how we got there. We soon learned language and then how to walk nd run.

In my eighties I am still learning. I am told that to duplicate my brain into a computer using the latest in circuits, chips, and material, it would take a building the size of the empire state building in New York city to house it. This is my scientific mind.

When I was six years old, I was enrolled into the first grade at the Odd elementary school at Odd, West Virginia. In the public school there and at the Kennett Consolidated school of Kennett Square, Pennsylvania for the next twelve years, I was exposed to the teachings of Plato, Socrates, Aristotle, Darwin, Marks, Dewey, Freud, and Dr. Spock.

I wanted to, 'do my own thing' and I became self-centered. I began to steal, and lie. Then Jesus came into my heart and I now had a spiritual mind that began to desire the sincere milk of the word and I began to grow.

I still have all three minds. The one I feed determines everything.

AUGUST 1
Power Of Influence

While I was dating my wife, Jan, her dad told of his days in a foster home on the Eastern shore of Maryland. His family had lived in Baltimore and because of serious problems he and the rest of the children were placed in foster homes.

He told of an old man and woman that took him in and cared for him. He said that the old man would get on his knees and pray each night before retiring.

I pictured that man in my mind and thought about him many times after. I didn't know him, hadn't met him, didn't know his name, and didn't know how he looked, but he'd had a positive spiritual impact on my life.

Many times I have slipped into my prayer closet and spent time with the Lord on my knees when I thought of him. I was indirectly influenced by that old gentleman and he was never aware of it.

We never know what influence and impact we are having on folks around us. The Bible speaks about believers, *"Ye are our epistle written in our hearts, known and read of all men"* (2 Cor. 3:2).

Most of us have been influenced by reading the accounts of their experiences in their biographies. Many have surrendered their lives to a call to the ministry or the mission field by reading or hearing of God's work in their lives.

Peter influenced a group of people by a decision he made. He said, *"I go a fishing. They say unto him, We also go with thee. They went forth, and entered into a ship immediately; and that night they caught nothing"* (John 21:3).

This shows that our influence can be good or bad.

AUGUST 2
Friendly Fireside Chat

Franklin Delano Roosevelt was well known for his fireside chats. He talked to the nation from his heart. This took place from 1933 to 1944, and he urged the American people to work together to win the second world war.

He asked the people to buy war bonds and they did. Billions of dollars' worth. He asked the coal miners to call off their strike for patriotic reasons. Thirty different times he got through to the people with a tender but firm message. His "chats" were very effective.

Now, my dear friend, would you let me chat with you for a moment about something more important than Roosevelt's themes? Can a person know for certain that they will go to heaven when they die? Can one be 100% sure?

To have this settled and know for sure would be worth so much to all of us. It would be of more value than to be the richest person on earth. Jesus said, *"For what shall it profit a man, if he shall gain the whole world, and lose his own soul?"* (Mark 8:36)

If we can really know, then how? The only source of information we have about heaven is from the Bible. It is not a matter of what the Baptist, Methodist, Catholic, Pentecostal, Jews, Muslims, or any other of the many religious group believe.

The Bible says, *"These things have I written unto you that believe on the name of the Son of God; that ye may know that ye have eternal life, and that ye may believe on the name of the Son of God"* (1 John 5:13).

We can know for sure, and we can know now. Getting into heaven is not automatic. *"Ye must be born again"* (John 3:7).

AUGUST 3
God And Barbers

A man went to a barber shop to have his hair cut. The conversation with the barber covered a variety of subjects. Suddenly, the subject of God came up. The barber said, "Look man, I don't believe that God exists as you say He does."

"Why do you say that?" asked the client.

"Well, it's so easy, you just have to go out in the street to realize that God does not exist. Oh, tell me, if God existed, would there be so many sick people? Would there be abandoned children? If God existed, there would be no suffering nor pain. I can't think of a God who permits all of these things."

The client stopped for a moment thinking but he didn't want to respond so as to start an argument. The barber finished his job and the client went out of the shop.

Just after he left the barber shop he saw a man in the street with very long unkempt hair.

Then the client again entered the barber shop with the shaggy haired man and he said to the barber, "You know what? Barbers do not exist."

"How come they don't exist?" asked the barber. "Well, I am here and I am a barber."

"No!" the client exclaimed. "They don't exist because if they did there would be no people with long hair like this man who walks in the street."

"Ah, barbers do exist, what happens is that people do not come to me."

"Exactly!" affirmed the client. "That's the point. God does exist, but people do not come to Him and that's why there's so much pain and suffering in the world."

Jesus said, *"Come unto me, all ye that labour and are heavy laden"* (Matthew 11:28).

AUGUST 4
Drawing Near To God

"Draw nigh to God, and he will draw nigh to you" (James 4:8).

This is one of the many light switch verses in the Bible waiting to be flipped. The nearer we come to God, the more graciously will He reveal Himself to us.

When the prodigal comes home, his father runs to meet him. When the wandering dove returns to the ark, Noah puts out his hand to pull her in unto him. When the tender wife seeks her husband's society, he comes to her on wings of love. Come then, dear friend, let us draw nigh to God who so graciously awaits us, yea, comes to meet us.

Did you ever notice that passage in Isaiah 58:9? There the Lord seems to put Himself at the disposal of His people, saying to them, "Here I am." As much as to say—"What have you to say to me? What can I do for you? I am waiting to bless you." How can we hesitate to draw near? God is nigh to forgive, to bless, to comfort, to help, to quicken, to deliver.

Jesus said, *"Come unto me, . . . and I will give you rest"* (Matthew 11:28). Let it be the main point with us to get near to God. This done, all is done. If we draw near to others, they may before long grow weary of us and leave us; but if we seek the Lord alone, no change will come over His mind, but He will continue to come nearer and yet nearer to us by fuller and more joyful fellowship.

Fanny Crosby said it well:
Draw me nearer, nearer, blessed Lord
To the cross where Thou hast died;
Draw me nearer, nearer, nearer, blessed Lord,
To Thy precious, bleeding side.

AUGUST 5
Hummingbirds And Evolution

In the tropical rain forest there are species of flowers, which, because of their peculiar design, can be pollinated only by hummingbirds with bills of matching design. One flower is curved, preventing insect pollination. Only one particular species of hummingbird with a matching curved bill can penetrate to the stigma and can thus pollinate the flower.

The other is a large flower, 6 to 8 inches long, which can be pollinated only by the Sword Bill Hummingbird whose bill is longer than its body length. Each of these flowers is dependent for its very existence, therefore, on the hummingbird that pollinates it. And each hummingbird, as well, is dependent for its existence on the flower that it pollinates—the bird must have the flowers' nectar to sustain its life.

The tiny birds must hover at the flower's opening with wings beating 1200 times per minutes, and heart beating 398 times per minute.

The hummingbird uses such an enormous amount of energy hovering, that it must feed every 3 to 5 seconds! Evolution requires millions of years for each transmutation according to Darwin to progress from a simple amoeba to a creature as amazingly complex as a hummingbird.

Consider, too, the astronomical odds against a specific species of flower and a specific species of bird, from two totally different kingdoms, appearing on the scene at the very same instant.

But the stark reality is that if both flowers and hummingbirds were not there together, fully developed and fully functioning at the very same moment in time, both species would die! The hummingbird without the flowers' nectar would fall to its death and the flowers would wilt shortly thereafter, having no pollinator to keep them alive. God covered every base and dotted every eye in creation.

AUGUST 6
It's Only A Quarter

Several years ago a preacher moved to Houston, Texas. Some weeks after he arrived, he had occasion to ride the bus from his home to the downtown area. When he sat down, he discovered that the driver had given him a quarter too much change. As he considered what to do, he thought to himself, 'You better give the quarter back. It would be wrong to keep it.' Then he thought, 'Oh, forget it, it's only a quarter. Who would worry about this little amount? Anyway the bus company already gets too much fare; they will never miss it. Accept it as a gift from God and keep quiet.'

When his stop came, he paused momentarily at the door, then handed the quarter to the driver and said, "Here, you gave me too much change."

The driver with a smile, replied, "Aren't you the new preacher in town? I have been thinking lately about going to worship somewhere. I wanted to see what you would do if I gave you too much change."

When the preacher stepped off the bus, he literally grabbed the nearest light pole, held on, and said, "O God, I almost sold your Son for a quarter."

Our lives are the only Bible some folks will ever read. Not only are there people around us who are checking us out, but sometimes the Lord gives us occasion to prove ourselves to Him. Temptations and trials are common to all believers, and God promises He will always provide the strength and help to do the right thing. (1 Cor. 10:13).

James also gives us a great promise, *"Blessed is the man that endureth temptation: for when he is tried, he shall receive the crown of life"* (James 1:12).

AUGUST 7
Prayer At A Ballgame

I don't believe in Santa Claus, but I'm not going to sue somebody for singing a Ho-Ho-Ho song in December. I don't agree with Darwin, but I didn't go out and hire a lawyer when my high school teacher taught his theory of evolution. Life, liberty or your pursuit of happiness will not be endangered because someone says a 30-second prayer before a football game.

So what's the big deal? They're just talking to a God they believe in and asking Him to grant safety to the players on the field. "But it's a Christian prayer," some will argue. Yes, and this is the United States of America, a country founded on Christian principles.

Christian churches outnumber all others better than 200-to-1. So what would you expect—somebody chanting Hare Krishna? If I went to a football game in Jerusalem, I would expect to hear a Jewish prayer. If I went to a soccer game in Baghdad, I would expect to hear a Muslim prayer.

If I went to a ping pong match in China, I would expect to hear someone pray to Buddha. And I wouldn't be offended. It wouldn't bother me one bit.

"But what about the atheists?" is another argument.

What about them? Nobody is asking them to be baptized. We're not going to pass the collection plate. Just humor us for 30 seconds. If that's asking too much, bring a Walkman or a pair of ear plugs. Go to the bathroom. Visit the concession stand. Call your lawyer.

Unfortunately, one or two will make that call. One or two will tell thousands what they can and cannot do. I don't think a short prayer at a football game is going to shake the world's foundations.

AUGUST 8
Who Do You Know

Hilding Halverson tells of when his son was a small boy playing with his buddies in the back yard, and overhearing them talking one day—and the conversation was very amusing.

One of the boys said 'My dad can whip your dad.' He says "I heard one boy proudly say, 'My dad knows the mayor of our town!' Then I heard another say, 'That's nothing—my dad knows the governor of our state!'

Wondering what was coming next in the 'program of bragging,' I presently heard a wonderfully familiar voice (that of my own little son), saying, 'That's nothing—my dad knows God!'

"I swiftly slipped away from my place of eavesdropping with tears running down my cheeks. I dropped on my knees in my room and prayed earnestly and gratefully, "Oh, God, I pray that my boy will always be able to say, 'My dad knows God.' ""

We do tend to take pride in who we know, don't we?

"I went to school with Michael Jordan."

"I once shook hands with Johnny Cash."

I personally enjoy telling folks that I had my picture made with President Regan, and had Governor Lester Maddox at my church when he was running for president.

I also like to talk about having Col. Harlan Sanders come by our table to chat with us at his wife's restaurant in Kentucky.

There is a sense in which we take on some of the prestige and the importance of those whom we know.

Of all the people we know, it would be great if we can say, I know God and I'm on a first name basis with Him.

"And hereby we do know that we know him, if we keep his commandments" (I John 2:3).

AUGUST 9
Loving Life And Seeing Good Days

Peter gives us a seven fold formula in this third chapter of I Peter. In verse ten he says, *"For he that will love life and see good days let him."*

Peter is reading minds in this passage. This is what everybody is looking for. He must have just finished reading the sermon on the mount. He is talking millennial language, "Peace on earth and good will toward all men."

These are the words the angels spoke when they appeared at the birth of Jesus. They were announcing that love and peace will result in a relationship with Jesus.

The first step is, *"Let him refrain his tongue from evil, and his lips that they speak no guile."* James tells us we can control horses with bits in their mouths, and ships with a small helm, but the tongue is like a fire out of control.

Second, *"Let him eschew evil, and do good."* If I am going to do this I must know the difference between the two. Solomon wrote, *"There is a way that seemeth right unto a man, but the end thereof are the ways of death"* (Proverbs 16:25).

Third, one must pursue and work toward peace, *"Let him seek peace, and ensue it."*

Fourth, *"Let him speak as of the oracles of God."* Thus sayeth the Lord, not 'I think', or 'I believe'.

Fifth, *"If any man minister, let him do it as of the ability which God giveth."* God gives different gifts. We must find our gifts and apply them.

Sixth, *"Yet if any man suffer as a Christian, let him not be ashamed."* We are to be bold in identifying with Him.

Finally, *"But let him glorify God on this behalf."* We glorify God in all things.

AUGUST 10
Pardon Refused

It was somewhere near the year of 1830 that a man named George Wilson killed a government employee who caught him in the act of robbing the mails. He was tried and sentenced to be hanged. President Andrew Jackson reviewed his case and issued him a pardon. To everybody's surprise Wilson refused to accept the pardon. The legal ramifications of the case ended up in the supreme court. Chief Justice Marshall, perhaps one of the greatest justices of all time wrote the opinion of the court. "A pardon is a slip of paper, the value of which is determined by the acceptance of the person to be pardoned. If it is refused, it is no pardon. George Wilson must be hanged." And he was.

Our Bible teaches that every man is guilty and has been sentenced to eternal death. It also teaches that Jesus has made the payment for sin and offers a free pardon to all who will receive it. *"And he is the propitiation for our sins: and not for ours only, but also for the sins of the whole world"* (1 John 2:2). John also wrote, *"He that believeth on him is not condemned: but he that believeth not is condemned already, because he hath not believed in the name of the only begotten Son of God"* (John 3:18).

Jesus offered pardon to multitudes and many refused to accept His offer. All the disciples offered a pardon to all that would believe and accept the offer of salvation. Paul offered it to Agrippa, and he said, "Almost thou persuadest me to be a Christian," but he turned down the offer and went into eternity lost forever.

Most of the people of the world are refusing this same free pardon from God.

AUGUST 11
The Truth About Prohibition

Between 1919 and 1933, it was illegal to make and sell liquor in the United States. It was called the Prohibition Era. The following observations about that era are from the Cornerstone Challenge, December 1988:

We have all heard the stories about how prohibition was such a failure because even during that time when alcoholic beverages were illegal, there were black marketers, illegal whiskey was made in back rooms, and gangsters like Al Capone and others made a mockery of the laws of the country.

But let's take a look at the facts.

During the Prohibition: (1919-1933)
- Crime decreased by 54%
- The death rate due to alcohol decreased by 43%
- 97% percent of the 98 Keely Alcoholic Clinics closed for lack of patients
- All 60 Neil Cure Clinics closed due to lack of patients afflicted with alcoholism
- Insanity decreased by 66%

Post Prohibition Era:
- Drunkenness increased 350% shortly after Prohibition ceased
- Crime immediately spiraled and continued to do so until it is now rampant
- Some 50% of all traffic accidents are alcohol related
- There are 10 million known alcoholics in America today
- Of the known alcoholics, 3.5 million are 14-17 years of age

We often hear about how deadly and harmful drugs are. One of the most, if not the most deadly drugs is that of alcoholic beverages.

Not only is it legalized but the government taxes it in order to increase its revenue. Solomon said, *"Wine is a mocker, strong drink is raging: and whosoever is deceived thereby is not wise"* (Proverbs 20:1).

And *"Look not thou upon the wine when it is red, when it giveth his colour in the cup, when it moveth itself aright. At the last it biteth like a serpent, and stingeth like an adder"* (Proverbs 23:31-32).

AUGUST 12
Too Good To Be True
(2 Kings 7:1-11)

The Bible is filled with some almost unbelievable stories. When I read this account of the intervention of the Lord and the abundant provision of food for the lepers and the starving people of the city of Samaria, I think of the words of the old country preacher who said, "I declare, if that wasn't in the Bible, I wouldn't believe that."

Well, it is in the Bible and it did happen just as the Bible says. The people in the city of Samaria were desperate. The army of Benhadad, surrounded the city and cut off their food supply. The people were starving. Except for just a few horses, they had eaten everything.

A woman came crying to the king with her heart-breaking story. She and her friend had agreed that they would kill their sons and eat them. They had killed and eaten the first boy, but the second woman backed out and would not go along with her bargain. Elisha gave a bold message of hope.

"Tomorrow," he said, "at this time, there will be an abundance of food."

Another drama was unfolding just outside the city gate. Four lepers were also starving. Their food supply had also been cut off. As they discussed their options, they reasoned, "We could go into the city, but there is no food there; we can sit here until we die, or we could go to the enemy camp and beg for food."

They hobbled over to the camp and were amazed to find it totally deserted. However, what they did find was stores of food, clothing, animals, silver, and gold in abundance. This was too good to be true. There was exceeding, abundantly, above all they could ask or even think (Ephesians 3:20).

AUGUST 13
Tracing Your Ancestry

The following conversation was overheard at a party attended by high society people: "My ancestry goes all the way back to Alexander the Great," said one lady.

A second lady said, "I don't know how far my family goes back, all of our records were lost in the Flood."

Someone said, "Every family tree has some sap in it. The theory of relativity says if you go back far enough, we're all related."

It's true the concept of the "brotherhood of man" is a biblical concept. Despite the differences around the world, despite the different cultures, despite the different skin tones, we are all related.

Paul said to the men of Athens: *"And hath made of one blood all nations of men for to dwell on all the face of the earth, and hath determined the times before appointed, and the bounds of their habitation; That they should seek the Lord, if haply they might feel after him, and find him, though he be not far from every one of us: For in him we live, and move, and have our being"* (Acts 17:26-28a).

Why would Paul make such a statement? Perhaps to say that if you trace your ancestry back only to the time of Abraham, you live in a divided world because you are either a Jew or a Gentile. But, if you trace your ancestry back even further, we are once again united in the realization that we are part of one human family, created by God to be in fellowship with Him.

Our realization of the brotherhood of man ultimately affects not only our relationship with one another, but our relationship with God as well. One day God will reunite all people into one family again, forever.

AUGUST 14
The Night Jesus Came

Twas the night Jesus came and all through the house,
Not a person was praying, not one in the house.
The Bible was left on the shelf without care,
For no one thought Jesus would come there.

The children were dressing to crawl into bed,
Not once ever kneeling or bowing their head.
When out of the east there rose such a clatter,
I sprang to my feet to see what was the matter.

Away to the window I flew like a flash,
Tore open the shutters and lifted the sash.
When what to my wondering eyes should appear,
But Angels proclaiming that Jesus was here.

The light of His face made me cover my head
Was Jesus returning just like He'd said.
And though I possessed worldly wisdom and wealth,
I cried when I saw Him in spite of myself.

In the Book of Life which He held in His hand,
Was written the name of every saved man.
He spoke not a word as he searched for my name,
when He said "it's not here" my head hung in shame.

The people whose names had been written with love,
He gathered to take to his Father above.
With those who were ready He rose without sound,
While all of the others were left standing around.

I fell to my knees but then it was too late,
I'd waited too long and thus sealed my fate.
I stood and I cried as they rose out of sight,
Oh, if only I'd known that this was the night.

In the words of this poem the meaning is clear
The coming of Jesus is now drawing near.
There's only one life and when comes the last call,
We'll find out that the Bible was true after all.

AUGUST 15
What Are You Still Carrying

Two monks on a pilgrimage came to the ford of a river. There they saw a girl dressed in all her finery, obviously not knowing what to do since the river was high and she did not want to spoil her clothes.

Without more ado, one of the monks took her on his back, carried her across and put her down on dry ground on the other side. Then the monks continued on their way. But the other monk after an hour started complaining, "Surely it is not right to touch a woman; it is against our vows to have close contact with women. How could you go against the rules for monks?"

The monk who had carried the girl walked along silently, but finally he remarked, "I set her down by the river an hour ago, why are you still carrying her?"

One of the hardest things we must do is to let go of something from the past. Someone does us wrong and seeks forgiveness, but we want to keep carrying the memory. Or maybe we made a mistake and we can't seem to stop beating ourselves up, despite the fact that we have done what God says to do to be forgiven.

We don't need to keep carrying the memory and the guilt. In fact, it often seems more difficult to forgive ourselves than to forgive others.

Paul wrote, *"Even as Christ forgave you, so also do ye"* (Col. 3:13) and, *"Brethren, I do not count myself to have apprehended: but this one thing I do, forgetting those things which are behind, and reaching forth unto those things which are before, I press toward the mark for the prize of the high calling of God in Christ Jesus"* (Phil. 3:13-14).

AUGUST 16
What Are you Worried About

I heard about a patient in a mental hospital who was holding his ear close to the wall, listening intently. The attendant finally approached.

"Shh!" whispered the patient, beckoning him over.

The attendant pressed his ear to the wall for a long time. "I can't hear a thing," he said.

"I know," replied the patient, "it's been like that all day!"

Have you ever worried so much about things going wrong that you begin to worry when everything goes right? Worry probably does more than anything else to keep us from having peace of mind.

Psychologists have come up with some statistics about our worries. They say that 40% of the things we worry about never happen, 30% of the things we worry about have already happened (and thus can't be changed), 12% of our worries focus on health concerns, and 10% of our worries are over insignificant things.

That means that over 80% of our worries are about things which are unimportant, or that we have absolutely no control over.

Dr. Curtis Hutson used to tell about the man who came downstairs and found a burglar gathering up the valuables. As the thief was about to flee, the man said, "Please wait right there for a few minutes, my wife has been expecting you for the last ten years and I don't want her to be disappointed."

So, what have you been worrying about lately? We are not to worry about anything, but pray and ask God for our needs. Paul wrote *"Be careful for nothing; but in every thing by prayer and supplication with thanksgiving let your requests be made known unto God. And the peace of God, which passeth all understanding, shall keep your hearts and minds through Christ Jesus"* (Phil. 4:6-7).

AUGUST 17
Heart Problem

The story is told of a woman who went to her first show at an art gallery and was looking at the modern art paintings. One was a huge canvas that had black with yellow blobs of paint splattered all over it. The next painting was a murky gray color that had drips of purple paint streaked across it.

The lady walked over to the artist and said, "I'm having trouble understanding your paintings."

"I paint what I feel inside me," explained the artist.

The lady stated, "Have you ever tried Alka-Seltzer?"

Jesus talked a lot about "what's inside of us." Truly, as someone once expressed, "The heart of the matter is the matter of the heart."

We can't fix what's on the outside until we fix what's wrong on the inside. Jesus was very plain about this, *"Woe unto you, scribes and Pharisees, hypocrites! for ye make clean the outside of the cup and of the platter, but within they are full of extortion and excess.... cleanse first that which is within the cup and platter, that the outside of them may be clean also.... ye are like unto whited sepulchers, which indeed appear beautiful outward, but are within full of dead men's bones, and of all uncleanness"* (Matthew 23:25-27).

And, every day, all of us do exactly what the artist above said—we express what's on the inside. We express it in the words that we speak.

"For out of the abundance of the heart the mouth speaketh. A good man out of the good treasure of his heart bringeth forth good things: and an evil man out of the evil treasure bringeth forth evil things" (Matthew 12:34-35).

Alka-Seltzer isn't the cure. For some, radical heart surgery is the answer. *"Create in me a clean heart, O God"* (Psalm 51:10).

AUGUST 18
Five More Minutes To Live

A young man stood before a large audience on the scaffold! The noose had been adjusted around his neck. In a few more moments he would be in eternity. The sheriff took out his watch and said, "If you have anything to say, speak now; you have but five minutes to live." What awful words for a young man, in full health and vigor, to hear.

He burst into tears and said with sobbing, "I only had one little brother. He had beautiful blue eyes and flaxen hair. How I loved him! I got drunk. I found my little brother picking strawberries. I got angry without reason; and killed him with a blow from a rake. I knew nothing about it till I awoke on the day after and found myself in prison. Whiskey had done it! It has ruined me! I have only one thing to say to the young people before I go to stand in the presence of my Judge. Never, never, touch anything that can intoxicate! Whiskey did it!"

How long, how long shall our nation be crazed with rum? When, oh when, will the American people wake up? Oh that the professed people of God would vote as they pray.

What about the multitudes of innocent people who are killed by drunkards? We protect and license a man who deals out death and destruction, and hang a man who gets drunk and kills his neighbor.

Who was most to blame—this young man, or the saloon-keeper who made him crazy, or the government that gave the saloon-keeper license? The Bible warns, *"Woe unto him that giveth his neighbour drink, that puttest thy bottle to him, and makest him drunken also, that thou mayest look on their nakedness"* (Habakkuk 2:15).

AUGUST 19
Why God Created Children

To those of us who have children, whether they are our own, grandchildren, nieces, nephews, or students...here is something to make you chuckle. Whenever your children are out of control, you can take comfort from the thought that even God's perfection did not extend to His own children.

187

After creating heaven and earth, God created Adam and Eve. And the first thing he said was "Don't!"

"Don't what?" Adam replied.

"Don't eat the forbidden fruit." God said.

"Forbidden fruit? We have forbidden fruit? Hey Eve...we have forbidden fruit!!!!!"

"No Way!"

"Yes way!"

"Do not eat the fruit!" said God.

"Why?"

"Because I am your Father and I said so!" God replied, wondering why He hadn't stopped creation after making the elephants. A few minutes later, God saw His children eating an apple and got upset!

"Didn't I tell you not to eat the fruit?" God asked.

"Uh huh," Adam replied.

"Then why did you?" said the Father.

"I don't know," said Eve.

"She started it!" Adam said.

"Did not!"

"Did too!"

"Did not!" Having had it with the two of them, God's punishment was that Adam and Eve should have children of their own. Thus the pattern was set.

But there is reassurance in the story! If you have persistently and lovingly tried to give children wisdom and they haven't taken it, don't be hard on yourself. If God had trouble raising children, what makes you think it would be a piece of cake for you?

Remember that He said, *"Train up a child in the way he should go: and when he is old, he will not depart from it"* (Proverbs 22:6). He also gave a word to the kids, *"Children, obey your parents in the Lord: for this is right"* (Ephesians 6:1).

AUGUST 20
The Twenty Commandments

The Lord gave Moses the ten commandments on Mount Sinai as recorded in the book of Exodus, *"And he wrote upon the tables the words of the covenant, the ten commandments"* (Exodus 34:28). He then gave them to him again as recorded in Deuteronomy 10:4: *"And he wrote on the tables, according to the first writing, the ten commandments."*

They were:
- Thou shalt have no other gods
- No graven images or likenesses
- Not take the LORD's name in vain
- Remember the Sabbath day
- Honour thy father and thy mother
- Thou shalt not kill
- Thou shalt not commit adultery
- Thou shalt not steal
- Thou shalt not bear false witness
- Thou shalt not covet

Some suggested that we need to add ten more.
- **11th–**Thou shalt not worry, for worry is unproductive
- **12th–**Thou shalt not be fearful, for most of the things we fear never come to pass
- **13th–**Thou shalt not cross bridges before you come to them, for no one has yet succeeded in accomplishing this
- **14th–**Thou shalt handle only one problem at a time, and leave the others to the Lord
- **15th–**Thou shalt not take troubles to bed with you, for they make very poor bedfellows
- **16th–**Thou shalt not try to carry the problems of the world on your shoulders, for nobody (except for One) has a back that is broad enough
- **17th–**Thou shalt be a good listener, for God often speaks to us through the mouths of others
- **18th–**Thou shall not try to relive yesterday; for good or ill, it is forever gone
- **19th–**Thou shalt firmly dismiss feelings of frustration, for 90% of it is rooted in self-pity
- **20th–**Thou shalt count thy blessings, realizing that our biggest blessings are composed of many small ones

AUGUST 21
A Dying Girl's Request

An evangelist said: "A little girl of eight years was sent on an errand by her parents. While on her way she was attracted by the singing of a gospel meeting in the open air. The conductor of the meeting was so struck with the child's earnestness that he told her about Jesus.

She being the child of unbelievers did not know much about Him, but the gentleman told her of His love to her. On returning home, her father asked her what had detained her. She told him, and he beat her, forbidding her to go to any such meeting again.

Later she went on another errand. She was so taken up with what she had heard about Jesus that she forgot all about her message. She saw the same gentleman, who again told her more about the Saviour.

On her return home she told her father, as before, where she had been, and that she had found Jesus. Her father was enraged, and kicked the poor little creature until the blood came. She never recovered from this brutal treatment.

Just before she breathed her last she called to her mother and said, 'Mother, I have been praying to Jesus to save you and father.' Then pointing to her little dress she said, 'Mother, cut me a piece out of the blood-stained dress.'

The mother, wondering, did so.

'Now,' said the dying child, 'Christ shed His blood for my sake, and I am going to take this to Jesus to show Him that I shed my blood for His sake.'

Thus she died, holding firmly the piece of her dress stained with her own blood. The testimony of that dear child was the means of leading both father and mother to Christ."

AUGUST 22
A Letter To Dad

A father passing by his son's bedroom was astonished to see the bed was nicely made, and everything was picked up. Then, he saw an envelope, propped up prominently on the pillow. It was addressed, "Dad." He opened the envelope and read the letter, with trembling hands.

Dear Dad,

It is with great regret and sorrow that I'm writing you. I had to elope with my new girlfriend, because I wanted to avoid a scene with Mom and you.

I've been finding real passion with Stacy, and she is so nice, but I knew you would not approve of her, because of all her piercing, tattoos, her tight motorcycle clothes, and because she is so much older than me.

But it's not only the passion, Dad she's pregnant. Stacy said that we will be very happy. She owns a trailer in the woods, and has a stack of firewood for the winter.

We share a dream of having many more children. Stacy has opened my eyes to the fact that marijuana doesn't really hurt anyone.

We'll be growing it for ourselves, and trading it with the other people in the commune. Meanwhile, we'll pray that science will find a cure for AIDS so Stacy can get better. She sure deserves it!

Don't worry Dad, I'm 15, and I know how to take care of myself. Someday, I'm sure we'll be back to visit, so you can get to know your grandchildren.

Love, your son,
John

P.S. Dad,

None of the above is true. I'm over at Tommy's house. I just wanted to remind you that there are worse things in life than the report card that's in my center desk drawer. I love you! Call when it is safe for me to come home.

AUGUST 23
Growing Old

Many people worry about growing old, and this is hard for them to cope with, mentally, or otherwise. It is only natural for us to want to live as long as we can with a reasonable portion of good health, and there is nothing wrong with this. But, why worry when we can pray and trust the Lord for our needs to be met?

Just think or a moment, if you know the Lord as your personal Saviour, you are getting closer to your eternal Home by the minute, in fact, by the second, and the best lies ahead for all the saved.

God's precious promises should expel from our mind all worry and gloom. 2 Cor. 4:18 says, *"While we look not at the things which are seen, but at the things which are not seen: for the things which are seen are temporal; but the things which are not seen are eternal."*

Think of what awaits us, His children, according to 1 Peter 1:4, *"An inheritance incorruptible, and undefiled, and that fadeth not away, reserved in heaven for you."*

As we all very well know, we are living in the land of the dying. Praise God, we who know the Lord, one day will go to the land where there is no death, no sickness, no suffering, no afflictions of any kind.

1 Cor. 2:9 says, *"But as it is written, Eye hath not seen, nor ear heard, neither have entered into the heart of man, the things God hath prepared for them that love Him."* We need to accept His will, and adjust to it, and have the right attitude, as Job said, *"Though He slay me, yet will I trust in Him"* (Job 13:15a).

—Evangelist Rutherford E. Layne

AUGUST 24
The Bullet

"Be not hasty in thy spirit to be angry: for anger resteth in the bosom of fools." (Ecclesiastes 7:9)

A magazine recently carried the strange story of a man who became so angry with his neighbor that he grabbed his gun and took a shot at him. The shot missed the neighbor and embedded in a nearby tree.

Fifty years later and after a lot of water had gone under the bridge the neighbor decided to cut the tree down. He began to cut away with his chain saw. The chain cut into the bullet and hurled it into the man's head and killed him instantly.

It would be interesting to know how a jury and a judge would handle a case like this in our modern court system. It will be even more interesting to know if God will hold the first man responsible for violating the commandment, "Thou Shalt Not Kill."

According to the words of Jesus in the sermon on the mount, he was already guilty of murder for the fifty years. He said, *"Ye have heard that it was said by them of old time, Thou shalt not kill; and whosoever shall kill shall be in danger of the judgment: But I say unto you, That whosoever is angry with his brother without a cause shall be in danger of the judgment"* (Matthew 5:21-22a).

The angry man could certainly be forgiven, and washed in the blood of Christ, however his anger and malice would likely have built up hardness of heart and caused him to refuse the gospel and reject Christ and end up at the Great White Throne judgment. and finally in the lake of fire.

AUGUST 25
Counterfeits

An incident took place back in 1887 in a small neighborhood grocery store when Emanuel Nenger, gave the cashier a $20 bill to pay for some turnip greens. When the cashier placed the bill in the cash drawer she noticed that some of the ink from the $20 came off on her hands which were wet from wrapping the greens. She'd known Mr. Nenger for years and was shocked.

She thought, "Is this man giving me a counterfeit $20 bill?" But she quickly dismissed the thought and gave him his change. But $20 was a lot of money so she notified the police who, went to Nenger's home where they found tools used to reproduce the counterfeit $20 notes.

They found an easel, paint brushes, and paints which he was using to meticulously paint the counterfeit money. He was a master artist. They also found three portraits that Nenger had painted that sold at public auction for a little over $16,000! It took him as much time to paint a $20 note as it did to paint those portraits.

That story reminds us of folks who spend a lot of effort creating an "image" which they can present to people. They will go out of their way to make you think they are someone they are not.

The irony is that it takes almost as much effort to create these "masks" as it does to develop the qualities themselves—which are infinitely more valuable!

Jesus said, *"Woe to you, scribes and Pharisees, hypocrites! For ye are like unto whited sepulchers, which indeed appear beautiful outward, but are within full of dead men's bones, and of all uncleanness. Even so ye also outwardly appear righteous unto men, but within ye are full of hypocrisy and iniquity"* (Matthew 23:27-28).

AUGUST 26
God's Embroidery

My mother used to sew a great deal. I would sit at her knee and look up from the floor and ask what she was doing. She informed me that she was embroidering. As from the underside I watched her work within the boundaries of the little round hoop, I complained to her that it sure looked messy from where I sat.

She would smile at me, look down and say, "Son, you go play for a while, and when I am finished with my embroidering, I will let you see it from my side."

I would wonder why she was using some dark threads along with the bright ones and why they seemed so jumbled from my view. A few minutes would pass and then I would hear Mother's voice say,

"Son, come and sit on my knee." This I did only to be surprised see a beautiful flower, or a sunset. I could not believe it, because from underneath it looked so messy. Then Mother would say to me, "My son, from underneath it did look messy but you did not realize that there was a plan on the top. I was only following it. Now look at it from my side and you will see what I was doing."

Many times through the years I have looked up to heaven and said, "Father, what are You doing?"

He has answered, "I am embroidering your life."

I say, "But it looks like a mess to me. Why can't they all be bright?"

The Father seems to tell me, "'My child, you go about doing My business, and one day I will bring you to Heaven and put you on My knee and you will see the plan from My side."

God bless you in the days to come!

AUGUST 27
World Peace

Is there ever going to be unity and harmony in the world? The angels that came to the shepherds to announce the birth of Christ spoke of *"Glory to God in the highest, and on earth peace, and good will toward men."* That would be a wonderful time.

History records periods when the world was controlled by one king. The Assyrian, Babylonian, Persian, Greek, and Roman empires are examples of this. We live in a strange period illustrated by the account of an English princess (Diana), with an Egyptian boyfriend, crashes in a French tunnel, driving a German car, with a Dutch engine, driven by a Belgian who was drunk on Scottish whisky, followed closely by Italian Paparazzi, on Japanese motorcycles; treated by an American doctor, using Brazilian medicines.

You may be reading this on a computer assembled in China, that uses Taiwanese chips, and a Korean monitor, assembled by Bangladeshi workers in a Singapore plant, transported by Indian lorry-drivers, hijacked by Indonesians, unloaded by Sicilian longshoremen, and trucked to you by Mexican illegals.

There is coming a time when there will be one kingdom, with one King reigning over the whole earth. Our Bible has never been wrong and it spells out how things are going to be. Christ is going to come with a great army of saints and angels and arrest the Devil and confine him in a bottomless pit for a thousand years. He will set up His kingdom and reign with a rod of iron, or complete control.

The Apostle Paul explains, *"Then cometh the end, when he shall have delivered up the kingdom to God, even the Father; when he shall have put down all rule and all authority and power. For he must reign, till he hath put all enemies under his feet"* (1 Cor. 15:24-25).

Glory!

AUGUST 28
God And A Spider

During World War II, a US marine was separated from his unit on a Pacific Island. Alone in the jungle, he could hear enemy soldiers coming. Scrambling for cover, he found his way up a ridge to several small caves.

He realized that once the enemy soldiers swept up the ridge, they would quickly search all the caves. He prayed, "Lord, if it be Your will, please protect me." After praying, he lay quietly listening to the enemy begin to draw close.

Then he saw a spider begin to build a web over the front of his cave. As he watched, the spider layered strand after strand of web across the opening of the cave.

195

He thought, "What I need is a brick wall and what the Lord has sent me is a spider web. God does have a sense of humor."

As the enemy drew closer he watched from the darkness of his hideout and could see them searching one cave after another. As they came to his, he got ready to make his last stand. To his amazement, however, after glancing in the direction of his cave, they moved on.

Suddenly, he realized that with the spider web over the entrance, his cave looked as if no one had entered for quite a while.

"Lord, forgive me," prayed the young man. "I had forgotten that in you a spider's web is stronger than a brick wall."

We all face times of great trouble. When we do, it is so easy to forget the victories that God would work in our lives, sometimes in the most surprising ways.

As the great leader, Nehemiah, reminded the people of Israel when they faced the task of rebuilding Jerusalem, *"The God of heaven he will prosper us"* (Nehemiah 2:20).

AUGUST 29
God Will Use Us

God can use me? The world might say there are many reasons why God wouldn't want to use you or me. But don't worry:

Moses stuttered. David's armor didn't fit. John Mark was rejected by Paul. Hosea's wife was a prostitute. Amos' only training was in the school of fig-tree pruning. Solomon was too rich. Abraham was too old. David was too young. Timothy had ulcers. Peter was afraid of death. Lazarus was dead. John was self-righteous. Naomi was a widow. Paul was a murderer. So was Moses. So was David. Jonah ran from God. Miriam was a gossip. Gideon and Thomas both doubted. Jeremiah was depressed and suicidal. Elijah was burned out. John the Baptist was a loudmouth. Martha was a worrywart. Mary was lazy. Samson had long hair. Noah got drunk.

Did I mention that Moses had a short fuse? So did Peter, Paul, and lots of other folks.

But God doesn't require a job interview. He doesn't hire and fire like most bosses, because He's more our Dad than our Boss. He doesn't look at financial gain or loss. He's not prejudiced or partial, not judging, grudging, sassy, or brassy, not deaf to our cry, not blind to our need.

Satan says, "You're not worthy."

Jesus says, "So what? I AM."

Satan looks back and sees our mistakes.

God looks back and sees the cross. He doesn't calculate what you did in '78. It's not even on the record. Sure. There are lots of reasons why God shouldn't want us. But if we are utterly in love with Him, if we hunger for Him more than our next breath, He'll use us in spite of who we are.

Step out of your limitations into the unlimited nature of God.

AUGUST 30
In His Hands

A basketball in my hands is worth about $19. A basketball in Michael Jordan's hands is worth about $33 million. It depends whose hands it's in.

A baseball in my hands is worth about $6. A baseball in Mark McGwire's hands is worth $19 million It depends whose hands it's in.

A tennis racket is useless in my hands A tennis racket in Pete Sampras' hands is a Wimbledon Championship. It depends whose hands it's in.

A rod in my hands will keep away a wild animal. A rod in Moses' hands will part the mighty sea. It depends whose hands it's in.

A sling shot in my hands is a kid's toy. A sling shot in David's hand is a mighty weapon. It depends whose hands it's in.

Two fish and 5 loaves of bread in my hands is a couple of fish sandwiches. Two fish and 5 loaves of bread in God's hands will feed thousands. It depends whose hands it's in.

Nails in my hands might produce a birdhouse. Nails in Jesus Christ's hands will produce salvation for the entire world. It depends whose hands it's in.

As you see now, it depends whose hands it's in. So put your concerns, worries, fears, hopes, dreams, families and relationships in God's hands because, you see, it depends whose hands it's in.

As Paul pleaded, *"I beseech you therefore, brethren, by the mercies of God, that ye present your bodies a living sacrifice, holy, acceptable unto God, which is your reasonable service"* (Romans 12:1).

Again, *"Neither yield ye your members as instruments of unrighteousness unto sin: but yield yourselves unto God, as those that are alive from the dead, and your members as instruments of righteousness unto God"* (Romans 6:13).

AUGUST 31
The Other Side Of The Coin

I have much to be thankful for.

For the teenager who is not doing dishes but is watching TV, because that means he is at home and not on the streets.

For the taxes that I pay, because it means that I have a job.

For the mess to clean after a party, because it means that I have been surrounded by friends.

For the clothes that fit a little too snug, because it means I have more than enough to eat.

For my shadow that watches me work, because it means I am out in the sunshine.

For a lawn that needs mowing, windows that need cleaning, and gutters that need fixing, because it means I am blessed with a home.

For all the complaining I hear about the government, because it means that we have freedom of speech.

For the parking spot I find at the far end of the parking lot, because it means I am capable of walking and that I have been blessed with transportation.

For my huge heating bill, because it means I am warm.

For the lady behind me In church that sings off key, because it means that I can still hear.

For the pile of laundry and ironing, because it means I have clothes to wear.

For weariness and aching muscles at the end of the day, because it means I have been capable of working hard.

For the alarm that goes of in the early morning hours, because it means that I am still alive.

And finally...

For way too much e-mail, because it means I have friends who are thinking of me.

"Giving thanks always for all things unto God and the Father in the name of our Lord Jesus Christ" (Ephesians 5:20).

SEPTEMBER 1
How To Get In

A man dies and goes to heaven. Of course, St. Peter meets him at the Pearly Gates.

St. Peter says, "Here's how it works. You need 100 points to make it into Heaven. You tell me all the good things you've done, and I give you a certain number of points for each item, depending on how good it was. When you reach 100 points, you get in."

"Okay," the man says, "I was married to the same woman for 50 years and never cheated on her, even in my heart."

"That's wonderful," says St. Peter, "that's worth three points!"

"Three points?" he says. "Well...I attended church all my life and supported its ministry with my tithe and service."

"Terrific!" says St. Peter. "That's certainly worth a point."

"One point? I started a soup kitchen in my city and worked in a shelter for the homeless veterans."

"Fantastic, that's good for two more points," he says.

"Two points!" the man cries. "At this rate, the only way I will get into heaven is by the Grace of God!"

"Bingo! 100 points! Come on in!"

Jesus made this very plain when He said, *"I am the way, the truth, and the life: no man cometh unto the Father, but by me"* (John 14:6).

Paul explains it when he wrote, *"For by grace are ye saved through faith; and that not of yourselves: it is the gift of God: Not of works, lest any man should boast"* (Ephesians 2:8-9) and again, *"But by the grace of God I am what I am: and his grace which was bestowed upon me was not in vain; but I laboured more abundantly than they all: yet not I, but the grace of God which was with me"* (1 Cor. 15:10).

SEPTEMBER 2
On Your Hands And Knees

There was a man telling his friend that he and his wife had a serious argument the night before.

"But it ended," he said, "when she came crawling to me on her hands and knees."

"What did she say?" asked the friend.

The husband replied, "She said, Come out from under that bed, you coward!"

We husbands like the idea of our wives coming to us on their hands and knees. We are quick to memorize Ephesians 5:22, *"Wives, submit yourselves unto your own husbands, as unto the Lord."* And the New Testament does teach the headship of the husband.

But it is not a leadership patterned after Genghis Khan (though you might think so to hear some men talk). Rather, it is a leadership patterned after Jesus Christ.

In fact, the verse prior to the one quoted above gives an important principle, *"...submitting yourselves one to another in the fear of God."* This is the principle of mutual submission.

We need to understand what Jesus was teaching when He washed the disciples feet and said, *"For I have given you an example, that ye should do as I have done to you"* (John 13:15).

In exclaiming this matter Paul stressed the fact that, *"Christ also loved the church, and gave himself for it;"* (Ephesians 5:25).

The man is to be an example of Christ in the home, taking the role of Christ, as the woman fills her role as the church. When both parties understand that they are given this role to help people around them see and understand that their role is part of a higher purpose than just themselves.

He later explains that, *"This is a great mystery: but I speak concerning Christ and the church"* (Ephesians 5:32).

SEPTEMBER 3
A Pretend Heart Attack

The story is told of a married couple enjoying their luxury fishing boat together. The husband was concerned about what might happen in an emergency.

So one day he said to his wife, "Please take the wheel, dear. Pretend that I am having a heart attack. You must get the boat safely to shore." So she did.

Later that evening, the wife walked into the living room where her husband was watching television. She sat down next to him, switched the TV channel, and said to him, "Please go into the kitchen, dear. Pretend I'm having a heart attack. You must set the table, cook the dinner, and wash the dishes."

It's not a very pleasant thing to pretend such a thing, but there are some concerns we should have. I wouldn't consider it at all out of place for an insurance salesman to ask the question, "If you were to die today, would your family be taken care of?"

If I were to have a heart attack tonight and die, would I be prepared to stand before God? As I grow older, I become more aware of the fact that each day is a blessing from God, and I am not promised even one more.

"Go to now, ye that say, To day or to morrow we will go into such a city, and continue there a year, and buy and sell, and get gain: Whereas ye know not what shall be on the morrow. For what is your life? It is even a vapour, that appeareth for a little time, and then vanisheth away" (James 4:13-14).

I know it requires a degree of seriousness that may make one uncomfortable, but just for a moment, pretend that you are having a heart attack. Are you prepared?

SEPTEMBER 4
Heirs of God

Watchman Nee an oriental pastor tells the story about a new convert who came to see him and who was in deep distress.

The new convert said, "Pastor, no matter how much I pray, no matter how much I try, no matter how hard I try, I simply cannot seem to be faithful to my Lord. I have trouble with doubt and I think I am losing my salvation. I want to be able to relax and have peace about my standing with the Lord."

The pastor wisely pointed over beside him on the floor where his pet lay. "Do you see this old dog? He is my dog and he is house trained. He never makes a mess. He is obedient to me and never talks back. He is a pure delight to me. Out in the kitchen, I have a son. He is my baby. He makes a mess at the table. Sometimes he throws food. He dumps his meal all over himself and fowls his clothes. Sometimes this all happens at once and he then is a total mess. But guess who is going to inherit my kingdom? Not my faithful old dog, but my son. He is my heir! You as a convert belong to our Lord Jesus Christ," he told the new convert. "It is for you He died. You are a son."

"Wherefore thou art no more a servant, but a son; and if a son, then an heir of

God through Christ" (Galatians 4:7). *"Behold, what manner of love the Father hath bestowed upon us, that we should be called the sons of God: therefore the world knoweth us not, because it knew him not"* (1 John 3:1).

This didn't happen by your perfection, but by His grace."

SEPTEMBER 5
Let Go And Let God

The old story is told of a man who fell off the edge of a cliff. On the way down he grabbed a branch which temporarily stopped his fall. The canyon fell straight down for a thousand feet.

There was no way for him to climb up the steep wall of the cliff. So he began yelling for help, "Help! Help! Is anyone up there?"

No one heard him. He was about to give up when he heard a voice.

"Jack, Can you hear me?"

"Yes! I can hear you!"

"I am the Lord."

"The Lord? You mean, God?"

"That's Me."

"God, please help me!"

"I am going to help you. Now, here's what I want you to do. Listen carefully."

"I'll do anything, Lord. Just tell me what to do."

"Okay. Just let go of the branch and I'll catch you."

"Are you sure?"

"I said, let go of the branch. Just trust Me. Let go."

There was a long silence. Finally Jack yelled, "Help! Help! Help! Is anyone else up there?"

I wonder how many of us have felt like Jack? We say that we want to know the will of God, but when we find out what it is, we can't handle it. Sounds too scary, too difficult. We decide to look elsewhere.

When He says, "Let go of the things that stand between you and Me, and trust Me with your life," it sounds pretty scary. But when we let go, we find freedom and safety in His hands. Remember that Jesus loves us! When Jesus told Peter to cast the net on the other side, Peter said, "but Lord we have fished all night and caught nothing, but never the less at Thy word," then they had more fish than they could handle.

SEPTEMBER 6
The People Perish

An old preacher accepted a church in the country, hoping and believing that he could bring it back to the vibrant work that it had once been. He began to preach, pray, program, and struggle to see the Lord's blessing on his congregation.

Nothing seemed to motivate the people. He had a sign placed across the front of the auditorium. It was a quotation of Solomon's words, *"Where there is no vision, the people perish"* (Prov. 29:18).

After a long time of burden and tears, the pastor gave up and told the church that he felt that he had failed and it would be best for him to resign and allow them to get another man to lead them. While he was concluding his farewell remarks, a piece of the sign fell with a loud noise to the floor.

The shocked congregation stared at the sign. The "W" had fallen and the remainder of the sign read, "here there is no vision, the people perish."

This story has the same ring as the words of the Lord to Micah in the Old Testament, *"Therefore night shall be unto you, that ye shall not have a vision; and it shall be dark unto you, that ye shall not divine; and the sun shall go down over the prophets, and the day shall be dark over them"* (Micah 3:6).

It would be well to remember the time when the people Israelites were bitten by snakes and the Lord told Moses to put a brass serpent on a pole. The dying people were told to look upon the snakes and believe, and they would be healed. Many looked and lived. The song writer wrote, *"Look and live, my brother, live, look to Jesus now, and live."*

SEPTEMBER 7
Sin Eating Fish

On Rosh Hashanah (Jewish New Year) it is customary for Jews to go to the ocean, pray, and throw bread crumbs onto the water, so that the fish can symbolically eat their sins. Some people have been known to ask what kind of bread should they throw.

Rabbi Dick Israel of Boston, Massachusetts has suggested the following (mind you, with tongue in cheek):

For Complex Sins—Multi-Grain,

For Sins Committed in Haste—Matzah,

For Truly Twisted Sins—Pretzels,
For Substance Abuse—Poppy Seed,
For Committing Arson—Toast,
For the Ill-Tempered—Sourdough,
For the Silliest—Nut Bread,
For Having a Hole Where Your Heart Should Be—Bagels,
For Acting like a Madman—Crackers,
For Cutting Remarks—Sliced Bread,
For Flaunting Wealth in the form of Fancy Cars—Rolls.

While it may sound silly to have fish "eat" our sins, it serves to remind us that people will go to great lengths to try to relieve the guilt of sin.

We all know too well what it feels like to be burdened with sin, to live with regret, wishing "if only I could do it all over again" and knowing that we can't. The solution is found not in fish, but only in Jesus Christ, in his sacrifice and our willingness to submit to what he has done for us.

John writes: *"If we say that we have no sin, we deceive ourselves, and the truth is not in us. If we confess our sins, he is faithful and just to forgive us our sins, and to cleanse us from all unrighteousness"* (1 John 1:8-9).What a beautiful promise that Christians can take comfort in!

So hold onto your bread (make a sandwich!), and turn to Jesus to know the joy of forgiveness. "Go and sin no more" (John 8:11).

SEPTEMBER 8
What The Blind Man Saw

Two men, both seriously ill, occupied the same hospital room. One man was allowed to sit up in his bed for an hour each afternoon to help drain the fluid from his lungs. His bed was next to the room's only window. The other man had to spend all his time flat on his back.

Every afternoon when the man in the bed by the window could sit up, he would pass the time by describing all the things he could see outside the window. The man in the other bed began to live for those one hour periods.

The window overlooked a park with a lovely lake. Ducks and swans played on the water and children sailed their model boats. As the man by the window described all this in exquisite detail, the man on the other side of the room would close his eyes and imagine the picturesque scene. One morning, the nurse arrived to find the lifeless body of the man by the window, who had died peacefully in his sleep.

As soon as it seemed appropriate, the other man asked if he could be moved next to the window. The nurse was happy to make the switch, and after making sure he was comfortable, she left him alone.

Slowly, painfully, he propped himself up on one elbow to take his first look at the real world outside. He strained to slowly turn to look out the window beside the bed. It faced a blank wall. The man asked the nurse what could have compelled his deceased roommate to describe such wonderful things outside this window.

The nurse responded that the man was blind and could not even see the wall. She said, "Perhaps he just wanted to encourage you."

SEPTEMBER 9
How Gullible Are We?

A freshman at Eagle Rock Junior High won first prize at the Greater Idaho Falls Science Fair, April 26, 1997. He was attempting to show how conditioned we have become to the alarmists practicing junk science and spreading fear of everything in our environment.

In his project he urged people to sign a petition demanding strict control or total elimination of the chemical "dihydrogen monoxide."

And for plenty of good reasons, since it can:
   1. cause excessive sweating and vomiting
   2. it is a major component in acid rain
   3. it can cause severe burns in its gaseous state
   4. accidental inhalation can kill you
   5. it contributes to erosion
   6. it decreases effectiveness of automobile brakes
   7. it has been found in tumors of terminal cancer patients

He asked 50 people if they supported a ban of the chemical dihydrogen monoxide. Forty-three said yes, six were undecided, and only one knew that the chemical was...water!

The title of his prize winning project was, "How Gullible Are We?" The conclusion is obvious.

Religion is another area where people have a tendency to be gullible.

205

Extreme examples can be found in David Koresh's followers and the Heaven's Gate cult.

But it can happen any time we believe someone without checking out God's Word to see if what is being taught is the truth.

Faith does not mean blindly accepting whatever anyone (even a preacher) says. John warned, "Beloved, believe not every spirit, but try the spirits whether they are of God; because many false prophets are gone out into the world" (1 John 4:1).

Use God's Word to discern between what is true and what is false. And if you feel like living dangerously today, pour yourself a big tall glass of dihydrogen monoxide.

SEPTEMBER 10
Jukes Verses Edwards

Max Jukes lived as a backwoodsman in the American frontiers. He is described as "a hunter and fisher, a hard drinker, jolly and companionable, averse to steady toil, working hard by spurts and idling by turns." He had a numerous progeny, some of them almost certainly illegitimate.

Max Jukes was not a believer. He married a non-Christian. 709 descendants have been studied (540 blood descendants; 169 people who married into the family). Dugdale estimated a total of 1200 Jukes.

Out of these 1200:
* 280-310 died as paupers;
* 140-150 criminals—sent to the penitentiary—7 murderers and 60 were thieves. Of the 20 who learned a trade, 10 learned it in a state prison.
* 100 became drunks;
* 300 died prematurely.

Of the 540 blood descendants of the Juke sisters:
* 52.4% of the females were "harlots"—immoral women.
* 128 out of the 709 descendants of Jukes were prostitutes. 50 averaged 15 years of prostitution.
* 142 Jukes received state aid for an average of about 5 years.

On today's economic scale this family cost the state over 6 million dollars. There is no record that they ever made any positive contribution to society.

Jonathan Edwards, on the other hand, was a believer. He married a

Christian. In 1925 there was a reprint of Winship's 1900 report on 1394 descendants of Jonathan Edwards. Practically none were lawbreakers.

More than 100 became lawyers, 30 became judges, 100 became preachers, missionaries, and theological professors. More than 100 became college professors, 13 became university presidents, 62 became physicians, 60 attained prominence in authorship or editorial life, with 135 books of merit 80 elected to public office, including 3 mayors, 3 governors, several were members of congress, 3 senators, and 1 vice president, (Aaron Burr), 1 comptroller of the U.S. treasury and 75 became army or navy officers.

SEPTEMBER 11
Amazing 911 Facts

The World Trade Center
The twin towers of the World Trade Center were a place of employment for some 50,000 people. With the missing list of just over 5,000 people, that means 90% of the folks targeted survived the attack.

The Pentagon
Some 23,000 people were the target of a third plane aimed at the Pentagon. The latest count shows that only 123 lost their lives. That is an amazing 99.5% survival rate.

American Airlines Flight 77
This Boeing 757 that was flown into the outside of the Pentagon could have carried up to 289 people, yet only 64 were aboard. Luckily 78% of the seats were empty.

American Airlines Flight 11
This Boeing 767 could have had up to 351 people aboard, but only carried 92. Thankfully 74% of the seats were unfilled.

United Airlines Flight 175
Another Boeing 767 that could have sat 351 people only had 65 people on board. Fortunately it was 81% empty.

United Airlines Flight 93
This Boeing 757 was one of the most uplifting stories yet. The smallest flight to be hijacked with only 45 people aboard out of a possible 289 had 84% of its capacity unused.

Yet these people stood up to the attackers and thwarted a fourth attempted destruction of a national landmark, saving untold numbers of lives in the process.

Out of potentially 74,280 Americans directly targeted by these cowards, 93% survived the attacks. That's a higher survival rate than heart attacks, breast cancer, kidney transplants and liver transplants - all common, survivable illnesses.

The hijacked planes were mostly empty, the Pentagon was hit at its strongest point, the overwhelming majority of people in the World Trade Center buildings escaped, and a handful of passengers gave the ultimate sacrifice to save even more lives.

SEPTEMBER 12
My Drug Problem

The other day, someone at a store in our town read that a methamphetamine lab had been found in an old farmhouse in the adjoining county and he asked me a rhetorical question, "'Why didn't we have a drug problem when you and I were growing up?"

I replied, "I had a drug problem when I was young. I was drug to church on Sunday morning. I was drug to church for weddings and funerals. I was drug to family reunions and community socials no matter the weather. I was drug by my ears when I was disrespectful to adults. I was also drug to the woodshed when I disobeyed my parents, told a lie, brought home a bad report card, did not speak with respect, spoke ill of the teacher or the preacher, or if I didn't put forth my best effort in everything that was asked of me. I was drug to the kitchen sink to have my mouth washed out with soap if I uttered a profane four-letter word. I was drug out to pull weeds in mom's garden and flower beds and cockleburs out of dad's fields. I was drug to the homes of family, friends, and neighbors to help out some poor soul who had no one to mow the yard, repair the clothesline, or chop some firewood; and, if my mother had ever known that I took a single dime as a tip for this kindness, she would have drug me back to the woodshed."

Those drugs are still in my veins; and they affect my behavior in everything I do, say, and think. They are stronger than cocaine, crack, or heroin; and, if today's children had this kind of drug problem America would be a better place. Amen!

SEPTEMBER 13
My Typical Day

I wanted to let you know that I have been diagnosed with A.A.A.D.D.—Age Activated Attention Deficit Disorder.

This is how it goes:

I decide to do the laundry, start down the hall and notice the newspaper on the table. OK, I'm going to do the laundry...but first I'm going to glance through the newspaper.

After that, I notice the mail on the table. OK, I'll just put the newspaper in the recycle stack...but first I'll look through the pile of mail and see if there are any bills to be paid. Now where is the checkbook? Oops...there's the empty glass from yesterday on the coffee table. I'm going to look for that checkbook...but first I need to put the glass in the sink.

I head for the kitchen, look out the window, notice my poor flowers need a drink of water, I put the glass in the sink and...there's the remote for the TV on the counter. "What's it doing here?" I'll just put it away. But first I need to water those plants.

I head for the door and...Aaaagh! Stepped on the dog. Dog needs to be fed. Okay, I'll put the remote away and water the plants...but first I need to feed the dog.

By the end of the day, the laundry is not done, the newspapers are still on the floor, the glass is still in the sink, the bills are not paid, the checkbook is still lost, the dog ate the remote control...and, when I try to figure out how come nothing got done today, I'm baffled because I know I was busy all day!

I realize this condition is serious. I'd get help, but first, I think I'll check my e-mail!

SEPTEMBER 14
Mocking God

The Bible says, *"Be not deceived; God is not mocked: for whatsoever a man soweth, that shall he also reap"* (Galatians 6:7). Here are some men and women who mocked God—

John Lennon—during his interview with a magazine, said: "Christianity will end, it will disappear. I am certain. Jesus was ok, but his subjects were too simple. Today we are more famous than Him." Lennon, after saying that the Beatles were more famous than Jesus Christ, was shot six times.

Tancredo Neves—President of Brazil during the Presidential campaign, said if he got 500,000 votes, not even God would remove him from presidency. He got the votes, but got sick a day before taking office, and died.

Cazuza—bi-sexual Brazilian composer, singer and poet, during a show in Rio, while smoking his cigarette, puffed out some smoke into the air and said: "God, that's for you." He died at the age of 32 of AIDS in a horrible manner.

The man who built the Titanic—after its completion, a reporter asked him how safe the Titanic would be. With an oath he said: "Not even God can sink it." The result: I think you all know what happened.

Marilyn Monroe—She was visited by Billy Graham during a presentation of a show. He said the Spirit of God had sent him to preach to her. After hearing what the Preacher had to say, she said: "I don't need your Jesus." A week later, she was found dead in her apartment.

Bon Scott—The ex-vocalist of the AC/DC. On one of his songs sang: "Don't stop me, I'm going down all the way, down the highway to hell." On the 19th of February 1980, he was found dead; choked by his own vomit.

SEPTEMBER 15
No Nursing Home For Me

There will be no nursing home in my future…

When I get old, I'm going to get on a Princess Cruise Ship. The average cost for a nursing home is $200 per day. Reservations at Princess with a long term discount and senior discount price is $135 per day. That leaves $65 a day for gratuities which will be $10 per day.

I will have 10 meals a day if I can waddle to the restaurant, and room service, which means I can have breakfast in bed every day of the week.

Princess has as many as three swimming pools, a workout room, free washers and dryers, and shows every night. They have free toothpaste and razors, and free soap and shampoo. They will even treat you like a customer, not a patient. An extra $5 worth of tips will have the entire staff scrambling. I will get to meet new people every 7 or 14 days.

TV broken? Light bulb need changing? Need to have the mattress replaced? No problem! They will fix everything and apologize for your inconvenience. Clean sheets and towels every day, and you don't even have to ask for them.

If you fall in the nursing home and break a hip, you are on Medicare. If you fall and break a hip on the Princess ship, they will upgrade you to a suite for the rest of your life.

Now hold on for the best! Do you want to see South America, the Panama Canal, Tahiti, Australia, New Zealand, Asia, or name where you want to go? Princess will have a ship ready to go.

So don't look for me in a nursing home, just call shore to ship.

P.S. When you die, they just dump you over the side at no charge.

SEPTEMBER 16
Paid In Full

For many months he had admired a beautiful sports car in a dealer's showroom, and knowing his father could well afford it, he told him that was all he wanted.

As graduation day approached, the young man awaited signs that his father had purchased the car. Finally, on the morning of his graduation his father called him into his private study. His father told him how proud he was to have such a fine son, and told him how much he loved him. He handed his son a beautifully wrapped gift box.

Curious, but somewhat disappointed, the young man opened the box and found a lovely, leather-bound Bible. Angrily, he raised his voice at his father and said, "With all your money, you give me a Bible?" and stormed out of the house, leaving the holy book.

Many years passed and the young man was very successful in business. He had a beautiful home and wonderful family, but realized his father was very old, and thought perhaps he should go to him.

Before he could make arrangements, he received a telegram telling him his father had passed away, and willed all of his possessions to him. When he arrived at his father's house, regret filled his heart. He began to search his father's important papers and saw the Bible, just as he had left it years ago.

With tears, he opened the Bible. As he did, a car key dropped from an envelope taped behind the Bible. It had a tag with the dealer's name, the same dealer who had the sports car he had desired. On the tag was the date of his graduation, and the words...**Paid In Full.**

In our Bible, *"The gift of God is eternal life through Jesus Christ the Lord"* (Romans 6:23).

SEPTEMBER 17
Rapper Death Music

David Cloud pointed out that Rapper music is violent in nature and leaves a trail of tragic death.

Jam Master Jay, rapper with the popular group Run-DMC, was shot to death in his recording studio at age 37 by an unknown assailant.

Rapper Michael Menson, of the group Double Trouble died at age 29 when a gang soaked him in gasoline and set him afire. Double Trouble had a hit that same year titled "Street Tuff."

MC Rock, rapper with The Almighty RSO, was stabbed to death at age 28.

Trouble T-Roy (Troy Dixon), rapper with Heavy D and the Boyz, fell off a balcony after a concert at age 22.

Brandon Mitchell, rapper with Wreckx-N-Effect, died at about age 20. He was shot in an argument over a woman.

Charizma, rapper with Peanut Butter Wolf, was shot to death at age 20.

Deah Dame, rapper with Damian Dame, died in a car crash at age 35.

Mr. Cee, rapper with R.B.L. Posse (Ruthless By Law), was murdered.

Rapper Seagram Miller was shot to death in Oakland, California, He was 26.

Fat Pat (Patrick Hawkins), rapper who recorded immoral songs, was shot to death at age 26.

Malcolm Howard, rapper with 4 Black Faces, was shot to death execution style at roughly age 30.

MC Big L (Lamont Coleman), rapper with Diggin' In the Crates Crew, was shot to death outside his home at age 23.

Rapper MC Ant was shot to death at roughly age 35.

Matthew Roberts of Blaggers I.T.A. died at age 36 of drug related causes.

SEPTEMBER 18
The Dead Duck

A boy visiting his grandparent's farm was given a slingshot to play with in the woods. He practiced in the woods, but he could never hit a target.

Heading back to dinner he saw Grandma's pet duck. Just out of impulse, he let fly, hit the duck square in the head, killing it. In a panic, he hid the duck in the wood pile, then saw his sister watching.

Sally had seen everything. After lunch grandma said, "Sally, let's wash the dishes."

But Sally said, "Grandma, Johnny told me he wanted to do dishes, didn't you Johnny?" And then she whispered to him, "Remember, the duck?" Johnny did the dishes.

Later Grandpa asked if the children wanted to go fishing, and Grandma said, "I'm sorry but I need Sally to help make supper."

But Sally smiled and said, "Well, that's all right Johnny told me he wanted to help." Sally went fishing and Johnny stayed.

After several days doing both his chores and Sally's, he couldn't stand it any longer. He confessed to Grandma. She knelt down, gave him a hug, and said, "Sweetheart, I know, I was standing at the window, and I saw the whole thing. But because I love you, I forgave you. However, I was wondering how long you would let Sally enslave you."

The Lord knows our past. He also knows that the enemy has been throwing it in our face and making us a slave to the past failure. Jesus Christ was standing at the window and He saw the whole thing. But because He loves you, He is ready to forgive you.

Perhaps He's wondering how long you'll let the enemy make a slave out of you. The great thing about God is that He not only forgives, but He forgets.

SEPTEMBER 19
Recall Notice

The Maker of all human beings is now recalling all units, regardless of make or year, due to a serious defect in the central component of the heart. This is due to a malfunction in the original prototype units code-named Adam and Eve, resulting in the reproduction of the same defect in all subsequent units. This defect has been technically termed "Subsequential Internal Non-Morality," or more commonly known as S.I.N.

Symptoms include: Loss of direction, Foul vocal emissions, Amnesia of origin, Lack of peace and joy. Selfish or violent behavior, Depression in the mental component, Fearfulness, Idolatry, and Rebellion.

The Manufacturer, who is not at fault for this defect, is providing factory-authorized repair free of charge to correct this, SIN defect.

The Repair Technician, Jesus, has most generously offered to bear the entire burden of the staggering cost of these repairs. There is no additional fee required.

The number to call for repair is: P-R-A-Y-E-R. Once connected, please upload your burden of SIN through the REPENTANCE procedure. Next, download ATONEMENT from the Repair Technician, Jesus, into the heart component.

No matter how big or small the SIN defect is, Jesus will replace it with: Love, Joy, Peace, Patience, Kindness, Faithfulness, Gentleness, Self-control; Please see the operating manual, the B.I.B.L.E. for further details.

WARNING: Continuing to operate the human being unit without correction voids any manufacturer warranties, exposing the unit to dangers and problems too numerous to list and will result in the human unit being permanently impounded.

DANGER: The human being units not responding to this recall action will have to be scrapped in the furnace.

Please assist where possible by notifying others of this important recall notice, and you may contact the Father any time by "kneemail".

—GOD.

SEPTEMBER 20
The Father's Decision

A pastor once gave a brief introduction of his childhood friend. With that, an elderly man entered the pulpit to speak.

"A father, his son, and a friend of his son were sailing off the Pacific Coast," he began, "when a fast approaching storm blocked any attempt to get back to shore.

"The waves were so high he could not keep the boat upright, and the three were swept out into the ocean." The old man hesitated, making eye contact with two teenagers who were looking somewhat interested in his story.

He continued, "Grabbing a rescue line, the father had to make the most excruciating decision of his life…to which boy he would throw the line. He only had seconds to decide.

"The father knew his son was a Christian. He also knew that his son's friend was not. As the father yelled out, 'I love you son!" he threw the line to his son's friend. He pulled the friend back to the boat. His son disappeared into the black of night. and was never recovered."

The teenagers were sitting up in the pew, waiting for the next words from the old man. "The father," he continued, "knew his son would step into eternity with Jesus, therefore, he sacrificed his son. How great is the love of God that He should do the same for us." With that, the old man sat back down in his chair.

Immediately, the two teenagers were at the old man's side. "Did the other boy become a Christian?" they asked.

"That story gives me an understanding of what it must have been like for God to give up His Son for me," he explained. "You see…I was the father in the story and your pastor was my son's friend."

SEPTEMBER 21
Stuart Hamblin Story

Back in the 50's a well-known radio host in Hollywood named Stuart Hamblin noted for his drinking and womanizing, wrote a song, "I won't go hunting with you Jake, but I'll go chasing women."

Along came a young preacher holding a tent revival. Hamblin had him on his radio show to poke fun at him. To gather material for his show, Hamblin attended the revival meetings.

The preacher announced, "There is one man in this audience who is a big fake."

Hamblin was convinced he was the one the preacher spoke of. The sermon haunted him until he showed up drunk at the preacher's hotel door around 2 AM demanding that the preacher pray for him!

But the preacher said, "This is between you and God and I'm not going to get in the middle of it." But he invited Stuart in and they talked until about 5 AM and Stuart dropped to his knees and cried out to God.

Stuart quit drinking, quit chasing women and soon began to lose favor with the Hollywood crowd. He was fired by the radio station for refusing to accept a beer company commercial. He tried writing a couple of "Christian" songs but the only one that had much success was "This Old House" written for Rosemary Clooney.

A friend asked how he could give up the old life and he answered, "it is no secret." His friend said, "That's a catchy phrase. You should write a song about it." And as they say, "The rest is history."

The song Stuart wrote was "It Is No Secret."

It is no secret what God can do.
What He's done for others, He'll do for you.
With arms wide open, He'll welcome you.
It is no secret, what God can do.

SEPTEMBER 22
Take My Son

A wealthy man loved to collect rare works of art. They had Picassos and Raphaels. When the Vietnam conflict broke out, the son went to war and died in battle while rescuing another soldier. Just before Christmas, there was a knock at the door.

A young man with a large package said, "Sir, I am the soldier for whom your son gave his life. He was carrying me to safety when a bullet struck him and he died instantly. He often talked about your love for art." The young man held out this package. "I think your son would have wanted you to have this." It was a portrait of his son, painted by the young man.

The man died a few months later. There was to be a great auction of his paintings. Many influential people gathered to purchase a painting.

On the platform sat the painting of the son. The auctioneer started "We will start the bidding with this picture of the son."

Someone shouted, "We want to see the famous paintings. Skip this one."

But the auctioneer persisted. "Will somebody bid for this painting. Who will start the bidding? $100, $200?"

Another voice angrily, "We didn't come for that painting. We came to see the Van Gogh's, the Rembrandts. Get on with the real bids!"

But still the auctioneer continued. "The son! Who'll take the son?"

216

Finally, a voice came from the very back of the room. The longtime gardener of the man said. "I'll give $10 for the painting."

"$10 is the bid, won't someone bid $20?"

"Going once, twice, SOLD for $10! I'm sorry, the auction is over. I was told that whoever bought that painting would inherit everything. The man who took the son gets everything!"

Jesus is the Son.

SEPTEMBER 23
The Wooden Bowl

A frail old man went to live with his son, daughter-in-law and 4 year old grandson. The old man's hands trembled, his eyesight blurred and his step faltered. The family ate together, but the elderly grandfather's shaky hands and failing sight made eating difficult. Peas rolled off the spoon onto the floor and milk spilled on the table cloth.

The son and daughter-in-law became irritated. "We must do something with Grandpa," so the husband and the wife set a small table in the corner.

There Grandpa ate alone while the rest of the family enjoyed their dinner. Since Grandpa had broken a dish or two, his food was served in a wooden bowl. When the family glanced in Grandpa's direction, sometimes he had a tear in his eye.

Still the only words the couple had for him were sharp admonitions when he dropped his fork or spilled food. The 4 year old watched it all.

One evening before supper, the father noticed his son playing with wood scraps on the floor. He asked the child sweetly, "What are you making?"

Just as sweetly the boy responded, "Oh, I am making a little wooden bowl for you and Mom to eat your food when I grow up."

The words so struck the parents that they were speechless. Then tears started to stream down their cheeks. Both knew what must be done.

That evening the husband took the Grandfather's hand and gently led him to the family table. For the remainder of his days he ate every meal with the family.

For some reason, neither the husband nor wife seemed to care any longer when a fork dropped, milk spilled, or the tablecloth soiled. *"For whatsoever a man soweth, that shall he also reap"* (Galatians 6:7).

SEPTEMBER 24
Things I've Learned

I've learned that you can do something in an instant that will give you heartache for life.

I've learned that you should always leave loved ones with loving words. It may be the last time you see them.

I've learned that either you control your attitude or it controls you.

I've learned that my best friend and I can do anything or nothing and have the best time.

I've learned that sometimes when I'm angry I have the right to be angry, but that doesn't give me the right to be cruel.

I've learned that just because someone doesn't love you the way you want them to doesn't mean they don't love you with all they have.

I've learned that no matter how good a friend is, they're going to hurt you every once in a while and you must forgive them for that.

I've learned that it isn't always enough to be forgiven by others. Sometimes you have to learn to forgive yourself.

I've learned that no matter how bad your heart is broken the world doesn't stop for your grief.

I've learned that we don't have to change friends if we understand that friends change.

I've learned that you shouldn't be so eager to find out a secret. It could change your life forever.

I've learned that two people can look at the exact same thing and see something totally different.

I've learned that your life can be changed in a matter of hours by people who don't even know you.

I've learned that credentials on the wall do not make you a decent human being.

SEPTEMBER 25
This Stuff Has Got To Stop

Have you noticed Stairs are getting steeper? Groceries are heavier. And, everything is farther away.

I am dumbfounded to discover how long our street had become!

People are less considerate now. They speak in whispers all the time! I also think they are much younger than I was at the same age.

On the other hand, people my own age are so much older than I am. I ran into an old friend the other day and she has aged so much that she didn't even recognize me.

I glanced at my own refection in the mirror this morning, Well, REALLY NOW—even mirrors are not made the way they used to be!

Another thing, everyone drives so fast these days! You're risking life and limb if you happen to pull onto the freeway in front of them. All I can say is, their brakes must wear out awfully fast.

Clothing manufacturers are less civilized these days. Why else would they suddenly start labeling a size 10 or 12 dress as 18 or 20? Do they think no one notices these things no longer fit around the waist, hips, and thighs?

The people who make bathroom scales are pulling the same prank, but in reverse. Do they think I actually "believe" the number I see on that dial? HA! I would never let myself weigh that much! I'd like to call up someone in authority to report what's going on—but the telephone company is in on the conspiracy too: they've printed the phone books in such small type that no one could ever find a number in here!

We are under attack! Unless something drastic happens, pretty soon everyone will have to suffer these awful indignities.

SEPTEMBER 26
Good Lesson

A young lady relates an experience she had in a seminary class given by her teacher, Dr. Smith. She says Dr. Smith was known for his elaborate object lessons.

One particular day, she walked into the class and knew they were in for a fun day. On the wall was a big target and on a nearby table were many darts.

Dr. Smith told the students to draw a picture of someone that they disliked and he would allow them to throw darts at the person's picture. Her girlfriend drew a picture of a girl who had stolen her boyfriend. Another friend drew a picture of his little brother. Then a student drew a picture of one who had cheated them out of some money. Sally drew a picture of a former friend, putting a great deal of detail into her drawing.

She was pleased at the overall effect she had achieved.

The class lined up and began throwing darts, with much laughter and hilarity. Some of the students threw their darts with such force that their targets were ripping apart.

Dr. Smith, because of time limits, asked the students to return to their seats, and he began removing the target from the wall. Underneath the target was a picture of Jesus.

A complete hush fell over the room as each student viewed the mangled picture of Jesus; holes and jagged marks covered His face and His eyes were pierced.

Dr. Smith said only these words, *"Inasmuch as ye have done it unto the least of these my brethren, ye have done it unto me"* (Matthew 25:40).

"He that saith he is in the light, and hateth his brother, is in darkness even until now. He that loveth his brother abideth in the light" (1 John 2:9-10a).

SEPTEMBER 27
He Understands

A farmer had some puppies to sell. He painted a for sale sign and began nailing it to a post. As he drove a nail into the post, he felt a tug on his overalls. He looked down into the eyes of a little boy. "Mister," he said, "I want to buy a puppy."

"Well," said the farmer, "these puppies come from fine parents and cost a lot of money." The boy reaching deep into his pocket, he pulled out a handful of change and held it up to the farmer.

"I've got thirty-nine cents. Is that enough?"

"Sure," said the farmer. With that he let out a whistle. "Here, Dolly!" he called. From the dog house ran Dolly followed by four little balls of fur. The boy pressed his face against the chain link fence. As the dogs got to the fence, the boy noticed something else in the doghouse.

Slowly another puppy appeared; this one smaller. Down the ramp it slid. Then in a somewhat awkward manner the little pup began hobbling toward the others.

"I want that one," the little boy said, pointing to the runt.

The farmer knelt down at the boy's side and said, "Son, you don't want that puppy. He will never be able to run and play with you like these other dogs would."

The little boy stepped back, reached down, and rolled up one leg of his trousers. He revealed a steel brace running down both sides of his leg. Looking back up at the farmer, he said, "I don't run well myself, and he will need someone who understands."

The world is full of people who need someone who understands. Jesus said, *"For we have not an high priest which cannot be touched with the feeling of our infirmities"* (Hebrews 4:15).

SEPTEMBER 28
Let's Say Amen

"**Amen**" means to ponder or give some thought to.

If you have food in the refrigerator, clothes on your back, a roof overhead and a place to sleep, you are richer than 75% of this world.

If you have money in the bank, in your wallet, and spare change in a dish someplace, you are among the top 8% of the world's wealthy.

If you woke up this morning with more health than illness, you are more blessed than the million people who will not survive this week.

If you have never experienced the danger of battle, the loneliness of imprisonment, the agony of torture, or the pangs of starvation. you are ahead of 500 million people in the world.

If you can attend a church meeting without any fear of harassment, or arrest, or torture, or death, you are more blessed than three billion people in the world.

If your parents are still alive and still married, you are very rare, even in the United States.

If you hold up your head with a smile on your face and are truly thankful, you are blessed because the majority can, but most do not.

If you can hold someone's hand, hug them or even touch them on the shoulder, you are blessed because you can offer healing touch.

If you can read this message, you just received a double blessing in that someone was thinking of you; furthermore, you are more blessed than over two billion people in the world that cannot read at all.

> Count your blessings, name them one by one,
> Count your blessings, see what God has done!
> Count your blessings, name them one by one,
> And it will surprise you what the Lord has done.

SEPTEMBER 29
Nothing to Them

During the Great Depression in Missouri, John Griffin was the controller of a railroad drawbridge across the Mississippi River. One day he decided to take his eight year old son Greg with him to work. At noon he drew the bridge up to allow ships to pass and sat on the observation deck with Greg for lunch.

Suddenly he heard the whistle of a train approaching. He looked at his watch and noticed it was 1:07 and time for the Memphis Express, with four hundred people on board roaring toward the raised bridge. He leaped from the observation deck and ran back to the control tower. Just before throwing the switch he looked down to check on any ships coming through and to his horror, noticed that Greg had fallen into the gears that operated the bridge. His left leg was caught in the cogs of two main gears.

John's mind raced to think of a plan to rescue his son, but at the same time the train was barreling down on the bridge. He knew there was no way to save him without wrecking the train and the loss of four hundred lives.

He knew what he had to do. He buried his head in his hands and pulled the switch. As the train roared by he saw businessmen casually reading the evening paper. Finely dressed women were sipping coffee the dining car. No one looked at the mangled body of his son in the gear box. John looked at the speeding train and yelled, "I sacrificed my son for you people, don't you care?"

These were the same words of Lamentations 1:12, *"Is it nothing to you, all ye that pass by?"* It was the same when people walked by the cross and saw Jesus hanging there for them.

SEPTEMBER 30
Twenty-Six Guards

A missionary told this story in his home church in Michigan:

"While serving at a field hospital in Africa, I traveled by bicycle through the jungle to a nearby city for supplies. This was a two day journey requiring camping overnight along the way.

"On one of these journeys, I arrived in the city to collect money from a bank, purchase medicine, and then begin my journey back to the field hospital.

"Upon arrival in the city, I observed two men fighting, one of whom had been seriously injured. I treated him for his injuries and at the same time talked to him about the Lord. I then traveled two days, camping overnight, and arrived home without incident. Two weeks later I repeated my journey.

"Upon arriving in the city, I was approached by the young man I had treated.

"Five friends and I followed you into the jungle, knowing you would camp overnight. We planned to kill you and take your money. But we saw that you were surrounded by 26 armed guards. My five friends also saw them, and we all counted them."

At this point in the sermon one of the men in the congregation interrupted the missionary and asked if he remembered the exact day this happened.

The missionary told him the date, and the man who interrupted told this story: "On the night of your incident in Africa, it was morning here and I felt the urge to pray for you. In fact, the urging of the Lord was so strong, I called men in this church to meet with me here to pray for you. Would those men who met with me on that day stand up?"

The men who met to pray stood up. The missionary counted 26.

OCTOBER 1
A Big Difference

Liberal and modernistic religions teach that we are all part of one big family and eventually will be together with God in Heaven forever and ever. We all wish that were true but as the old adage goes, that's too good to be true. According to the Bible, we have a different father.

The believer says "Our father which art in heaven." We "are born of God" (John 1:13). The unbelievers, "Ye are of your father the devil" (John 8:44).

Our father lives to delight His children. The devil lives to deceive and devour.

We have a different family. The believer: "Now are we the sons of

God"(1 John 3:2). We are brothers and sisters of the same loving, wonderful Father in the same family. We are to love one another (1 Peter 1:22), pray for one another (James 5:16), be kind to one another (Ephesians 4:32), encourage one another (Hebrews 3:13), edify, build up one another (1 Thess. 5:11), and by love serve one another (Galatians 5:13).

The unbeliever: The works of the flesh are Adultery, fornication, uncleanness, lasciviousness, idolatry, witchcraft, hatred, wrath, strife, envying, murders, drunkenness and such like (Gal 5:19-20).

We have a different focus. The believer: *"Set your affections on things above, not on things on the earth"* (Colossians 3:2).

The unbeliever: *"For men shall be lovers of their own selves, covetous, boasters, proud, blasphemers, disobedient to parents, unthankful, unholy, without natural affections, trucebreakers, false accusers, incontinent, fierce, despisers of those that are good"* (2 Tim 3:2-3).

We have a different future. The believer: *"And if I go and prepare a place for you, I will come again, and receive you unto myself; that where I am, there ye may be also"* (John 14:3).

The unbeliever: *"And in hell he lifted up his eyes, being in torments"* (Luke 16:23).

OCTOBER 2
Your Sunday Best

I'm really stirred up. I just came from church, but the way folks were dressed, you would have thought we were at the county fair. I attended a funeral recently and the dearly departed was dressed better than the bereaved.

It used to be that people dressed up for church, weddings, funerals and other special occasions. Now nobody bats an eye at the way folks cover their hide or don't cover it.

I know the old argument "What's on the inside is important not what's on the outside" but the label on a can also tells you what's inside.

My wife used to buy those unlabeled, dented cans for a quarter at the grocery store, but I got tired of eatin' cat food casserole.

My wife went to a bridal shower where the bride and other guests wore tacky jeans and shorts. She was out of place in her nice skirt and dress shoes.

People tell me to loosen up cause times have changed. And that's the problem! A sense of decency has been lost in this generation and no one seems to care but old fogeys like me. We've come a long way, but in the wrong direction.

Nakedness in public is the norm and not just the younger folks. I see older people who know better showing too much skin. Mothers and Grandmothers ought to be ashamed for leading girls astray.

The Bible says the older women are to teach the younger and brother they've done exactly that, but they have put the emphasis on modern apparel and not modest apparel.

And preacher, dress up. Comb your hair, tuck in your shirt and put on a tie. It ain't gonna kill you to look professional.

—*Brother Ritechus N. Dignation.*

OCTOBER 3
The Benefits of Aging

For years I have dreaded getting old. As I approach mid-eighties I have begun to think of the blessings involved.

I was changing from an American Airlines to the Philippine Airline for a flight to Manila. The young ticket agent saw my age on my driver's license and said with her pretty smile, "Oh, you old man, I let you get on with the wheel chairs and the babies." Then she said, "We have you in row ninety-five, too far back for old man, I move you up to row fifteen." She marked my ticket as priority boarding.

Everywhere I went in the Philippian Islands, they called me to the desk and asked with an oriental smile, "You need wheel chair?"

The plane in Las Angeles had 384 seats, and I was the first passenger to board. When I came home I began to approach the desk and ask for priority boarding. At the time of this writing I have been the first passenger on sixty-eight flights.

I like my pitiful Social Security check each month, Medicare, and Health Spring, the thirty-five cent coffee at McDonalds, and the senior discount at almost every place we eat.

I am always happy also to be able to park in the handicap zone in motels and restaurants. I love having valet parking when I go to our church on Sunday and having the car right outside the door when the service is over. I don't even have to tip the fellows.

Then of course I am getting closer to my trip to Heaven, where eye hath not seen nor ear heard of the things He has prepared for those of us who love Him. Bring it on.

OCTOBER 4
A Well Rounded Life

Solomon in his tremendous wisdom spells out in Proverbs 3 a recipe for a life of success and victory.

In the first verse he speaks of a relationship to the Father. He begins with the word, "My son" and establishes a father and son relationship.

He speaks second about the Law of God, putting emphasis on our relationship to the Bible.

Then he touches on our response to both of these. From that point on, he spells out a series of relationships that lead to a series of benefits.

First, there is relationship to authority (v.2,13), that leads to long life and peace. *"Thy days shall be long upon the earth."*

Second, a relationship to others (v.3-4), that establishes a good reputation. *"favor and good understanding with God and man."*

Then a right relationship to God (v.5-6), that gives daily guidance. *"He shall direct thy path."*

Next a relationship to self that assures a strong healthy body (v.7-8) *"shall be health to thy navel and morrow to thy bones."*

After that our relationship to money is given (v.9-10). That provides abundance of God's blessings. *"Thy barns shall be filled with plenty."*

He then covers our relationship to difficulties (v.11-12), that spells out a reminder that God has our best interest at heart. *"for whom the Lord loveth."*

And finally, a comment on our relationships to our responsibilities (v.27), to the Lord and then also to our neighbor. *"withhold not good from them to whom it is due."*

In all seven of these promises of blessings, the ball is in our court. He is waiting for us to *"draw nigh to God, and he will draw nigh to you"* (James 4:8).

It is our serve, God is waiting for us to make our move.

OCTOBER 5
Brush Fires And Bond Fires

When a fire is burning out of control it usually sends out embers that start smaller brush fires and soon a whole area is ablaze. Recent fires in southern California drive home that point in a big way.

It works that same way when things get out of control in our lives. We spend a lot of time running around putting out the smaller fires while the big fire keeps starting new ones. It's usually a losing battle. We would do well to deal with the source first, then deal with the smaller situations.

I have found that when folk come to me with problems they usually spend a lot of my time and theirs telling me about incidents and happenings. She said, or he did, or they acted in a certain way. I usually ask, "when are we going to deal with the real problem."

They usually tell me about sins of commission rather than sins of omission, or what they are doing rather than things they are not doing.

I then explain that they have given me the results of their problem but have not mentioned the problem yet. When Biblical principles are ignored there will be results.

Husbands and wives will have continual conflict. Moms and Dads who ignore Biblical principles will pay price in the struggle to raise children.

The benefits of following scriptural teachings result in better decisions and a better outcome. These results will show up, not only in the spiritual, but also the physical, the mental, the emotional, the social, the domestic, and the financial areas of our lives.

Jesus said, *"But seek ye first the kingdom of God, and his righteousness; and all these things shall be added unto you"* (Matthew 6:33).

OCTOBER 6
Cleaning Up The Choir

When I accepted the pastorate of a church several years ago, I became aware that they had not had any teaching on separation and Biblical standards for the workers.

The former pastor was Southern Baptist and led the church in reaching out to win souls but had no convictions on personal separation.

Our choir had a great sound but they looked awful. Several tall girls stood on the front row of the choir in mini-skirts. They looked more like Broadway dancers than Baptist choir girls.

Some of the men had long shaggy hair, and a number of folks smoked openly. The Lord only knows what else.

The choir leader informed me that it would cost us over half the choir to get it corrected.

Still my convictions demanded that something be done. I called the choir together and told them of my dream of an "ideal choir". The "ideal choir" would not have smokers, men with long hair, and ladies that wore mini-skirts.

It got a little strained. It was March of that year. I explained that by January of the next year we would have the new choir. I continued by explaining that we appreciated them and that I hoped that they would help us clear up these areas and remain a great choir for the Lord.

I also explained that if they could not go along with the standards, they would have the option to drift out in a month or two or three, but by the first of the year something would have to be done.

Slowly and gradually the problem was resolved and by January 1st our choir was "my ideal choir". *"Be not conformed to this world: but be ye transformed by the renewing of your mind"* (Romans 12:2).

OCTOBER 7
Three Ways To Die

Travelling through the central part of our country one will often see three crosses in a field, on a hillside, or somewhere easily seen from the highway. These have been erected to remind people what happened at Calvary where Jesus died to pay for the sins of the whole world.

Luke gives us the whole story in one short sentence. *"And there were also two other, malefactors, led with him to be put to death"* (Luke 23:32). These also are a reminder that we too are going to die. The Bible tells us. *"And as it is appointed unto men once to die, but after this the judgment"* (Hebrews 9:27).

We do not know when, how, or where we will die, but we know that we are going to die. Not only are we reminded that all people are going to die, but we see three ways that people die. The first is a person dying in sin. He was not only paying for his sin on the cross, but he also will be paying for all eternity. His sin problem came to him by inheritance. It started with

Adam and passed on to him from his grandfather, then his father, then to him.

The second man died to sin. He saw that there was nothing he could do to correct or make up for his sin so he cried out to the Saviour, *"Lord, remember me when thou comest into thy kingdom"* (Luke 23:42). Jesus gave him a promise assuring him he would be with him in the kingdom.

The third man was Jesus Himself. He died for sin. John explained, *"And he is the propitiation for our sins: and not for ours only, but also for the sins of the whole world"* (1 John 2:2).

OCTOBER 8
God At Work

An account is given of a man visiting in a bronze factory. The workmen were laboring on massive panels for doors. They were cleaning the surfaces, trimming the edges, filling cavities, touching and retouching the outlines, shaping, smoothing, and polishing one part after another, going back over each one again and again.

The visitor asked, "How do you know when you're through?"

"We are never through," replied a workman, "We stop when they take the panels away."

One of the hardest lessons for a Christian to learn is that God is continually working on us. A recent song says "He's still working on me, to make me what I ought to be".

The second verse of that song says, "In the mirror of His Word, reflections that I see, Make me wonder why He never gave up on me. He loves me as I am, and helps me when I pray, Remember He's the Potter, I'm the clay.

Isaiah said, *"O LORD, thou art our father; we are the clay, and thou our potter; and we all are the work of thy hand"* (Isaiah 64:8).

The problems of life, times of sickness, and various problems and circumstances are designed by the Lord to shape us in His mold until we fulfill His will.

The teachings of Scripture about church, prayer, study, giving, and going are all part of God's program for helping us to be conformed to the image of His Son.

In fact that very truth is spelled out in the following verses. *"All scripture is given by inspiration of God, and is profitable for doctrine, for reproof, for correction, for instruction in righteousness: That the man of God may be perfect, throughly furnished unto all good works"* (2 Timothy 3:16-17).

OCTOBER 9
Hart To Heart

One of the most unusual true stories that I have heard was the story of a wealthy family in North Carolina who had a small eleven year old son with epilepsy. They were embarrassed by him, and he interfered with their social life, so they hired another family to raise him for them.

He moved to the home of his new parents and became a member of their family. As the boy grew, his "parents" began to realize that how very gifted he was in singing.

In a very unique way he was exposed to a couple of other very wealthy families who took an interest in him. They arranged for voice training and furnished the money to cover the lessons. He sang in church, school assemblies, and different events in his circles.

It was arranged for him to sing at the Metropolitan Opera in New York City. He traveled to Switzerland, Italy, Monte Carlo, and many other well-known places of great music.

He appeared on the Johnny Carson show, with Carol Burnett, Tiny Tim, and many others. Roy Acuff of the Grand Ole Opry became a personal friend.

Then he met Mr. U.G. Robinson who introduced him to Jesus Christ. In a big, citywide tent revival, listening to Evangelist E.J. Daniels he surrendered his talent and dedicated himself to sing for the glory of the Lord.

He soon became known throughout the Christian world as well. Dr. John Rice and later Curtis Hutson began to invite him to sing in the National Sword Conferences. That opened the door for him to hundreds of churches.

His name—Ray Hart.

His favorite album, "Hart to Heart."

OCTOBER 10
Get Your Heart Fixed

Barry Greening was the music director at Franklin Road Baptist Church. Some time ago he suffered a heart attack and had to have major heart surgery. Barry recuperated very quickly from the surgery and was back on the platform in just a few weeks.

His first Sunday back he quoted the Psalmists to the delight of our people and stated *"My heart is fixed, O God, my heart is fixed: I will sing and give praise"* (Psalm 57:7).

David was talking about something quite different when he made that statement. He was talking about Paul's parallel statement in the New Testament when he said *"Let every man be fully persuaded in his own mind."*

Isaiah also touched on this thought when he wrote, *"Thou wilt keep him in perfect peace, whose mind is stayed on thee: because he trusteth in thee"* (Isaiah 26:3).

We need to have our hearts fixed and completely settled on the matter of our salvation. No one could have peace without being completely settled about their eternal destiny.

The Bible is clear on the assurance of salvation. *"These things have I written unto you that believe on the name of the Son of God; that ye may know that ye have eternal life, and that ye may believe on the name of the Son of God"* (1 John 5:13), and also on the matter of the inspiration of the Bible, the deity of Christ, His virgin birth and the fact that God answers prayer.

We also need to be settled on giving, on church attendance and witnessing to others about Christ. Psalm 57:7, *"My heart is fixed, O God, my heart is fixed: I will sing and give praise."*

OCTOBER 11
Is Your Candle Lit?

To most people life is a drag. Many do not know where they are going and will not know where they are if they get there. It doesn't have to be that way.

In the days following the death, burial and resurrection of our Lord Jesus Christ, most of the followers of our Lord were discouraged, disillusioned and wondering what to do next. Their hopes had been dashed. The Shepherd was now gone. The sheep were scattering.

They had hoped that He would lead them to victory over the cursed Romans who had enslaved them. They remembered that He had asked them to go to the upper room and wait for the enduring of power from the Holy Spirit.

While they tarried in obedience, He came and set them ablaze for God. Without buildings, without money, without TV cameras, cell phones, or without computers, they turned the world upside down.

The Lord is ready to touch our lives individually with this same fire. He is waiting for us to make ourselves available to Him.

Paul the apostle said, *"I beseech you therefore, brethren, by the mercies of God, that ye present your bodies a living sacrifice, holy, acceptable unto God, which is your reasonable service. And be not conformed to this world: but be ye transformed by the renewing of your mind, that ye may prove what is that good, and acceptable, and perfect, will of God"* (Romans 12:1-2).

He wants us to yield ourselves unto Him as an instrument of righteousness (Romans 6:13).

A drab boring life can be filled with purpose and excitement. You don't have to go another day without the touch of God's fire. He promised, *"Ye shall receive power, after that the Holy Ghost is come upon you"* (Acts 1:8).

OCTOBER 12
Into All The World

Several years ago we were mailing our Church paper to all the rural box holders in our town and surrounding areas.

One fellow wrote a letter to the editor of our local paper and stated, "I am greatly alarmed about a certain religious institution in our community that has its own bus company and gathers people for its services, has its own school, its own newspaper, its own banking system, (we sold bonds to finance our buildings), its own broadcast, etc., etc."

He continued, "I call upon this church to confine its religious extremities within the four walls of its building and stay out of the affairs of our community."

That is exactly what Satan would like for us to do. That is also what the liberal media, and socialistic minded people are hoping to accomplish.

Things have not changed much since the days of Jesus when the scribes and Pharisees, along with the political leaders of that day ordered them not to spread their teachings any further in their communities. They said, "Did not we straitly command you that ye should not teach in this name? and, behold, ye have filled Jerusalem with your doctrine" (Acts 5:28). Peter answered, "We ought to obey God rather than man" (Acts 5:29).

I like what Dr. J.B. Buffington used to do in Lakeland, Florida. About twice each year he would buy a two-page advertisement in the centerfold of the local newspaper and publish a sermon on abortion, homosexuality, alcoholism, prostitution, or some other social issue. A lot of people complained to the newspaper and insinuated that he had no right to place his ads.

The world would certainly be happy if we would keep our religion to ourselves, but the Great Commission commands us to go and tell others.

OCTOBER 13
The Mountain Top

Our favorite game when I was a boy was King of the Hill. We would find a pile of sawdust or a big mound of dirt. One of us would climb to the top and yell, "ready". The other fellows at the bottom of the hill would come tearing up the hill to push us off the top and declare themselves, "King of the Hill".

After becoming a Christian I discovered that every time I got on top of the Spiritual mountain and got all my circumstances under control, my enemies, the world, the flesh and the devil, immediately would attack my position and try to push me back down to defeat and failure through lust of the flesh, lust of the eyes, and the pride of life.

The Book of Judges characterizes most of our lives. There are seven mountains and seven valleys. Victory and defeat, up and down, up and down, yo-yo Christianity.

David asked, *"Lord, who shall abide in thy tabernacle? Who shall dwell in thy holy hill?"* (Psalm 15:1) The Apostle Paul reminds us that daily victory is there for the taking. *"But thanks be to God who giveth us the victory through our Lord Jesus Christ. Therefore, my beloved brethren, be ye steadfast, unmovable, always abounding in the work of the Lord, forasmuch as ye know that your labour is not in vain in the Lord"* (1 Corinthians 15:57,58).

Dr. Bill Harvey used to sing a great old song, "I want that mountain for it belongs to me."

It surely does belong to us and we should all consider the words of the Lord to Joshua and the people of Israel, *"Go up and possess the land which the Lord thy God hath given thee"* (Deut. 23:9).

OCTOBER 14
A Successful Marriage

Just before walking his daughter down the aisle to give her away in marriage, a father gave her some good sound advice.

"Remember", he told her, "Your marriage is like two horses pulling the same wagon. To go forward both horses must be pulling in the same direction. If one pulls one way and one pulls in the opposite direction, they will not get very far. For a marriage to be a success both must pull together in the same direction."

Some tell us that happy homes are the result of a 50/50 relationship. Other say it will take 100% and 100%. One couple I talked with experienced some serious problems and had separated. I asked about the interest level in getting things back together. The fellow said he was 1000% interested in getting things back together. The girl in a matter of fact way stated that her interest was 0%. Of course, they didn't make it.

One thing is certain. If two people will give 100% to the Lord and implement Biblical principles of dedication, loyalty and selflessness into their lives, they will be rewarded with a beautiful and happy marriage.

The Bible gives clear directions on the husbands role in marriage as well as the wife's responsibilities. It also give direction about how to succeed in raising children.

To keep the matter simple, two people must each be right with the Lord, follow the Bible teachings, and really work at it.

To have an attractive lawn, a beautiful garden, or a neat looking car someone has to put some energy and effort into the situation.

Marriages can be beautiful and blessed of the Lord, but neglect and taking things for granted will cause it to end up on the rocks in no time.

OCTOBER 15
Think About This

Someone said, the sad paradox of our time in history is that we have taller buildings, but much shorter tempers; wider freeways, but narrower viewpoints; we spend more, but have less; we buy more, but enjoy it less. We have bigger houses and smaller families; more conveniences, but less time. We have more degrees, but a lot less sense; more knowledge, but less wisdom; more experts, yet more problems; more medicine, yet less health of the whole person. We have multiplied our possessions, but reduced our values. We talk too much, love too seldom, and hate too often. We've learned how to make a living, but not a life; We've added years to life, not life to years. We've been all the way to the moon and back, but have trouble crossing the street to meet the new neighbor. We've conquered outer space, but not inner space. We've cleaned up the air, but polluted the soul and the minds of our kids. We've split the atom, but not our prejudice. We have higher incomes, but lower morals. We've become long on quantity, but short on quality.

These are the times of tall men and short character; steep profits and shallow relationships.

These are the times of proclaimed world peace, but domestic and civil warfare; more leisure, but less joy; more kinds of food, but less nutrition.

These are days of two incomes, but more divorce; of fancier houses, but broken homes. It is a time when there is much in the show window yet little in the moral stockroom; a time when technology can bring this thought to you, and a time when you can choose either to make a difference through Christ Jesus. We are to be doers of the word and not hearers only (James 1:22).

OCTOBER 16
A Little Red Dot

Mr. Mike Coe, a pilot for American Airlines and a former deacon of our church, is certified as a teacher of the Larry Burkette Financial Concepts. In Mike's seminar at our church, he gave all of us a little red dot to put on the face of our watch. He said, "We look at our watch an average of 85 times a day."

The red dot was to remind us that God Owns It All; our house, our car, our bank account, our retirement, our body, and we are to be stewards for Him.

The Bible bears that out by saying, *"The earth is the Lord's and the fullness thereof"* (Psalm 24:1).

"For every beast of the field is Mine, and the cattle upon a thousand hills" (Psalm 50:10).

"The silver is mine, the gold is mine, saith the Lord of hosts" (Haggai 2:8).

He created us and redeemed us at Calvary and made a double claim on us. *"For ye are bought with a price: therefore glorify God in your body, and your spirit, which are God's"* (1 Cor. 6:20).

We are twice His, first through creation and second, through salvation.

Jesus told a story of a wealthy man who trusted his servants with his investment money. Two of the servants were diligent and gained a profit for their master. He rewarded them with the words, "well done." Each was given a generous reward. The third man disobeyed and was careless about his responsibility. He suffered a great loss.

We would do well to ask ourselves are we giving God what is rightfully His? We also would do well to get a little red dot and put it on our watch and remember several times a day whose we are.

OCTOBER 17
I've Gotta' Get My Name In That Book

Recently a mother called our church office and said that her small boy had come home from church and asked if he could get his name in that book.

"What kind of book do you have at the church?" she asked.

She told us that her boy said to her, "Momma, if you don't get your name in that book, you can't go to heaven. You have to go down to that other place."

One of our teachers had gotten her message across. The mother asked if someone might come by the house and talk with the boy.

One of our staff went by the house and sure enough, the boy got his name in that book.

There are thousands of good well-meaning people who do not have their names in that book. Jesus said, *"Rejoice that your names are written in heaven"*(Luke 10:20). Our Bible also says, *"Whosoever was not found written in the book of life was cast into the lake of fire"* (Rev. 20:15).

It is necessary that each person sign up and make a reservation for heaven. The reservation assures us of a place.

For years I have travelled to different cities to hold meetings in churches. It has been a great comfort to walk up to the reservation desk and tell them my name and have them hand me a key to my room.

The song writer has well written:

"There's a new name written down in glory, and it's mine,
Oh yes it's mine. And the white robed angels sing the story,
a sinner has come home "There a new written down in glory,
and it's mine, Oh yes it's mine. With my sins forgiven
I am bound for heaven, never more to roam."

OCTOBER 18
Tithing: Old Or New Testament?

After a message on the importance of giving in Knoxville, TN., a young preacher approached me and asked, "Bro. Wallace are you an Old Testament tither, or a New Testament tither?"

"I do not know." I though a moment. "Is there a difference?"

He asked me about my take home pay. I shared with him that the church family paid me $100.00 each week. This was the mid-1950s.

"When you get your pay then you give $10.00?" he asked.

"That's it," I told him, "$100.00 then $10.00, then $100.00 and another $10.00.

"You're and Old Testament tither," he commented.

"Now, what is a New Testament tither?" I asked.

"Well you give $10.00 and the Lord gives you $100.00, then you give another $10.00 and He gives you another $100.00."

"I don't see any difference," I explained.

"How long have you been living at the $100.00 level?" he asked. I shared with him that was my salary since I came to the church.

"How are you doing financially?" he asked. I told him that we were about to starve. "You will continue to starve too, until you start giving the New Testament way," he said. "Why don't you give $20.00 each week so the Lord can give you $200.00, or $30.00 so the Lord will give you $300.00?" he suggested.

I looked at that young preacher and told him, "You just got yourself a convert." From that day until the present, we have never had a problem with finances.

Paul explained this principle when he said, *"He which soweth sparingly shall reap sparingly, and he that soweth bountifully shall also reap bountifully"* (2 Cor. 9:6).

OCTOBER 19
Nice Guys Need Salvation Too!

Tom Bright was one of the friendliest and well-liked fellows that I had ever met, but he was a lost sinner.

Bill Baker, Vice-President of a large bank in our city and a deacon in our church, took me to see Tom. Bill had presented the gospel to Tom over and over again, but he could not get him to make his decision to accept Christ as his Saviour. Several of our men had witnessed to him, also, and I had talked to him a number of times myself.

Several times he was right to the point of conversion, but he would always freeze up. He would apologize each time for not receiving Christ. He told me several times, "I know I should not put this off."

One Sunday, Tom showed up for church. Then he began to come every Sunday. His faith began to build and his interest became obvious. Then the sudden death of his wife's best friend brought the break we were all hoping for.

A small group of us had gathered in the family room at the local hospital and the teenage son of the young mother who had just died walked over to him and said, "Tom do you think you would like to trust Jesus now?"

With tears running down his cheeks, he invited the Lord Jesus to come into his heart and save him. We tallied the number of times he had been witnessed to by some of our men at the church. It was over one hundred. Tom came forward in church to take a stand for Christ and to be baptized. I'm so glad we didn't give up on Tom!

"For I am not ashamed of the gospel of Christ: for it is the power of God unto salvation" (Rom. 1:16).

OCTOBER 20
Old Mother Wolf

Some years ago Walt Disney produced a film about a she wolf with several little cubs. The mother wolf was killed and several days later the little wolves were seen trying to get nourishment from the body of their dead mother. This was a very sad scene. How can the dead give life to the children?

Thousands of churches that once gave a life giving message to their children no longer do so! The children go regularly each week to get fed but go away still hungry and unsatisfied. Liberal theologians and social gospel preachers proved to be clouds without water, trees without fruit, and as the old Indian remarked, "heap, lot of wind but no rain."

One such preacher, smoking his pipe, sat in his office and instructed me on how to come forward on Palm Sunday to present myself for baptism and church membership. Five others were coming, also. This was the only Sunday in the year that they did this. Nothing was said about salvation. Later a young man led me to Christ at work.

If I were Satan I would allow the church to die too, but I certainly wouldn't let the members find it out. Just let them go through the motions, continuing to serve on the committees, channeling their money in the offerings and anything else that would keep them from helping people go to Heaven.

Church is intended to be a maternity ward where spiritual babies are born into the family of God, but so many have become funeral homes. There is some good news! There are lots of Bible believing, Gospel preaching churches around ready to satisfy the spiritual hunger of babes in Christ.

"Desire the sincere milk of the word, that ye may grow thereby" (I Peter 2:2).

OCTOBER 21
Par Bar Westward

In Bible college one of the young preachers stated with excitement that he had been invited to preach in a local church nearby. He asked some of us students what we thought might be a good text for him to expound on. One of our young embryo preachers suggested "Why don't you preach on that text in I Chronicles 26:18 that says "At Par bar westward, four at the causeway, and two at Par bar." Everybody got a big laugh out of the whole thing. It was a fun time for all of us.

One day I realized that all Scripture is equally inspired. I Chronicles 26:18 is just as much a part of God's Word as John 3:16 or the 23rd Psalm.

I got my Bible out and began to meditate and pray over that verse. It wasn't long before I had six tremendous words to build a message from the Lord. I saw direction in that verse.

One was posted "westward to guard at the causeway."

Then decision: someone had to decide who would serve and where they would do it.

There were degrees of responsibility. It was mentioned that some were "small" and some were "great."

There is Duty in the verse. Some were "over" others.

Then there was dedication. Some were, "sanctified or set apart to the work."

Finally, diligence. They were expected to give their best.

I was really blessed when I realized that there are hundreds of verses in the Bible that have great truth, ready to open and flow when we meditate therein day and night.

We all could greatly profit from Paul's words to Timothy, *"Mediate upon these things; give thyself wholly to them; that thy profiting may appear to all"* (I Tim 4:15).

OCTOBER 22
Be Positive Today

I woke up early today, excited over all I get to do before the clock strikes midnight. I have responsibilities to fulfill today. My job is to choose what kind of day I am going to have.

Today I can complain because the weather is rainy, or I can be thankful that the grass is getting watered for free.

Today I can feel sad that I don't have more money, or I can be glad that my finances encourage me to play my purchases wisely and guide me away from waste.

Today I can grumble about my health, or I can rejoice I am alive.

Today I can lament over all that my parents didn't give me when I was growing up, or I can feel grateful that they allowed me to be born.

Today I can cry because roses have thorns, or I can celebrate that thorns have roses.

Today I can mourn my lack of friends, or I can excitedly embark upon a quest of being friendly.

Today I can whine because I have to go to work, or I can shout with joy because God has given me the power to create wealth.

Today I can murmur because I have to do housework, or I can feel honored because the Lord has provided shelter for my mind, body and soul.

Today stretches ahead of me, waiting to be shaped. And here I am, the sculptor who gets to do the shaping.

What today will be like is up to me. I get to choose what kind of day I will have! Have a great day…unless you have other plans? I sat down with a pencil and paper and wrote down one hundred and twenty-five things that did not happen to me.

OCTOBER 23
Predestined To Be Glorified

"**P**redestination" is a term that has reference only to believers. The word "pre" means beforehand. Destination refers to the climax, the final point or to the end.

I recently flew on Southwest Airlines from Baltimore, MD to Nashville, TN. When I purchased my ticket I made a "pre" arrangement that guaranteed, or promised me delivery to Nashville Tennessee. No provision was made for seating. I picked out my seat near a window and close to the front after I got on the plane.

I had no prior arrangements for the snack. The stewardess came by, and there on the spot, I decided to accept a fruit bar, a cup of coffee, and a bag of sugar peanuts for my grandson who would be waiting with his grandmother at the airport in Nashville. The pre-arrangement was only for my destination and did not cover how smooth or bumpy the flight might be. My ticket just covered the destination. Only those of us who have pre-arranged to get a ticket were allowed to get on the plane and come to our destination.

When I accepted Christ as my Saviour and placed my trust in Him, my destination for Heaven was also settled. Whether I find happiness and victory along the way will be determined by other decisions that are made day by day.

I will need to decide about church attendance, Bible study, prayer, giving and such. These matters, however, will not affect my destination. "Pre" destination is a wonderful Bible truth in its simplicity.

Paul said, speaking only to Christians who have their ticket for Heaven, *"Moreover whom he did pre-destinate, them he also called and whom he called, them he also justified: and whom he justified, them he also glorified"* (Romans 8:30).

OCTOBER 24
Procrastination

When Charlie Jones decided to clean up his attic, he was greatly surprised to find a ticket stub from a shoe repair shop. He had taken some shoes in for repairs over 30 years before and forgotten to go back and get them. Charlie decided to have some fun. He took the ticket to the repair shop and placed in on the counter and said, "I'd like to pick up my shoes." The old shoe maker looked at the stub, turned and walked back into his repair shop and was gone for about ten minutes.

When he finally came back Charlie, remarked with a smirk, "Couldn't find them could you?"

"Oh, yes I found them," replied the shoemaker with a serious look on his face, "They will be ready next Thursday."

We often say "I've been laying off to do that, I'm going to get around to it." Dr. Tom Malone used to say that the folks in his area would tell him they were "aimin' to do it." He said, "I wish just one time they would quit aimin', and go on and shoot."

Many a person has lost their soul because they planned to get saved some other time. Dr. Bill Rice used to say, "The road to Hell is paved with good intentions." It would be wise to heed the admonition, "Never put off till tomorrow what you should do today.

The Bible says it best, *"Now is the accepted time; today is the day of salvation"* (2 Cor. 6:2). And Isaiah declared, *"Come now, and let us reason together, saith the LORD: though your sins be as scarlet, they shall be as white as snow; though they be red like crimson, they shall be as wool"* (Isaiah 1:18).

OCTOBER 25
Quick Thinking

Senator Will Rice, the father of Dr. John and Dr. Bill Rice used to tell the story of a man who was painting the dome of the Texas state capitol in Austin, Texas. The scaffold was thirteen tiers high and he was on the top painting the inside of the dome.

He looked around to see a man standing behind him with a gun pointed at him. The man who had escaped from a mental institution had climbed up the scaffold, and demanded that the painter jump down to the bottom and to certain death.

"Why do you want me to jump down there," the painter asked.

"Because I've never seen anybody jump down that far before," the crazy man answered, "Now jump."

"I'll bet you have never seen anybody jump back up this high from down there either, have you?" the painter asked the man.

"Well, no I haven't," he said.

"Well then, you wait right here and I'll go down there and jump back up from down there," the painter explained.

"Ok, you do that", said the crazy man, and the painter climbed down the ladder and out the door to find a policeman.

After telling that story, Senator Rice said to his sons, "Boys you must learn to think fast if you are to succeed in this life."

Our Bible tells us that believers have a special discernment and alertness given to us by the Holy Spirit within us. We need to keep tuned in at all times so that when the time or situation comes to react to it, we will be able to "think quick."

Peter advises us in 1 Peter 3:15 to *"be ready always"*.

OCTOBER 26
She Wanted To Write My Boss

I boarded a big jet liner coming out of Atlanta. It was past midnight and most of the passengers had turned out their light and settled back to sleep.

I turned on my light and got out my briefcase and began to catch up on some much needed work. "You are not going to work?" exclaimed the stewardess.

"Yes I am too!" I replied.

"If you give me the name of your boss," she said, "I will write and tell him what a hard worker you are."

"You can't write my boss," I told her. "You have to talk to him person to person."

"Why?" She asked.

Her eyes got real big when I told her "Because I'm a preacher, I work for the Lord."

"Oh," she said, and away she went. Paul the Apostle said, *"We then, as workers together with him"* (2 Cor. 6:1).

What a blessing it is to get orders directly from headquarters. What a blessing it is to be able to talk to the boss person to person any time you want to.

It is so sad that so many people work for another company and have a different boss. Some work for themselves, some for the world and some even for Satan. I suppose that these folks are busy trying to please their own boss.

Those who live their life and give all of their time to the world, the flesh and the devil should remember that "the wages of sin is death" (Romans 6:23).

"For ye are bought with a price: therefore glorify God in your body, and in your spirit, which are God's." (1 Cor. 6:20)

OCTOBER 27
Skin Of Our Teeth

Does our teeth have skin? Job says they do. He speaks of, *"escaping with the skin of his teeth"* (Job 19:20). He is saying that everything is lost. All that is left, just the skin on his teeth.

Paul touches on this when he talks about man's work being burned. *"But he himself shall be saved; yet so as by fire"* (1 Cor. 3:15). His reference is to the Judgment Seat of Christ where many of our works will be burned up and we will be spared only because we have Christ. How embarrassing not to have any reward.

When I sat with my high school graduating class, all I cared about was getting the diploma. After all I had invested 12 years of my life for that piece of paper. Freedom was just a few minutes away. The awards and scholarships were presented to a number of our classmates. Some received several recognitions, and a great deal of money for future education.

I got nothing but my diploma. Not one time did the principal embarrass me, or make me feel ashamed. He ignored me. After it was all over I began to feel really bad. I could have done better, if I had realized how bad I was going to feel, but it was too late now.

The Judgment Seat of Christ will be somewhat like that graduation service. Many will be given rewards for their work for the Lord. However many others will be passed over. As the songwriter put it, "I'll wish I had given Him more."

Some will get by with the skin of their teeth. Some will see their works burned, *"but he himself shall be saved; yet so as by fire"* (1 Cor. 3:15).

If this scene is to be changed we will need to get to it.

OCTOBER 28
Took Off His Socks And Went To Church

A successful business man from New Jersey related to me an incident that has blessed me ever since I heard it. He was on his way to church for the second night of a revival service. A burden from the message the night before was weighing heavy on him. The preacher had preached about concern for lost souls. He spoke of the responsibility of every believer to help sinners come to Christ.

A small, ragged looking boy standing on the street near the church caught his attention. He engaged him in conversation then invited him to come with him to the church service.

"I can't go in there mister, I ain't got no socks on," the little fellow remarked.

"Would you go in there with me, if I pulled my socks off?" he asked the boy.

The puzzled boy, challenged by the offer, looked him in the eye and said, "Yea, sir mister, I will go in with you." With that, my friend pulled off his socks and together they slipped into the service.

The message from the preacher found its way into the tender heart of the boy and soon he was kneeling at an old fashioned altar, confessing his need of the Saviour. He had lost all concern for the fact that he had no socks on.

I could not help thinking of how Christ stripped off His glory and position and came to live among us in order that we might go in with Him. *"But made himself of no reputation, and took upon him the form of a servant, and was made in the likeness of men:"* (Phil. 2:7), *"He humbled himself, and became obedient unto death, even the death of the cross"* (Phil. 2:8).

OCTOBER 29
Unchangeable Laws

At creation, God set into motion the laws of gravity, centrifugal force, aerodynamics, electricity, regularity, variety, law of reproduction, the sowing and reaping laws, and the second law of thermodynamics. Just like the God who gave them to us, they are immutable or unchangeable.

Men like John Newton, Benjamin Franklin, and the Wright brothers discovered some of these laws, but all of us are entitled to the benefit and the good that comes to human beings from them.

Now God gave us another set of laws when He gave the ten commandments to Moses. These tell us, Thou shalt not have any other gods, or make graven images of God, or take His name in vain or take His day ourselves.

Also, His law included, thou shalt not dishonor father or mother, or commit adultery, or kill, or steal, or lie, or covet what belongs to your neighbor.

The Apostle Paul spoke of those who are "A law unto themselves" or in other words, they make their own rules. He also pointed out that this set of laws is a teacher to help us understand that we have broken them and disqualified ourselves from going to Heaven. David wrote of some who have the *"law of God in his heart"* (Psalm 37:31). Again he said, *"Thou through thy commandments hast made me wiser than mine enemies: for they are ever with me"* (Psalm 119:98).

Mankind can be divided by whether he is governed by God's laws or makes his own laws to live by. One, of course, is humanism or egocentric philosophy. The other is Christ centered, or Christocentric.

Heaven or hell is decided by these two outlooks. God and His laws have not changed. We would do well to do it God's way.

OCTOBER 30
The Almighty—Sovereign Or Servant?

To many folks God is someone who does things for them. They want Him to heal them when they are sick or injured. They pray and ask Him to help them with their financial woes, help them with their problems, keep watch over their kids for them and keep the tornadoes, the fires, the hurricanes and the floods away from their house. Some even want Him to fill the cavities in their teeth.

Now the blessings of the Lord do include some of these benefits, but God is bigger than all that. The people who want to harness God and make Him pull their wagon need to take another look. He is an awesome God who says, "I am the Lord, and there is none, there is no God beside me" (Isaiah 45:5).

The song writer put it this way:

Oh Lord my God
When I in awesome wonder,
Consider all the wealth
Thy hands hath made.

Then sings my soul
My Saviour God to thee,
How great thou art,
How great thou art.

God owns it all. He created it, He has fearfully and wonderfully made us. He purchased our redemption with His own blood on the cross. With that accomplished, He wants to share it all with us. He would like to take us into His family and make us heirs and joint heirs as partners with Christ.

There are a few conditions. In the Word of God we read, *"For ye are bought with a price: therefore glorify God in your body, and in your spirit, which are God's"* (I Cor. 6:20).

Like the Apostle Paul we should recognize that we are bond servants of the Lord and ask, *"Lord, what will thou have me to do?"* (Acts 9:6).

OCTOBER 31
The Bio-Chip

Do you think scientists will ever be able to plant a computer chip in the human mind and gain access to instant knowledge?

Bio-engineers and computer scientists are attempting to grow a bio-chip. They hope to use a protein and an enzyme to create the miracle chip.

A storage unit measuring one cubit inch could store all available knowledge in existence today. They suggest that they might implant the chip into the mind of an expert or genius. It would then absorb all of their expertise and knowledge and then the chip would be reproduced, and transferred to students or clients who would become instant geniuses. It is suggested that through this type of implanting, damaged brains could be fixed so that blind eyes could see again, deaf ears could hear, and the dumb could speak, and the body could be programmed to heal itself in a hundred different ways.

It sounds as if we might be trying to do the work of the Lord, and maybe even replace Him. Is this a type of Tower of Babel thinking?

We might want to consider a spiritual implant instead. As the Apostle Paul said, *"Let this mind be in you, which was also in Christ Jesus"* (Phil. 2:5).

God promises that with our glorified bodies will have total knowledge in the life to come. I don't think this will ever be accomplished in this life so in the meantime I think it would be wise for us to follow the Biblical admonition, *"This book of the law shall not depart out of thy mouth; but thou shalt meditate therein day and night, that thou mayest observe to do according to all that is written therein: for then thou shalt make thy way prosperous, and then thou shalt have good success"* (Joshua 1:8).

NOVEMBER 1
The Millionaire's Will

When J. Pierpoint Morgan, the American financier and multi-millionaire died some years ago, his will consisted of 10,000 words and some 37 articles. When his will was read, many held their breath, wondering who and where the millions would be distributed. After the reading, there was no doubt in any mind that the famous man had made careful preparation and plans for his last desires and wishes. There was also no doubt as to what the most important part of the will was to him. He stated, "I commit my soul into the hands of my Saviour full of confidence that having redeemed me and washed me with His precious blood He will present me faultless before the throne of my Heavenly Father." He continued saying, "I entreat my children to maintain and defend at all hazards, and at any cost of personal sacrifice, the blessed doctrine of complete atonement of sins through the blood of Jesus Christ, once offered and through that above."

This sounded more like the will of God rather than the will of a man. While many trust in their millions, Morgan with millions, knew that trusting in the payment made on Calvary was his only hope of eternal life. He knew that, *"Forasmuch as ye know that ye were not redeemed with corruptible things, as silver and gold, from your vain conversation received by tradition from your fathers; But with the precious blood of Christ, as of a lamb without blemish and without spot"* (1 Peter 1:18-19).

His advice, instead of making millions, make preparation for death and eternity. He obviously believed the truth of the Bible verse that says, *"For what shall it profit a man, if he gain the whole world, and lose his own soul?"* (Mark 8:36).

NOVEMBER 2
Children And Home

What is wrong with our country, and with the professing church? Which of course brings us to the home. As goes the home, so goes the church and the nation. The problem? Children having too much input! There you have it, and I said it out loud, or dared to put in black and white!

Otto von Bismark said, "Universal suffrage is the government of a house by its nursery." When Bismark made his statement he of course was referring to limiting votes to qualified men. To qualify you had to be of his choosing!

Our own country for many years limited the right to vote to landowners, more exactly, male landowners. In the course of time this right has been extended to any person who is of age and can breathe.

Socrates wrote, "Could I climb the highest place in Athens, I would lift up my voice and proclaim: Fellow citizens! Why do ye turn and scrape every stone to gather wealth, and take so little care of your children, to whom one day you must relinquish it all?"

Again he said, "Children today are tyrants. They contradict their parents, gobble their food, and tyrannize their teachers." An unknown said, "Times change. Not too many years ago minding one's children didn't mean obeying them."

God gave Abraham a high compliment and great responsibility when He said in Genesis 18:19, *"For I know him, that he will command his children and his household after him, and they shall keep the way of the LORD, to do justice and judgment; that the LORD may bring upon Abraham that which he hath spoken of him."*

Lest you think I am anti-child, I bring to bear the words of Dostoevsky, "The soul is healed by being with children." Agreed. (Dr. Larry Lilly)

NOVEMBER 3
The Modem In Your Mind

The human mind is one of the most complex computers in existence today. To duplicate it would require the space of the Empire State Building. It has the capacity to store more than three terabytes of information. With a good modem in your P.C. at home you can be in touch with people anywhere in the world day or night.

The modem in the mind will do better than that. It will make connection to the Creator God in Heaven. Our Bible declares, *"His ears are open unto their prayers"* (1 Pet.3:12).

An article in a Jewish Christian magazine some time ago suggested that a Christian has a spiritual modem in the brain that gives access to God. The article pointed out that the brain of Albert Einstein has been preserved and they cannot detect any visible difference between it and the brain of an imbecile who was known to have an IQ of 25 or 30.

Could it be possible that intelligence and wisdom is transmitted from God to some more than others to accomplish His purpose here on the earth? Solomon's wisdom came directly from God and James tells us that anyone who desires wisdom can ask God and He will give it generously.

I recently bought a new state of the art modem for my computer and it connected to the internet immediately, but it could not get through to the Internet Service that we have our Web page on and subscribe to. It needed some special codes to enter the service that we subscribe to.

The Bible says that God heareth not sinners. It would be to your advantage to get your modem connected to the Lord's Internet service and then maintain it in good working order on a day by day basis.

NOVEMBER 4
The Tragedy Of The Dew

One would not ordinarily think of tragedy being associated with dew. The beauty of a shining, sparkling dew on a meadow at night, reflecting the moon is very beautiful, and anything but tragic.

You can imagine how all of us felt at a national meeting when a well-known speaker announced his topic, "The Tragedy of the Dew".

He explained the scientific process of evaporation. God's warm sun draws water quietly from the still farm pond all day long. Then he talked about condensation. During the cooling of the air in the evening, the process stops. The water and moisture that has not been lifted high enough, falls back to earth to form dew.

"Dew", said our speaker, "is water that started for heaven too late." The drop in temperature had suddenly slammed the door and that is tragic. Too late for heaven!

The warm Son of the love of God has been drawing people out of this earthly life for heaven for almost 2000 years by the process of repentance and faith, but we must take warning from Luke 13:25 where Jesus said, *"The master of the house will rise up and hath shut to the door."*

There are thousands of people who intend to go to heaven but have not started for heaven yet. Soon the door will close and many will find that they have waited too long.

Much sadder than "The Tragedy of the Dew", is the "The Tragedy of the Lost Soul". 2 Corinthians 6:2 says that *"now is the accepted time; behold, now is the day of salvation."*

The writer of the book of Hebrews warned, *"How shall we escape, if we neglect so great salvation; which at the first began to be spoken by the Lord, and was confirmed unto us by them that heard him"* (Hebrews 2:3).

251

NOVEMBER 5
Big Rocks

An expert in time management speaking to a group of business students used an illustration those students will never forget. As he spoke to the group of high-powered overachievers, he said, "Okay, time for a quiz," and he pulled out a one-gallon, mason jar.

He also produced about a dozen fist-sized rocks and carefully placed them, into the jar. When the jar was filled and no more would fit inside, he asked, "Is this jar full?"

Everyone in the class yelled, "Yes."

The time management expert replied, "Really?"

He reached under the table for a bucket of gravel. He dumped gravel in and shook the jar causing gravel to work into the spaces between the rocks. He then asked the group, "Is the jar full?"

"Probably not," one of them answered.

"Good!" he replied. He reached under the table and brought out a bucket of sand. He dumped sand in the jar and it went into the spaces left between the rocks and the gravel. Again he asked, "Is this jar full?"

"No!" the class shouted.

Again he said, "Good." Then, a pitcher of water which he poured in until the jar was filled. Then he asked the class, "What is the point of this illustration?"

One student said, "The point is, no matter how full your schedule, you can always fit in more!"

"No," the speaker replied. "That's not the point. This illustration teaches: If you don't put the big rocks in first, you'll never get them in at all."

What are the 'big rocks' in your life faith, time with loved ones, education, dreams? Remember to put these BIG ROCKS in first or you'll never get them in at all. Jesus said, *"But seek ye first the kingdom of God, and his righteousness"* (Matthew 6:33).

NOVEMBER 6
Time

Imagine there is a bank that credits your account each morning with $86,400. It carries over no balance from day to day. Every evening deletes whatever part of the balance you failed to use. What would you do? Draw out every cent, of course!

Each of us has such a bank. Its name is **Time**. Every morning, it credits you with 86,400 seconds. Every night it writes off whatever of this you have failed to invest to good purpose. It carries over no balance. Each day it opens a new account for you. Each night it burns the remains of the day. If you fail to use the day's deposits, the loss is yours. There is no going back, or drawing against the "tomorrow".

You must live on today's deposits. Invest it so as to get from it the utmost in health, happiness, and success! The clock is running. Make the most of today.

To realize the value of **One Year**, ask a student who failed a grade. The value of **One Month**, ask a mother who gave birth to a premature baby. The value of **One Week**, ask the editor of a weekly newspaper. The value of **One Hour**, ask the lovers who are waiting to meet. The value of **One Minute**, ask a person who missed the train. The value of **One Second**, ask a person who just avoided an accident. The value of **One Millisecond**, ask the person who won a silver medal in the Olympics.

Treasure every moment that you have! And treasure it more because you shared it with someone special, special enough to spend your time. And remember that time waits for no one.

Yesterday is history. Tomorrow is a mystery. Today is a gift. That's why it's called the present!

NOVEMBER 7
Tough Lawman Got Saved

Evangelist Wilbur Hurt tells of preaching a sermon on intercessory prayer in one of his revival meetings. A woman came to him and shared her burden for her father who was lost. She was quite concerned that he would die and go to hell. Her father was the sheriff in another county and Brother Hurt remembered that he was scheduled to have a revival meeting in that area four months into the future. The lady said, "I'm going to give myself to intercessory prayer for my dad for that entire four months period and I believe that God will save him."

On the first night of the meeting, the pastor pointed out a man in the congregation and said, "That fellow is the sheriff of our county." Brother Hurt said suddenly the women's statement came back to him. Surely that must be her dad. He was a hard looking fellow and very non responsive. He came back the second night and then the next and the next, in fact he came every night of the meeting and when someone asked him to go forward and be saved he bluntly said, "No."

On the last night of the meeting he lingered in the lobby until Brother Hurt and the Pastor came out. He wanted to talk. In the pastor's office in just a few moments after a clear presentation of the death, burial, and resurrection of Jesus Christ, the tough hard sheriff was on his knees asking God to save his poor lost soul.

"The effectual fervent prayer of a righteous man availeth much" (James 5:16b). The Word of God had done its work but Brother Hurt knew it was the four months of intercessory prayer with God by his daughter that made it happen.

NOVEMBER 8
True Value

A well-known speaker started off his seminar by holding up a $20 bill. In the room of more than 200 people, he asked, "Who would like this $20 bill?" Hands started going up.

He said, "I am going to give this $20 to one of you but first, let me do this." He proceeded to crumple the dollar bill up.

He then asked, "Who still wants it?" Still the hands were up in the air.

"Well," he replied, "What if I do this?" And he dropped it on the ground and started to grind it into the floor with his shoe. He picked it up, now all crumpled and dirty.

"Now who still wants it?" Still the hands went into the air. "My friends, you have all learned a very valuable lesson. No matter what I did to the money, you still wanted it because it did not decrease in value. It was still worth $20. Many times in our lives, we are dropped, crumpled, and ground into the dirt by the decisions we make and the circumstances that come our way. We feel worthless. But no matter what has happened or what will happen, you will never lose your value in God's eyes. To Him, dirty or clean, crumpled or finely creased, you are still priceless to Him."

"But God commendeth his love toward us, in that, while we were yet sinners, Christ died for us" (Romans 5:8).

Psalm 17:8 states that God will keep us, *"as the apple of [his] eye."* The worth of our lives comes not in what we do or who we are but by Whose we are! *"For ye are bought with a price: therefore glorify God in your body, and in your spirit, which are God's"* (1 Cor. 6:20).

NOVEMBER 9
Overcoming

The life and ministry of Jesus was divided into three periods of time.

There was a period of obscurity. Except for several things about the time of His birth and the brief appearance when He was twelve we know almost nothing.

Next there was the period of popularity. After He began to work miracles, every time He appeared in public He was mobbed with people who wanted to be healed.

Then there was the period of rejection. From the time He spoke of, *"eating His body and drinking His blood"* many walked away and followed Him no more.

In Mark chapter two, when it was discovered that He was in Capernaum a great crowd surrounded the place where He was. He began to preach to them. While He preached, four men came carrying a friend on a stretcher. They could get to Him because of the barriers. People were pushing and shoving trying to get closer themselves.

There will always be barriers. Nobody would move out of the way and help them get the man to Jesus. They went around to the side or back of the house and climbed upon the roof and made a hole to let them man down to Jesus who immediately healed him.

This is a story of overcoming obstacles. This is about victory in our prayer life, or getting more out of our Bible study, or finding fulfillment in our Christian life, and winning over temptation, or succeeding in our struggle in giving, or a breakthrough in soul winning, and rising above resentment, anger, bitterness, jealousy.

We do not need to give up in defeat because of the barriers and obstacles that will be present anytime we attempt to do anything for the Lord.

"Thanks be to God which giveth us the victory." (1 Cor. 15:57a)

NOVEMBER 10
21st Century Teacher

Let me see if I've got this right. You want me to go into that room with all those kids and fill their every waking moment with a love for learning. Not only that, I'm supposed to instill a sense of pride in their ethnicity, behaviorally modify disruptive behavior, observe them for signs of abuse and T-shirt messages.

I am to fight the war on drugs and sexually transmitted diseases, check their backpacks for guns and raise their self-esteem. I'm to teach them patriotism, good citizenship, sportsmanship and fair play, how and where to register to vote, how to balance a checkbook and how to apply for a job.

I am to check their heads occasionally for lice, maintain a safe environment, recognize signs of potential antisocial behavior, offer advice, write letters of recommendation for student employment and scholarships, encourage respect for the cultural diversity of others, and give the girls in my class 50 percent of my attention.

I am to make sure all students pass the state and federally mandated testing and all classes, whether or not they attend school on a regular basis or complete any of the work.

Plus, I am expected to make sure that all of the students with handicaps are guaranteed equal education, regardless of their mental or physical handicap. I am to communicate with each student's parent by letter, phone, newsletter and grade card.

I'm to do all of this with just a piece of chalk, a computer, a few books, a bulletin board, a 45 minute more-or-less plan time and a big smile, all on a starting salary that qualifies my family for food stamps in many states.

Is that all? And you want me to do all of this and expect me NOT TO PRAY?

NOVEMBER 11
A Glass Of Milk

One day, a boy selling goods from door to door to pay his way through school, found that he had only one dime left, and he was hungry. He decided he would ask for a something to eat at the next house.

However, he lost his nerve when a lovely young woman opened the door. Instead he asked for a drink of water. She thought he looked hungry so brought him a large glass of milk.

He drank it slowly, and then asked, 'How much do I owe you?"

"You don't owe me anything," she replied.

"Then I thank you from my heart." As he left that house, he not only felt stronger physically, but his faith in God was strengthened.

Many years later that same young woman became critically ill. The local doctors were baffled and sent her to a specialist to study her rare disease. Dr. Howard Kelly was called in for consultation.

When he heard the name of the town, a strange light filled his eyes. Immediately he rose and went to her room. He recognized her. He determined to do his best to save her life. He gave special attention to her case. After a long struggle, and special attention, the battle was won.

Dr. Kelly requested the business office to pass the bill to him for his final approval. He wrote something on her bill and it was sent to her room. She feared to open it, she was sure that it would take the rest of her life to pay for it all.

Finally she looked, and read these words...

"Paid in full with one glass of milk." She reaped what she had sown. *"Cast thy bread upon the water: for thou shalt find it after many days"* (Eccl. 11:1).

NOVEMBER 12
Adding Water To The Mudhole

A husband and wife were driving their car down a country lane on their way to visit some friends. They came to a muddy patch in the road and the car became bogged. After a few minutes of trying to get the car out by themselves, they saw a young farmer coming down the lane, driving some oxen before him. He stopped when he saw the couple in trouble and offered to pull the car out of the mud for $50.

The couple accepted and minutes later the car was free. The farmer turned to the husband and said,

"You know, you're the tenth car I've helped out of the mud today." The husband looks around at the growing fields and asks the farmer,

"When do you have time to plow your land? At night?"

"No," the young farmer replied seriously, "Night time is when I put the water in the hole."

There are some people who are always available to help solve problems, and there are others who spend their time making life more difficult for others (and sometimes the same person can do both!)

The New Testament is filled with warnings, though, about being a "stumbling block" to others, especially to children and young Christians.

"But whoso shall offend one of these little ones which believe in me, it were better for him that a millstone were hanged about his neck, and that he were drowned in the depth of the sea. Woe unto the world because of offences! For it must needs be that offences come; but woe to that man by whom the offence cometh!" (Matt. 18:6-7).

May your day be filled with opportunities to help others in need. But don't be guilty of adding any water to the mud hole!

NOVEMBER 13
Jordan, Gates and Wallace

Michael Jordan having "retired," with $40 million in endorsements, makes $178,100 a day, working or not. While sleeping 7 hours at night, he makes $52,000. If he goes to a movie he'll make $18,550 while there. He makes $7,415/hr. more than minimum wage.

If he wanted to save up for a new Acura NSX ($90,000), it would take him a whole 12 hours. He'll probably pay around $200 for a nice round of golf, but will accumulate $33,390 during that round.

Assuming he puts the federal maximum of 15% of his income into a tax deferred account (401k), his contributions will hit the federal cap of $9500 at 8:30 a.m. on January 1st.

If you were given a penny for every 10 dollars he makes, you'd be living at $65,000 a year. He'll make $15,600 during the Boston Marathon. While the common person is spending about $20 for a meal in his trendy Chicago restaurant, he'll pull in about $5600. This year, he'll make more than twice as much as all the U.S. past presidents for all of their terms combined. Amazing isn't it?

However. If Jordan saves 100% of his income for the next 450 years, he'll still have less than Bill Gates, and there are several men who have more than Gates.

Just as I was about to become envious, the Holy Spirit reminded me that I am an heir of God and a joint heir with Jesus Christ (Romans 8:17). We own all the oil, coal, diamonds, gold and silver in the world, and the cattle on a thousand hills.

NOVEMBER 14
Dog Killer Becomes Pastor

We have all heard and read the captions, "From Prison to the Pulpit" and "from Crime to Christ." Dr. Oliver B. Green announces his testimony message as "From Disgrace to Grace." Billy Sunday was promoted as the ball player who was promoted to the big leagues.

While visiting hillside tribe villages in Northern Thailand I was really excited to meet a young pastor who was doing an outstanding job ministering to his people. I was even more interested, because one of the widows from my church had made a donation to build the church and living quarters for the young pastor.

The missionary, also from our church, told me that the same young pastor had given up his job raising dogs when the Lord called him to pastor his church. When I asked the reason, he told me that he butchered them and sold them for people to eat. Eating dog meat, grasshoppers, and grub worms, was a way of life to these people, but since his conversion he was not comfortable with his old ways, and gave it up.

His willingness to give up his business and trust the Lord to supply his livelihood, had brought him support from the missionary, a new church and house, had relaxed his congregation, and made a lot of dogs happy.

He agreed with Paul when he said, *"If meat make my brother to offend, I will eat no flesh while the world standeth"* (I Cor. 8:13). Paul also had said, *"But meat commendeth us not to God: for neither, if we eat, are we the better; neither, if we eat not, are we the worse. But take heed lest by any means this liberty of yours become a stumblingblock to them that are weak"* (1 Cor. 8:8-9).

NOVEMBER 15
Not Who He Seemed To Be

From the Sunshine Coast, Queensland comes a true story. Recently a routine police patrol parked outside a local neighborhood tavern. Late in the evening the officer noticed a man leaving the bar so intoxicated that he could barely walk.

The man stumbled around the car park with the officer quietly observing. After what seemed an eternity and trying his keys on five vehicles, the man managed to find his car which he fell into. He was there for a few minutes as a number of other patrons left the bar and drove off.

Finally he started the car, switched the wipers on and off (it was a fine dry night), flicked the indicators on and off, tooted the horn and then switched on the lights. He moved the vehicle forward a few inches, reversed a little and then remained stationary for a few more minutes as more patrons left in their vehicles.

At last he pulled out of the car park and started to drive slowly down the road. The police officer, having patiently waited all this time, now started up the patrol car, put on the flashing lights, promptly pulled the man over and carried out a Breathalyzer test. To his amazement the breathalyzer indicated no evidence of the man having consumed alcohol at all!

Dumbfounded, the officer said "I'll have to ask you to accompany me to the Police station this breathalyzer equipment must be broken."

"I doubt it," said the man, "Tonight I'm the designated decoy."

"I know thy works, and tribulation, and poverty, (but thou art rich) and I know the blasphemy of them which say they are Jews, and are not, but are the synagogue of Satan" (Rev. 2:9). A lot of people are not what they appear.

NOVEMBER 16
Creation Contest

One day a group of scientists got together and decided that man had come a long way and no longer needed God. So they picked one scientist to go and tell God that they were done with Him.

The scientist walked up to God and said, "God, we've decided that we no longer need you. We're to the point that we can clone people and do many miraculous things, so why don't you just go on and get lost."

God listened very patiently and kindly to the man and after the scientist was done talking, God said, "Very well, how about this, let's say we have a 'man-making' contest."

To which the scientist replied, "OK, great!"

God added, "Now, we're going to do this just like I did back in the old days with Adam."

The scientist said, "Sure, no problem." and bent down and grabbed himself a handful of dirt.

God just looked at him and said, "No, no. You go get your own dirt!"

The story makes a good point. True, scientists are not able to create life, but in all their attempts to duplicate God's feat, they overlook one very important point—God started with nothing!

Everything around us was not just rearranged, it was "created." God spoke, and the world came into existence. Every time we think we can accomplish great things (maybe even as great as God), we need to remind ourselves of that truth.

Take nothing and try to make something out of it, and you will realize just how far short of God's omnipotence you fall. *"Through faith we understand that the worlds were framed by the word of God, so that the things which are seen were not made of things which do appear"* (Hebrews 11:3).

NOVEMBER 17
He Led Her To Christ In A Bathtub

Dr. Jack Hyles tells of an experience that took place while he was in a Bible Conference in Houston, Texas. He returned to his room at the motel and found the door open. There was singing from the bathroom. He checked the key number to see whether or not he was in the right room. He called into the room. "Who's there?"

A maid answered, explaining that she was cleaning the tub. Dr. Hyles asked her if she was a Christian.

She said, "Mercy no! I'm as mean as the devil!" While she continued to clean in the tub, on her knees, he gave her the Bible plan of salvation. While she cleaned the tub, the Lord cleaned her heart. Later, Dr. Hyles said that he was probably the only person who ever led a lady to Christ in the bathtub.

Wouldn't it be a terrible thing for a person to spend their life cleaning for other people and not ever be cleansed themselves? Thank God for the lady who got saved in the bathtub.

"Now ye are clean through the word which I have spoken unto you" (John 15:3). I have never had the opportunity to lead a person to Christ in a bathtub, but I have won someone to the Lord in a hospital bed, a jail cell, in an airplane seat, in a car, under a car, in a barn, in my office, at an altar, in a motel hall way, at a reception desk, in a Wal-Mart parking lot, under a China Berry tree, in a vestibule, at the front door, at the cash register, on the telephone, at a turtle farm, and many other places.

NOVEMBER 18
Heirs Of God

My friend Coach Ron Bishop flying from Guatemala to Atlanta, was asked by the stewardess if he might like to sit in first class. She gave him a seat across from two ladies with small babies. Then the stewardess came back and told them they could not have four people in two seats. She asked Ron if he would trade seats with one of them.

Oh boy, right between two fussing, crying babies. He was better off back in the tourist cabin. He asked one of the women where she was going.

"Boston," she replied, "my husband is a ball player, for the Red sox".

"Who is your husband," Bishop asked.

"Pedro Martinez," she answered. Wow, the 11 ½ million dollar per year pitcher for the Red Sox. Suddenly the children were beautiful. The coach asked if he might hold one on his lap.

That just changed the whole picture. Maybe when we get to feeling that we are not important and nobody cares, just remember, we are heirs of God and joint heirs with Christ.

Our father is preparing a mansion for us that cannot be described. He is the rightful owner of all the gold and silver in the world, along with the oil deposits, diamonds, and all other minerals in the earth.

"The silver is mine, and the gold is mine, saith the LORD of hosts" (Haggai 2:8).

"For every beast of the forest is mine, and the cattle upon a thousand hills." (Psalm 50:10).

We are in line to receive an inheritance, *"To an inheritance incorruptible, and undefiled, and that fadeth not away, reserved in heaven for you"* (1 Peter 1:4). Let's read the will again.

NOVEMBER 19
Cancer Is A Great Preacher

Bill McGill was dying with cancer. The killer disease had eaten its way through his lymph node system and was now working on his brain. The word they were using was "terminal." In spite of his condition he was upbeat and very alert. I spent a few minutes just chatting. We talked about people we both knew and things we enjoyed doing.

Then I asked him point blank, "Bill, If this thing gets you will you go to heaven?" When he hesitated with his answer, I quickly told him there were only three possible answers to that question. "Yes, I would, No, I wouldn't, or I don't know."

Bill quickly answered, "I don't know preacher. I sure would like to know," he added.

I asked him, "If I can show you from your own Bible exactly what to do and you knew if you did it you would go to Heaven, would you do it?"

"Why sure I would," said Bill, "I would be a fool not to." I shared several verses of the Bible with him. Then I told him the story of another fellow in a similar situation who had invited Christ into his heart. He listened intently. Then I saw the tears beginning to well up in his eyes. I knew he was ready. At my suggestion, he quietly prayed and invited Christ into his heart. Bill's mother had been listening the whole time. She suddenly began to shout and rejoice.

She had prayed for years and now her prayers had been answered. Sometime later Bill died and went to Heaven. That cancer might have been the best thing that ever happened to Bill. Maybe that's why Paul said, *"Therefore I take pleasure in infirmities"* (2 Cor.12:10).

NOVEMBER 20
Who Or What To Blame

Flip Wilson made the accusation "The devil made me do it" famous. We humans are experts at placing blame for our shortcomings on someone or something else.

Dr Larry Lilly says, "In my work with prisoners and ex-prisoners I hear, too much, that "they" are the cause of all my woe. "Prison has made me into what I have become." Sounds philosophical doesn't it? It's not true. No more than being born in Germany makes you a Nazi.

Dr. Henry Brandt said, "Other people don't create your spirit, they only reveal it." So much for Adams, "the woman thou gavest me," excuse.

God brings people and circumstances into our lives to reveal the real us. It's true, some person, sets in motion a series of painful events, that bring out some negative aspect of our personality. This sets in motion thoughts and actions that reveal who we are and what we are, and what we are becoming, Unchecked anger can lead to murder. Porn can lead to rape, even murder. Rage can lead to suicide.

So, what to do? Accept God's statements about you as true. This is not all bad. God's statements about you communicate to you that you are loved, that God wants to be around you. God brings painful things into our life to show us what we are, where we are going and to cause us to do one of two things: Place the blame or change. It's that simple.

Changing mates, places or jobs seldom makes any lasting difference. Changing our mind, how we think about people and things, changing our heart, will lead to a change in actions, resulting in a change in how people think and feel about us and how they react to us.

Simple? Yes. Easy? No.

NOVEMBER 21
Can Anybody See God?

A small boy once approached his slightly older sister with a question about God.

"Susie, can anybody ever really see God?" he asked.

Susie curtly replied, "No, of course not, silly. God is so far up in heaven that nobody can see him."

Time passed, but his question still lingered so he approached his mother: "Mom, can anybody ever really see God?"

"No, not really," she gently said. "God is a spirit and he dwells in our hearts, but we can never really see him."

Not long afterwards, his saintly old grandfather took the little boy on a fishing trip The sun was beginning to set with unusual splendor as the day ended. The old man stopped fishing and turned his full attention to the exquisite beauty unfolding before him.

On seeing the face of his grandfather reflecting such deep peace and contentment as he gazed into the magnificent ever-changing sunset, the little boy thought for a moment and finally spoke hesitatingly: "Granddad I wasn't going to ask anybody else, but I wonder if you can tell me the answer to something I've been wondering about. Can anybody really see God?"

The old man did not even turn his head. A moment slipped by before he finally answered. "Son," he quietly said. "It's getting so I can't see anything else."

"The heavens declare the glory of God; and the firmament sheweth his handywork. Day unto day uttereth speech, and night unto night sheweth knowledge. There is no speech nor language, where their voice is not heard. Their line is gone out through all the earth, and their words to the end of the world" (Ps. 19:1-4).

I long for the day when I can not only see God, but can see nothing else.

NOVEMBER 22
Praying And Longer Life

Dianne Hales, in an article written in Parade Magazine back in 2003 stated, "Dozens of studies have shown that individuals who pray regularly and attend religious services stay healthier and live longer than those who rarely or never do—even when age, health, habits, demographics and other factors are considered.

"A six year Duke University study of 4,000 men and women of various faiths, all over 64, found that the relative risk of dying was 46% lower for those who frequently attended religious services."

Perhaps the medical world will one day will heed the words of the Apostle Paul: Pray without ceasing (1 Thess. 5:17).

"Another Duke study of 4,000 people over 64, found that those who prayed regularly had significantly lower blood pressure than the less religious. A third study showed that those who attended religious services had healthier immune systems than those who did not."

Solomon, referring to the commandments said, *"For length of days, and long life, and peace, shall they add to thee"* (Proverbs 3:2).

Paul the Apostle who continually wrote of contentment, satisfaction, and fulfillment advised, *"Be careful for nothing; but in every thing by prayer and supplication with thanksgiving let your requests be made known unto God. And the peace of God, which passeth all understanding, shall keep your hearts and minds through Christ Jesus"* (Phil. 4:6-7).

Mary Kidder, in the chorus of her well-loved hymn penned the words:

> Oh, how praying rests the weary!
> Prayer will change the night to day;
> So when life seems dark and dreary,
> Don't forget to pray.

Hundreds of years before Christ, Isaiah the prophet spoke of the Lord saying, *"Thou wilt keep him in perfect peace, whose mind is stayed on thee: because he trusteth in thee"* (Isaiah 26:3).

NOVEMBER 23
Dead While You Live

Dr. Lee Roberson, the founder of the Tennessee Temple University of Chattanooga, Tennessee and pastor of Highland Park Baptist Church for so many years, gave a message entitled, "Dead at 25, Buried at 72".

He made reference to the multitudes who float through life without purpose, as some say from pillar to post, going where ever the winds carry them. These folks usually have very little thought as to where they will go when they die.

Then too, if they are Christians there is no concern for what they will face at the Judgment seat of Christ, or the position that will occupy in the millennium.

An old story was passed around several years ago concerning some deacons who always sat on the front row to evaluate the preacher's message. One of them died during one of the services. When the undertaker was called to remove the body, he carried out three of them before he got the right one.

An old preacher on the radio out of Detroit used to say, "Anything that is dead ought to be buried." He was referring to formal dead lifeless religion and reminded his listeners that Jesus was the way, the truth and the life.

My friend, Bill Webb, preached a message in a meeting in the Cincinnati, Ohio area called "Living Until You Die". He said Christ was the source of his life, the strength of his life, the satisfaction of his life, the standard of his life and the subject of his life.

He closed with a quotation from Paul the apostle. *"For me to live is Christ."* Jesus said, *"I am the resurrection and the life: he that believeth in me, though he were dead, yet shall he live"* (John 11:25).

NOVEMBER 24
Not One Rejection

The submarine *Squalas* developed a problem and sank to the bottom of the Atlantic Ocean. They were 240 feet below the surface and in an almost hopeless situation. The crew sent up smoke flares to attract attention to their plight location, hoping someone would see them. Another submarine did take notice. A ten ton diving bell was lowered repeatedly and all thirty-three of the ill-fated crewmen were rescued.

Not one said, "I'll think it over", "Maybe later", "I don't think I'm ready", "I'll wait for a more convenient time". Every one of them gratefully and without hesitation accepted the opportunity to escape from a certain death.

Jesus warned of an awful Hell for all eternity and any who turn down His offer of deliverance would cast into a lake of fire. John wrote, *"And whosoever was not found written in the book of life was cast into the lake of fire"* (Rev. 20:15). People refuse the offer of salvation because they do not believe they are really going to perish.

Paul wrote. *"In whom the god of this world hath blinded the minds of them which believe not, lest the light of the glorious gospel of Christ, who is the image of God, should shine unto them"* (2 Cor. 4:4).

The writer of Hebrews gives a plea, *"How shall we escape, if we neglect so great salvation; which at the first began to be spoken by the Lord, and was confirmed unto us by them that heard him"* (Hebrews 2:3).

It is simply a matter of believing. John also said, *"He that believeth on the Son hath everlasting life: and he that believeth not the Son shall not see life; but the wrath of God abideth on him"* (John 3:36).

NOVEMBER 25
Taps

We have all heard the haunting melody of "Taps." The song gives us that lump in our throats and tears in our eyes.

It began in 1862 during the Civil War, when Union Army Captain Robert Ellicombe was with his men near Harrison's Landing, Virginia. The Confederate Army was on the other side of the narrow strip of land. During the night, Captain Ellicombe heard the moans of a soldier who was severely wounded.

Not knowing if it was a Union or Confederate soldier, the Captain decided to risk his life and bring the stricken man back for medical attention. Crawling on his stomach through the gunfire, he reached the soldier and began pulling him toward the encampment.

When the Captain finally reached his own lines, he discovered it was a Confederate soldier, but he was dead. The Captain lit a lantern and caught his breath and went numb. He saw the face of his own son.

The boy had been studying music in the South when the war broke out. Without telling his father, the boy enlisted in the Confederate Army. The father asked permission to give his son a full military burial despite his enemy status. His request was partially granted. The Captain had asked if he could have a group of Army band members play a funeral dirge for his son.

The request was denied since the soldier was a Confederate. But, out of respect for the father, they did say they could give him one musician. The Captain chose a bugler. He asked the bugler to play the musical notes he had found on a piece of paper in the pocket of the dead youth's uniform.

This wish was granted. The haunting melody, which we now know as "Taps" used at military funerals, was born.

NOVEMBER 26
Daily Thanksgiving

I'm glad we set aside a Thursday in November every year to think about the Pilgrims, to eat turkey with our families and to count our many blessings and express our gratitude to God for His bounty.

Thanksgiving, however, ought to be a daily habit and a way of life. When I got out of my bed this morning I went to my place of prayer and began to tell the Lord how grateful I was for His loving kindness, tender mercies, amazing grace, wonderful love, blessed forgiveness, abundant life, peace that passeth all understanding, joy unspeakable, promise of a glorified body, privilege of someday living in the New Jerusalem and the opportunity to assist the Lord Jesus in His millennium reign on the earth.

Then I cried out with the Psalmist, *"O that men would praise the Lord for his goodness and for his wonderful works to the children of men!"* (Psalm 107:8). I have praised Him for His work of creation of the universe, inspiration of the Bible, salvation of the soul, sanctification of the life, preservation of the believer, glorification of our bodies and calumniation of the last days on the earth.

I then expressed my thankfulness to the Lord Jesus for volunteering to come to earth, His virgin birth, His virtuous life, His vicarious suffering, His victorious resurrection, His valuable intercession, His visible return and His vibrant reign on the earth.

I then ask God's blessings on our pastor, our widows and widowers, family members, and our sick folks. By this time all my mountains have become molehills and I was ready to face another day with gratitude in my soul. *"Oh that men would praise the Lord for his goodness and for his wonderful works to the children of men!"* (Psalm 107:8).

NOVEMBER 27
Create In Me A Clean Heart

Two bachelors were talking one day, and their conversation drifted from politics to sports to cooking.

One of them said, "I got a cookbook once, but I could never do anything with it."

The other one said, "Too much fancy work in it, huh?"

269

The first one said, "Yeah, it sure was. Every one of the recipes began the same way—'Take a clean dish.' "

Our relationship with God is much the same. God says, "Take a clean life", and we go, "Wait a minute, that's a problem." Because *"all have sinned, and come short of the glory of God"* (Romans 3:23). Our lives are not clean. We're stained by sin.

Making the matter even more difficult is the fact that we do not have the ability to cleanse ourselves: *"Who can say, I have made my heart clean, I am pure from my sin'?"* (Proverbs 20:9). The answer is, "No one." As the leper that came unto Jesus, saying, *"Lord, if thou wilt, thou canst make me clean. And Jesus put forth his hand, and touched him, saying, I will; be thou clean. And immediately his leprosy was cleansed"* (Matthew 8:2-3).

Fortunately, God offers cleansing through the blood of Jesus Christ. So our plea to God is that of David: *"Wash me throughly from my iniquity, and cleanse me from my sin…Create in me a clean heart, O God."* (Psalm 51:2,10a).

Isaiah put it this way, *"Though your sins be as scarlet, they shall be as white as snow; though they be red like crimson, they shall be as wool"* (Isaiah 1:18b).

May we all be willing to do what God says in order to receive the cleansing he offers. And praise be to God for his willingness to make clean what we cannot!

NOVEMBER 28
Taking God's Blessings For Granted

Two friends bumped into one another on the street one day. One of them was almost on the verge of tears.

His friend asked, "What has the world done to you?"

The sad fellow said, "Three weeks ago, an uncle died and left me forty thousand dollars."

"That's a lot of money."

"Then two weeks ago, a cousin I never even knew me eighty-five thousand."

"Sounds like you've been blessed…"

"You don't understand!. Last week my great-aunt passed away. I inherited a quarter of a million."

"Then, why do you look so glum?"

"This week…nothing!"

The trouble with receiving something on a regular basis is that we eventually come to expect it. Someone once suggested to me a way to test someone's character. Give him (or her) $5 a day for a month, then stop, and see what his reaction is. The natural tendency is that if we receive a gift long enough, we come to view it as an entitlement. We feel hurt, even angry, if we don't receive it any longer.

It's the same way with the blessings of God. I don't deserve the comfortable home I live in, the beautiful scenery around me, the clean water that I drink. But after receiving these gifts for years, I sometimes fail to be grateful. I've come to expect these good things. And when one of them is removed for a short while (like the water being cut off or electricity failing), I get upset.

Taking God's blessing for granted is a sin. Focus on what you have rather than on what you don't have, and see if it doesn't improve your attitude. *"Oh, that men would praise the LORD for his goodness, and for his wonderful works to the children of men!"* (Psalm 107:8).

NOVEMBER 29
Are You Important?

A famous football coach was on vacation with his family in Maine. When they walked into a movie theater and sat down, the handful of people applauded. He thought to himself, "I can't believe it. People recognize me all the way up here." Then a man came over to him and said, "Thanks for coming. They won't start the movie for less than ten people." Ouch! That'll deflate an ego in a hurry.

That's the trouble with thinking you're important. I heard about one man who was hesitant to go on vacation. When someone at work told him, "Don't worry. We can get by without you for a while," his response was, "I know, I just don't want anybody else to find that out!"

Humility, is one of the most difficult-to-find traits in our society. And one of the most important traits in the eyes of God. How often we try to raise our esteem in the eyes of men when we ought to be showing a servants attitude.

"When thou art bidden of any man to a wedding, sit not down in the highest room; lest a more honourable man than thou be bidden of him; And he that bade thee and him come and say to thee, Give this man place; and thou begin with shame to take the

271

lowest room; But when thou art bidden, go and sit down in the lowest room; that when he that bade thee cometh, he may say unto thee, Friend, go up higher: then shalt thou have worship in the presence of them that sit at meat with thee. For whosoever exalteth himself shall be abased; and he that humbleth himself shall be exalted" (Luke 14:8-11).

NOVEMBER 30
Let Your Words Be Few

A woman goes into the local newspaper office to see that the obituary for her recently deceased husband is properly written (she had always been known for her accuracy to details, second only to her famous sense of thrift). Only his beloved pickup truck remains to remind her of his presence.

The obit editor informs her that the fee for the obituary is 50 cents a word. She pauses, reflects and then says, "Well then, let it read, 'Billy Bob died.'

Although amused at the woman's cleverness, the editor says, "Sorry, ma'am, but there is a 7 word minimum on all obituaries."

This causes her to become a little flustered, and she thinks things over for a few seconds. "In that case," she says, "let it read, 'Billy Bob died, 1983 Pickup for sale.'

For reasons that go far beyond finances, we should learn to be a people of few words (and we should make those few words count).

Solomon had quite a few things to say on this subject: *"In the multitude of words there wanteth not sin: but he refraineth his lips is wise"* (Proverbs 10:19).

"Therefore let your words be few....a fool's voice is known by multitude of words" (Eccl. 5:2c-3b).

James speaks to this also, when he says, *"Even so the tongue is a little member, and boasteth great things. Behold, how great a matter a little fire kindleth! And the tongue is a fire, a world of iniquity: so is the tongue among our members, that it defileth the whole body, and setteth on fire the course of nature; and it is set on fire of hell"* (James 3:5-6).

Let your words be few. I would say a few more things, but...

DECEMBER 1
Worldly Minded

In 1924 Richard Loeb and Nathan Leopold two young men conceived and executed what they thought was the perfect crime—the murder of a school mate. Leopold said it was an experiment just as easy to justify as impaling a beetle on a straight pin.

An atheistic philosopher named Nietzsche had lectured and planted this thinking in the boys' minds. They were convicted and sentenced to life plus 99 years in prison.

Dr. Lee Roberson in his book *Preaching to America* published by the Sword of the Lord says: America is sick. We are seeing it in every city, every village, every state and we are seeing it in the nation's capital.

In Washington D.C. 383 murders in one year.

Half of our marriages end in divorce. In 30 years we've had 47 million divorces.

In 30 years—18 million babies killed by Abortion.

80,000 cases of child abuse in Georgia in 1 year. They were beaten, raped, starved, burned, etc.

3500 to 4000 churches close each year.

7500 Southern Baptist churches—no baptisms.

Children's defense fund reports that every 24 hrs:

437 teens are arrested for drunk driving.

1206 unwed teens have abortions.

1365 unwed teens have babies.

11,512 teens drop out of school.

3288 teens run away from home.

13,500 teens carry guns to school each year.

These figures have become increasingly worse since that book was written. The four cities with the highest crime and murder rate have the strictest gun laws and yet they are out of control.

Humanistic and secular philosophy being taught in our schools, along with God, prayer, and the Bible view of creation being expelled from the schools and government while evolution and socialistic philosophy is being taught in their place. We are experiencing the natural result.

DECEMBER 2
God's Wonderful Works

The psalmist gives four different scenario's and how God responded to them in Psalm 107.

People were wandering around without direction, hungry, and thirsty.

A second group were confused and in rebellion against God.

The third group were sick, had no interest in God, and about to die. A fourth people were being tossed back and forth in a stormy sea.

In each case they cried out to the Lord and the Lord stepped in and delivered them from their distresses. David then pleads, *"Oh that men would praise the LORD for his goodness, and for his wonderful works to the children of men!"* (Psalm 107:8,15,21,31).

God's works can be divided into seven categories. First there is the work of Creation. *"And, Thou, Lord, in the beginning hast laid the foundation of the earth; and the heavens are the works of thine hands"* (Hebrews 1:10).

Second, there is the work of Inspiration of the Bible. *"All scripture is given by inspiration of God, and is profitable for doctrine, for reproof, for correction, for instruction in righteousness"* (2 Timothy 3:16).

Third, the work of Salvation of the souls. *"For by grace are ye saved through faith; and that not of yourselves: it is the gift of God"* (Ephesians 2:8).

Fourth, the work of Sanctification of Believers. *"For this is the will of God, even your sanctification"* (1 Thess. 4:3).

Fifth, the preservation of our salvation. *"For I know...that he is able to keep that which I have committed unto him against that day"* (2 Timothy 1:12).

Sixth, the glorification of the believer's body. *"Who shall change our vile body...according to the working...to subdue all things unto himself"* (Phil. 3:21).

Seventh, the culmination of the end time. The Rapture and resurrection will finalize His work on earth.

DECEMBER 3
Do Unto Others

On a cold day in December in New York City some years ago, A little boy about 10 years old was standing before a shoe store, barefooted, peering through the window, and shivering with cold.

A lady approached the boy and said, "My little fellow, why are you looking so earnestly in that window?"

"I was asking God to give me a pair of shoes," was the boy's reply.

The lady took him by the hand and went into the store. She asked the clerk to get a half a dozen pairs of socks for the boy. She then asked if he would get her a basin of water and a towel. He quickly brought them to her. She took the little fellow to the back part of the store and, removing her gloves, knelt down, washed his little feet and dried them with a towel. By this time the clerk had returned with the socks. Placing a pair upon the boy's feet, she purchased him a pair of shoes.

She tied up the remaining pairs of socks and gave them to him. She patted him on the head and said, "No doubt, my little fellow, you feel more comfortable now?"

As she turned to go, the astonished lad caught her by the hand, and looking up in her face, with tears in his eyes, answered the question with these words: "Are you God's wife?"

Jesus told His disciples, *"For I was an hungered, and ye gave me meat: I was thirsty, and ye gave me drink: I was a stranger, and ye took me in...Verily I say unto you, Inasmuch as ye have done it unto one of the least of these my brethren, ye have done it unto me"* (Matthew 25:35-40).

DECEMBER 4
The Pearl Necklace

A little girl, waiting with her mother at the checkout stand, saw some white pearls in a pink box.

"Mommy, can I have them? Please?"

The mother checked the box and said, "They're almost $2.00. I'll think of some chores for you and you can save money to buy them for yourself. Your birthday's only a week away and you might get a dollar bill from Grandma."

After dinner, she did some chores and went to the neighbor and asked if she could pick dandelions for ten cents. Grandma did give her a dollar bill and now she had enough money. She got her pearls.

The only time she took them off was when she went swimming. Mother said if they got wet, they would ruin. Every night her daddy read her a story.

One night as he finished he asked Jenny, "Do you love me?"

"Oh yes, daddy."

"Then give me your pearls."

"Oh, daddy, not my pearls. You can have my white horse from my collection."

"That's okay, Honey."

About a week later, daddy asked again, "Do you love me?"

"Daddy, you know I love you."

"Then give me your pearls."

"Oh Daddy, not my pearls. You can have my doll."

The next night Jenny's chin was trembling. She lifted her hand up and there was her little pearl necklace. She finally said, "Here, daddy,"

With tears in his eyes, he reached out and took the imitation necklace, and reached into his pocket and pulled out a strand of genuine pearls. He was waiting for her to give up the fake so he could give her the genuine.

So it is, with our Heavenly Father. He is waiting for us to give up the cheap things in our lives so that he can give us beautiful treasures.

DECEMBER 5
Christologically Advantaged

Several years ago Dr. Larry Lilly wrote an article about Mary Parr who lived to be 113 years of age. At that time she was the oldest woman in America. She attributed her mental alertness, physical stamina, and longevity to the fact that she never married. She had no known survivors. She had given her energy to others by working for the Red Cross, and a Tuberculosis organization.

Most people hope for a long and happy life. Most do not have enough years or happiness. I think the years are pretty much in the hands of the Lord through genetic makeup.

Happy? Well, books are written about happiness and the secular and Christian Counselors make reasonable livings attempting to aid Adams' fallen children in their mad search for fleeting happiness.

Some attribute longer life to being "Chronologically Advantaged." "It's in the genes", they say. No matter how "chronologically advantaged" we may be, the time will come when the old ticker will give way to the demands of the way things are and we will go to meet our maker. I don't think the Bible teaches that there is any particular advantage to having lived a long time.

What matters is how we lived and for whom we have lived. If we have lived to ourselves and for ourselves, we shall die by ourselves. A lonely, fearful time, you may be sure, and it comes sooner than we think.

Christ not only makes the difference in life at any age, He makes all the difference when life is done, whatever the time on earth.

Several places in the Bible, reference is made to, "thy days shall be long on the earth." A relationship with the Lord and the resulting satisfaction surely will give us a Christological Advantage.

DECEMBER 6
The Cookie Thief

A woman was at an airport, with a good bit of time before her flight. She hunted for a book in the airport shops, bought a bag of cookies and found herself a seat. She got engrossed in her book but happened to see that the man sitting beside her smiled and took a cookie from the bag in between them, which she tried to ignore to avoid a scene.

So she munched the cookies and watched the clock. In a few moments the gentleman reached over and took another cookie from the bag. She was getting more irritated as the minutes ticked by.

Thinking, If I wasn't so nice, I would blacken his eye. With each cookie she took, he took one too. When only one was left, he smiled and reached over and took it, broke it in half and handed the other half to her She glared at him as she took it from his hand.

She thought this guy has some nerve. Why he didn't even show any gratitude! She had never known when she had been so irritated about anything.

Just then she heard them call her flight, she gathered her belongings and headed to the gate and on to the plane. As she got settled into her seat and stowed her carry-on bags, she reached in to get her book and there was her unopened bag of cookies.

If mine are here, she moaned in despair, The others were his, and he tried to share. Too late to apologize, she realized with grief, that she was the rude one, the ingrate, the thief.

How many times in our lives have we absolutely known that something was a certain way, only to be wrong. How do you admit wrong?

DECEMBER 7
Fulfilled Prophesies

The Bible contains over 2,000 detailed prophesies in the Old Testament alone. Except for the prophesies about things yet to come in the end time return of Jesus, every single one including political, religious, intellectual, and geographic events leading up to the return of Jesus Christ has been fulfilled to the smallest detail. In the writings of Buddha, Confucius, Lao-Tse, the Koran, not one single fulfilled prophesy can be found.

Someone has suggested that for only eight of the prophesies concerning the birth, life, death, resurrection, and such of Jesus to be fulfilled accurately, it would be more likely if silver dollars could be spread over the entire state of Texas four feet deep.

A plane would then be dispatched from the air base in Bangor Maine and remotely flown over Texas, and after flying thirty-eight minutes and twenty seconds, a silver dollar painted red would be thrown out to fall to earth.

Next a helicopter would be flown from Elgin Air Force base in Florida across Texas, and an order would be given thirty minutes after crossing the Texas border, for an air force captain to be blind-folded and parachuted to the ground.

When he lands, he must walk for one hour, then stoop down, still blindfolded, and pick up one coin. The chances of him picking up the red one would be thousands of times more likely than the eight prophesies fulfilled. And remember there were not eight, but more than 2,000.

We know that it is absolutely impossible for man to predict the future with 100% accuracy. Only God can do that. The Old Testament said He would be born in Bethlehem, come out of Egypt, and would be called a Nazarene. This simply could not be, yet it all came to pass.

DECEMBER 8
Balanced Christians

Solomon said, *"Give me neither poverty nor riches...lest I be full and deny thee... or lest I be poor, and steal"* (Proverbs 30:8b-9). Both poverty and riches are extremes. He didn't want to go off the deep end.

Jesus speaking to the scribes and pharisees said *"Ye blind guides, which strain at a gnat, and swallow a camel…ye make clean the outside of the cup and of the platter, but within they are full of extortion and excess"* (Matthew 23:24-25).

God is love and He is also a consuming fire. The priest in the Old Testament had a bell then a pomegranate intermittently around the hem of his garment. One was to be seen and the other to hear. (Exodus 39:26).

David wrote, *"Be not as the horse, or as the mule"* (Psalm 32:9). A horse is quick spirited, while the mule is stubborn. If the thread of a sewing machine is too tight it will snap, but if it is too loose, then it also will snap.

All sowing no reaping or all reaping and no sowing equals failure. All reaching and no teaching or all teaching and no reaching will not produce a good church or Sunday school class.

For a pastor to visit 90% of the time and study 5% of the time will make his sermons shallow and empty, but to study 90% of time and visit 5% of the time will make him deep and dusty.

We must have both zeal and knowledge. All work and no play makes Jack a dull boy. All play and no work will make Jack hungry.

Jesus spoke of the Pharisees being hypocrites and being full of excess (Matthew 23:24-25). Job said it well, *"Let me be weighed in an even balance, that God may know mine integrity"* (Job 31:6).

DECEMBER 9
The Secret of Greatness

"For we would not, brethren, have you ignorant of our trouble which came to us in Asia, that we were pressed out of measure, above strength, insomuch that we despaired even of life: But we had the sentence of death in ourselves, that we should not trust in ourselves, but in God which raiseth the dead" (2 Cor. 1:8-9).

While attending a Bible conference, I heard Dr. Lee Roberson announce that he would speak the next evening on "The Secret of Greatness." I arrived early the next evening with notebook in hand, ready to take down points of instruction. I wanted to be sure to get the facts straight from the man who knew what he was talking about.

After he was introduced to speak, he stood up, and said "I give you tonight the secret of greatness. It is found in one key word, the word is "Trouble." I was so disappointed not to get a systematic formula of instruction from Dr. Roberson based upon his years of experience and success. But the more he preached, the more I realized that what he was saying surely was the true secret of greatness.

People react to trouble in several different ways. Some grumble, others gripe, many growl, a few groan; then there are those who grieve and thank the Lord; then some grow. Trouble will never leave one the same. Trouble is nothing new.

The Bible, of course, is filled with stories of those in trouble. The Hebrew children had their fiery furnace. Daniel had his lions' den. Joseph was cast into prison. Paul was shipwrecked. Peter was sent to prison. John was exiled at Patmos. James had his head cut off. Samson had his eyes put out.

These were the greats of the Bible.

DECEMBER 10
Meaning Well

A man found a cocoon of a butterfly with a small opening. He sat watching for several hours as it struggled to force its body through that little hole. Then it seemed to stop making any progress. It appeared as if it had gotten as far as it could. He decided to help the butterfly. He took a pair of scissors and snipped off the remaining bit of the cocoon. The butterfly then emerged easily.

But it's body was swollen and small, and it's wings shriveled. He continued to watch because he expected that, at any moment, the wings would enlarge and expand to be able to support the body, which would contract in time. Neither happened! In fact, the butterfly spent the rest of its life crawling around with a swollen body and shriveled wings. It never was able to fly.

What the man did not understand was that the restricting cocoon and the struggle required for the butterfly to get through the tiny opening were God's way of forcing fluid from the body of the butterfly into its wings so that it would be ready for flight once it came from the cocoon.

Sometimes struggles are exactly what we need.

If God allowed us to go through life without obstacles, it would cripple us. We would not be as strong as we needed to be.

I asked for strength—and God gave me difficulties to make me strong.
I asked for wisdom—and God gave me problems to solve.
I asked for prosperity—and God gave me brain and brawn to work.
I asked for courage—and God gave me danger to overcome.
I asked for love—and God gave me troubled people to help.
I asked for favors—and God gave me opportunities.
I received nothing I wanted—I received everything I needed!

DECEMBER 11
Conquering Anger

Alexander the Great was one of the few men in history who seemed to deserve his descriptive title. He was energetic, versatile, and intelligent. Although hatred was not part of his nature, several times he was tragically defeated by anger.

The story is told of one of these occasions, when a dear friend of Alexander, a general in his army, became intoxicated and began to ridicule the emperor in front of his men. Blinded by anger, Alexander snatched a spear from the hand of a soldier and hurled it at his friend. Although he had only intended to scare the drunken general, his aim was true and the spear took the life of his childhood friend. Deep remorse followed. Overcome with guilt, Alexander attempted to take his own life with the same spear, but he was stopped by his men. For days he lay sick, calling for his friend and chiding himself as a murderer.

Alexander the Great conquered many cities and vanquished many countries, but failed miserably to control his own spirit.

Anger is put into the same category as Adultery, fornication, uncleanness, lasciviousness, idolatry, witchcraft, hatred, variance, emulations, wrath, strife, seditions, heresies, envyings, murders, drunkenness, revellings, and such like. They are called the works of the flesh (Galatians 5:17-21). These bring regret, remorse and bitterness to our lives.

As Christians we have a tool that Alexander did not have. We have the Holy Spirit dwelling in us. He will help us overcome our flesh. To walk in the Spirit results in the fruit of the Spirit, love, joy, peace, longsuffering, gentleness, goodness, faith, meekness, temperance. These are obtained by yielding yourselves unto God, as those that are alive from the dead, and your members as instruments of righteousness unto God (Romans 6:13).

DECEMBER 12
Secular or Spiritual Mind

"But we speak the wisdom of God in a mystery, even the hidden wisdom, which God ordained before the world unto our glory" (1 Cor. 2:7).

Paul speaks of the battle for the mind. These are on two different frequencies. We all start with a scientific mind. It is the most complex arrangement in the universe, weighing about three pounds. If we compared it to giant computers and try to duplicate it, we would need the space of the empire state building.

It contains trillions of cells each capable of holding knowledge. Each is connected to tens of thousands of other cells by neurotransmitters. These supervise our hearing, seeing, smell, taste, behavior, thinking, feeling, wants, likes, dislikes, emotions, body functions, etc.

We all start blank and began a journey down the broad road of secularism or the narrow road of spiritual mindedness, according to our exposure.

The secular mind has accepted Evolution, Secularism, Humanism, Chas. Darwin, Karl Marks, John Dewey, Plato, Aristotle, Socrates, Thos. Paine, Voltaire, Wm. James, and Napoleon Hill, and been exposed to the media, Hollywood, secular education. art, fiction, drama, poetry, politics, and secular philosophy. Like a negative in a camera we are molded by what we hear and see.

The result is modernism, socialism, liberalism, communism, fascism, and the cults. The outgrowth is crime, abortion, pornography, homosexuality, greed, rape, living together without marriage. This is referred to as the natural mind in the Bible (1 Cor. 2:14).

The spiritual mind is Bible centered and directs one down the narrow road spoken of by Jesus (Matthew 7:14). Paul explains the difference in 1 Cor. 2:14-15. When Jesus comes into a believer's heart, the Spirit of the Lord opens our minds to the truth. This results in righteousness and produces the fruit of the Spirit (Galatians 5:22).

DECEMBER 13
Cause And Effect

The Lord set a number of basic laws into effect when He created the Heavens and the earth, such as the law of gravity, law of the harvest, and such. Among them He included, "Cause and Effect."

In each case we must do something to set God into motion. What an amazing thought, that we have the power to set almighty God into motion. The disciples had to obey the word of Jesus and pour water into the water pots to have it turn into wine. Their action brought reaction.

Moses' rod had to be raised to open up the red sea. Blood had to be applied to the door post to have the death angel pass over in Egypt. Rahab had to hang the scarlet cord out her window to save her family. The priests had to step into the water before it opened at Jordon. Naaman had to dip seven times in Jordon to be cleansed of his leprosy. The man with the withered hand had to stretch it forth, then it was healed.

Every miracle and answer to prayer is preceded by a condition. We must ask, then we receive, seek then find, knock, then it will be opened. We sow first then reap. We draw nigh to God and He draws nigh to us. We honor Him and He honors us. We call upon Him and He answers and shows us great and mighty things.

Sinners must believe and then they shall be saved. We bring our tithes into the storehouse and He opens the windows of Heaven for us. We come unto Him and He gives us rest. We honor father and mother and our days are long upon the earth. We confess our sins and He is faithful to forgive us.

DECEMBER 14
Champion's Creed

One of my closest friends and chairman of our deacons Jim Breene, a very successful business man at one of my three churches wrote to his grandchildren at Christmas time challenging them to be champions.

They were given in a book titled *A Hero In Every Heart* written by H. Jackson Brown, Jr. and sent to athletes.

His sixteen suggestions were:

1. Never underestimate your opponent.
2. Work on your weaknesses until they become your strong points.
3. Remember that a great effort is usually the result of a great attitude.
4. Dedicate yourself to a mighty purpose.
5. Win with humility, lose with grace.
6. Ignore those who discourage you.
7. Work to improve your moral and spiritual strengths as well as your physical ones.
8. Remember that how you conduct yourself off the field is just as important as how you conduct yourself on the field.
9. Talent is God-given—be humble. Fame is man-given—be thankful. Conceit is self-given—be careful.
10. Don't ask to be deprived of tension and discipline—these are the tools that shape success.
11. Do what has to be done, when it has to be done, and as well as it can be done.
12. Remember that when you're not working to improve, your competition is.
13. Always give your best.
14. Practice like a champion.
15. Play like a champion.
16. Live like a champion.

Jim told his grandchildren, "I hope you will print a copy of The Champion's Creed and put it someplace where you will see it every day so it can become a part of your life.

I challenge you to be a "CHAMPION" both at home, in school, on the athletic field and in your spiritual life. Great advice for all of us.

DECEMBER 15
Three Righteous Men

"Though these three men Noah, Daniel, and Job, were in it, they should deliver but their own souls be their righteousness, saith the Lord GOD" (Ezekiel 14:14).

Noah overcame the World and won over, *"the lust of the eyes"*. Daniel overcame the Flesh, and won over *"the lust of the flesh"*. Job overcame the

Devil, and won over *"the pride of life"*.

Noah is a symbol of salvation. Noah found grace in the eyes of the Lord (Genesis 6:8). He and his family were the only ones saved from the flood. We also see a symbol of fellowship. *"Noah walked with God"* (Gen 6:9). There is also a lesson in obedience. *"Noah did according unto all that the Lord commanded him"* (Genesis 7:5). Then he is an example of Faith. Noah believed God and responded when warned by God (Genesis 11:7).

Daniel is a symbol of separation. He *"purposed in his heart that he would not defile himself with the portion of the king's meat"* (Daniel 1:8). Believers have trouble with the flesh cycle. We knock down the sign that says it's wrong. Evil then becomes acceptable. Evil becomes popular. It then becomes unpopular not to. It then becomes lawful. It then becomes unlawful not to. It then becomes religious. Then God sends judgment.

Job is a symbol of steadfastness. He stayed true through it all. *"He was perfect and upright, and one that feared God, and eschewed evil"* (Job 1:1). *"There is none like him in the earth"* (Job 1:8). He was steadfast in prosperity. He was steadfast in adversity. He was steadfast in sorrow. He was steadfast in affliction. He was steadfast in family desertion. He was steadfast in doubt. He was steadfast in spirituality. *"In all of this Job sinned not."*

DECEMBER 16
The Bike Ride

Chuck Ebbs wrote, at first, I saw God as my observer, my judge, keeping track of the things I had done wrong, as so to know whether I merited heaven or hell when I die. He was sort of like a president.

But later on, when I met Christ, it seemed as though life were rather like a bike ride, but it was a tandem bike, and I noticed that Christ was in the back helping me pedal. He suggested we change places, and life has not been the same since.

When I had control, I knew the way. It was rather boring, but predictable. But when He took the lead, He knew delightful long cuts, up mountains, and through rocky places.

I worried and was anxious and asked, "Where are you taking me?" He didn't answer, and I started to learn to trust. I forgot my boring life and entered in to the adventure. He took me to people with gifts that I needed, gifts of healing, acceptance, and joy.

They gave me gifts to take on my journey, and we were off again. He said, "Give the gifts away;" so I did to the people we met, and I found that in giving I received. I did not trust Him, at first, in control of my life.

I thought He'd wreck it; but He knows bike secrets, knows how to make it bend to take sharp corners, knows how to jump to clear high rocks. And I'm learning to be quiet and pedal, and I'm beginning to enjoy the ride and the experiences. and the constant companion with, Jesus Christ.

And when I'm sure I just can't do any more, He just smiles and says… "Pedal."

DECEMBER 17
Tragedy Of Unbelief

Before the American forces dropped the Atomic Bomb on Nagasaki, Japan, planes flew over the city and sprinkled warning messages. These Japanese leaflets, restated to the residents the power of America and the Atom Bomb, reminded them what had happened at Hiroshima a few days before, and they told what would be the outcome if Japan did not surrender. The last three words of the message were: EVACUATE YOUR CITIES.

On August 9, 1945 two planes appeared above Nagasaki. *Bockscar,* the B-29 carrying the A-bomb known as "Fat man" released its deadly cargo at 11:01 a.m. local time, and within seconds over 50,000 people went out into eternity. Nagasaki and her residents had been warned. In fact, several survivors of the Hiroshima atomic blast had reached Nagasaki. Yet, except for many of the children who had been taken out of town, the people of Nagasaki chose to stay. The city had never been bombed before. Their choice cost them their lives, and for most, that choice left them in eternal doom.

In a spiritual sense, preachers give the warnings of eternal judgment from God's Word. Tracts, personal witness, good radio, television, and internet programming, daily contain the Truth of eternity. Yet a vast majority of people choose not to believe.

The book of Hebrews links "unbelief" with an evil heart (3:12), and later we are reminded that this was the cause of Israel's early failure in the Exodus. Forty years after wandering in the wilderness, Moses would remind a second generation of Israelites of the problem. *"Yet in this thing ye did not believe the LORD your God"* (Deut. 1:32).

Unbelief...It is found in every generation, and often with tragic results. *"He that believeth on him is not condemned: but he that believeth not is condemned already"* (John 3:18a).

DECEMBER 18
The Boy Who Shot His Brother

I had just gotten settled in as pastor of my new church when a call told of a family who needed comfort. They were at the emergency room with their nine year old son. He had been shot by his twelve year old brother.

When I arrived the Dad, Mom, and the twelve year old son were in the family waiting area. I prayed with them and did all I could to encourage and comfort them. The father shared with me that his concern was not so much for his boy who had been shot, but the boy who did the shooting.

His other son was in shock. He was staring at the wall with a blank look and not responsive to anything they said. I asked them to let me talk with the boy alone. I did everything I could to get response from the boy, but to no avail.

The next day I checked in with them and found the boy had snapped out of it and was doing fine. It seems that after I left another preacher came by and talked with the boy. He snapped right out of it. When I inquired as to what had taken place, they shared that the other preacher told the boy, "I know how you feel. I shot my brother when I was your age." When the boy heard that he tuned in and began to listen and then also began to talk to him.

How wonderful to know that Jesus understands our burdens. The Bible declares, *"For we have not a high priest which cannot be touched with the feelings of our infirmities; but was in all points tempted like as we are, yet without sin"* (Heb. 4:15).

DECEMBER 19
Failure Of Riches

In 1923, the world's most successful financiers met at a Chicago hotel. Financially, they "held the world by the tail"—anything that money could buy was within their grasp.

They were Charles Schwab, the president of the largest steel company; Samuel Insull, the president of the largest electric utility company; Howard Hopson, the president of the largest gas company; Arthur Cutten, the great wheat speculator; Richard Whitney, president of the New York Stock Exchange; Albert Fall, the Secretary of Interior in President Harding's Cabinet; Jesse Livermore, the greatest "bear" on Wall Street; Ivar Kreuger, head of the world's greatest monopoly; Leon Fraser, president of the Bank of International Settlements. Impressive. Who wouldn't like to change positions with one of them?

Twenty-five years later in 1948: Charles Schwab was forced into bankruptcy and lived his last five years on borrowed money. Samuel Insull died in a foreign land, a fugitive and penniless. Howard Hopson was insane. Arthur Cutten became insolvent and had died abroad. Richard Whitney had just been released from Sing Sing prison. Albert Fall had been pardoned from prison so he could die at home, broke. Jesse Livermore had died of suicide. Ivar Kreuger took his own life. Leon Fraser also committed suicide.

A vast amount of talent and potential went down the drain with these men. What happened? Their lives were out of balance and motivated to be rich! *"But they that will be rich fall into temptation and a snare, and into many foolish and hurtful lusts, which drown men in destruction and perdition"* (1 Timothy 6:9). They fell into temptations, a snare, foolish and hurtful lusts. Will drown in destruction and perdition.

"Better is a dry morsel, and quietness therewith, than a house full of sacrifices with strife" (Proverbs 17:1).

DECEMBER 20
One On One

Andrew brought his brother to Jesus. A little while later Peter invited a large group of Jewish people to accept Jesus Christ as the messiah they had long awaited and three-thousand of them did so. A few days later five thousand more were saved. Josephus the early Jewish historian wrote that twenty thousand people were saved that week, were baptized and joined that Church, and that eighty thousand were added that year. All because one man won one man.

Ed Kimble a shoe salesman won an eighteen year old boy to Christ named D. L. Moody. Moody then won over a million souls.

A humble woman Sunday school teacher won a junior boy to the Lord in Louisville, Ky. That boy was Lee Roberson, who is responsible for thousands upon thousands of souls being saved. Thank god for Mrs. Daisy Haws.

Ernie Habecker won me to the Lord by witnessing to me on the assembly line at a General Motors plant. I've seen thousands of souls saved because one fellow won his fellow worker to the Lord. I won a young Spanish teenager to Christ in Mexico. He surrendered to preach, went to Bible college then to Spain as a missionary. He's been there now for three terms. A great work has been established there.

I realize that I could not win a million people like Moody but I could win a young person to Christ, disciple him, help him through Bible college, and he could win several thousand or even a million. I won a fellow whose two sons are pastors and several of his grandsons also are pastors.

It all started when I was able to win the one fellow. The potential is unlimited. This is the closest thing to God's heart, and the reason He came to earth.

DECEMBER 21
Angelphilia

It's Christmas time. The attention of the world focuses on a time when God came down in the form of a baby to live among us and then die to pay for the sins of all mankind. Isaiah called Him Emmanuel, "God with us."

There is a great interest in the angels that appeared during the time of His birth. Angels appeared to Joseph, Mary, Zachariah, and the shepherd in the field. Angels appear in 34 of the 66 books of the Bible. They are mentioned 108 times in the Old Testament, and 165 times in the New Testament. Two-thirds of them are good angels and one third are fallen angels or demons (Hebrews 13:2). Both were created by God (John 1:10) prior to creation of the universe (Job 38:4).

The good angels appear in white (Acts 1:10) and usually as men. Some have wings and others do not. The reaction to their appearance is normally fear. They are called ministering spirits or messengers.

Paul tells us, *"Be not forgetful to entertain strangers: for thereby some have entertained angels unawares"* (Hebrews 13:2). A Bible scholar writing about Angels, used the term "Angelphilia" an extreme interest in angels.

We have all heard stories from people who claim to have had a heavenly visitor. Even I remember as a child, when my mother came running up the stairs in the middle of the night and wakened each of us six children, one at a time, asking if we were alright.

The next morning at breakfast we listened with awe as she told of seeing an shining angel standing on the foot of her bed. She thought he had come to take one of us to Heaven. I believe in and have a decided interest in angels.

DECEMBER 22
Standing For Jesus Christ

Sometimes there is "no room in the Inn" for churches and Christians. We are witnessing the attempt of the extreme radical Muslim groups such as Isis, Al-Shabaab, Al-Qaeda, Taliban, Hamas, to rid the world of Jesus and His influence. They are killing Christians including children in terrorist attacks around the world. Mostly their efforts are centered in the middle East and Africa and much of it on schools to do away with future influence. Their goal is to eliminate Christians from the world and establish Muslim law over the entire world.

In Herod's day thousands of children were killed because he wanted to eradicate Jesus Christ. Today this same attempt to eradicate Jesus Christ is underway. Monuments and memorials are torn down, the distribution of Bibles in public schools is ended, prayers at public events are stopped, Christian employees lose their jobs, and church buildings are prevented from being built.

But just as Herod's carnage failed to kill the Christ child, today's attackers will not succeed in eradicating the name of Jesus. Just as God warned the wise men not to return to Herod and told Joseph to take Mary and the Christ child to Egypt, today He provides the wisdom needed for many legal victories. We can rejoice this year over many triumphs that keep the name of Jesus before our nation.

This Christmas, we would encourage you to remember that we serve a living God. None of these attacks take Him by surprise. He is Lord of

Lords and King of Kings. *"Glory to God in the highest, and on earth peace, good will toward men"* (Luke 2:14).

As a Christmas gift back to God this year, make the decision to boldly declare His name and His message as proclaimed in His Book.

DECEMBER 23
History Of A Christmas Carol

What in the world do leaping lords, French hens, swimming swans, and especially the partridge who won't come out of the pear tree have to do with Christmas? Today I found out, thanks to the Internet.

From 1558 until 1829, Roman Catholics in England were not permitted to practice their faith openly. Someone during that era wrote this carol as a catechism song for young Catholics. It has two levels of meaning: the surface meaning plus a hidden meaning known only to members of their church.

Each element in the carol has a code word for a religious reality which the children could remember.

The partridge in a pear tree was Jesus Christ.

Two turtle doves were the Old and New Testaments.

Three French hens stood for faith, hope and love.

The four calling birds were the four gospels of Matthew, Mark, Luke and John.

The five golden rings recalled the Torah or Law, the first five books of the Old Testament.

The six geese a-laying stood for the six days of creation.

Seven swans a-swimming represented the sevenfold gifts of the Holy Spirit: Prophesy, Serving, Teaching, Exhortation, Contribution, Leadership, and Mercy.

The eight maids a-milking were the eight beatitudes.

Nine ladies dancing were the nine fruits of the Holy Spirit: Love, Joy, Peace, Patience, Kindness, Goodness, Faithfulness, Gentleness, and Self Control.

The ten lords a-leaping were the ten commandments.

The eleven pipers piping stood for the eleven faithful disciples.

The twelve drummers drumming symbolized the twelve points of belief in the Apostles' Creed.

So there is your history for today. The Bible uses this approach in the parables and through types and symbols to reveal truth to the believer and hide it from the unbeliever. Isaiah spoke of, "seeing yet not seeing."

DECEMBER 24
A Biblical View Of Christmas

Traditions have a way of spreading around the world much faster than the truth. Children hear about Santa Claus long before they hear about Jesus Christ. The Easter bunny gets far more attention than the resurrection. "Turkey Day" is replacing the theme of Thanksgiving. The stork bringing babies is still the explanation many people use to tell their children about where babies come from. The theory of evolution has been accepted worldwide as a substitute for the Bible account of creation.

To keep their children from becoming Christians many middle Eastern families pass along the legends that Jesus as a child turned several other children into goats until Mary persuaded Him to turn them back again.

Another legend tells that Jesus took a dead fish, placed it in the water and made it come back to life. Still another says that He made 12 clay pigeons on the Sabbath and when the elders scolded Him for it, He made them come back to life.

Now none of these things are true, but the sad part of it all is that these legends undermine the real miracles that Jesus did and the true things that Jesus said.

The real truth of Christmas is that God Himself came to earth in a very unique way to make a payment for the sins of the world that He might give us the gift of eternal life.

Isaiah the prophet, hundreds of years before the first Christmas foretold that Jesus would be born of a virgin and would be called "God" (Emanuel).

Now I don't know about anybody else but I am overwhelmed that God would come Himself to make arrangements for me to come to heaven and spend my eternity with Him. What a Christmas gift!

DECEMBER 25
Unwrapping The Gift Of God

Each Christmas morning my mind fills with memories of slipping downstairs with my five siblings at the first sign of daylight to see the bikes wagons, dolls, BB guns, sitting around under the tree.

One Christmas was really different because the order from Sears did not make it on time and Mom explained that Santa Claus had told her he was so far behind that he would be late, and that Mrs. Claus would make his delivery on New Year's Eve.

Sure enough Mrs. Claus came through right on schedule. Mom would always wrap socks, work shirts and pants and more for Dad and place them under the tree. All of us urged him to join in and open his gifts. He would always say, "I'll do it later." He never did.

Mom would wait several days then unwrap them and put them away for him. Years later I was preparing a message on "The Gift of God". My thoughts went back to those times and I could still see in my mind those unopened gifts. He was not a Christian and I saw the parallel.

The Bible says, *"The Gift of God is eternal life through Jesus Christ our Lord"* (Romans 6:23). I also remembered what James wrote, "Every good gift and every perfect gift is from above and cometh down from the Father of lights."

Satan makes every effort to keep God's gift wrapped up in tradition and false teachings. The Holy Spirit came to unwrap him so that people might see and know who He really is and accept the gift of God.

Jesus explained to Nicodemus that he would need to be born again in order to see or understand who He was and what He came to do.

DECEMBER 26
Little Robin Egg

It had been raining during the night and now the clouds were gone and the sun was shining. It was Kansas City, and I was walking down the sidewalk. Water was running down the edge of the street and into a sewer drain. A small pile of sticks had gathered if front of the drain and a small baby blue robin egg was laying on the sticks. It had been blown out of a nest by the wind of the storm.

I was amazed that it had not broken. I picked it up and rolled it around I my hand. Under normal circumstances that egg would produce a robin, which would produce three more eggs and three more robins. In ten years there would be 60,000 or more robins and another year over one million.

I realized that I held in my hand the potential for millions of robins, but that was not going to happen. This egg is now cold and dead.

I thought of the man who won a young fellow named Moody to the Saviour and he won over a million. Think of the humble unknown lady who won a junior boy to the Lord in her Sunday School class in Louisville, KY that grew up to be the late Dr. Lee Roberson. Who would have dreamed that little, "Jackie boy Hyles" would make such an astounding impact on the lives of so many thousands of people?

The potential for thousands and maybe even millions of souls and lives being saved from an awful hell through the life of a child sitting in a Sunday school class or riding on a church bus.

Only God knows what one of the teenagers in one of our families will accomplish for the Lord.

DECEMBER 27
The Grace Of God

Dr. Delma Lowery in his book *Building Steadfast Christians* gives an illustration of a fellow that he calls Billy Burpo. Every time Billy saw the preacher he threw stones at him, cursed him, and voiced his general dislike of him. The preacher never fought back, or tried to retaliate in any way. One day the preacher caught Billy with his head turned and slipped up behind him. There was a piece of two by four leaned up against the fence, but instead of using it to whack Billy up against the side of his head, which he deserved, the preacher threw his arms around Billy and held him tightly so he could not wiggle loose. He had in one of his hands a twenty dollar bill. He held it so Billy could see it and said, "Billy this is a gift, and I want you to have this because I love you."

This would be pure grace. Dr. Lowery then explained that this is exactly what God has done for sinners. Because of the sin of Adam, we are all born with a sinful nature and resent the restraint of the Bible and the God it reveals to us.

We deserve to be condemned to eternal damnation, but God

commended His love toward us in that while we were sinners, Christ died in our place. He now offers the gift of eternal life, which is far beyond twenty dollars.

It is natural for us to resent God and reject, refuse, and not want any part of God or the Bible, but once we see what His gift is all out, "we love Him because He first loved us."

This is all seen in the account of Paul who persecuted Christians, who became a zealous follower of Christ.

DECEMBER 28
Killing Giants

I have preached in several hundred church auditoriums during my years of ministry and each time the lights were on when I entered. Someone had already flipped a switch on the wall to make that happen. We all know that somewhere in that area is a hydroelectric plant that cost millions of dollars to build and hundred and maybe thousands of man hours to build the plant.

One day the turbines were turned on, electricity was created, it was sent by three phase wire to that area, transferred by a transformer to a smaller frequency, sent to a meter, then to a light switch on the wall. When that switch was triggered, the room filled with light. With that flip of the switch we got the benefit of all those hours and all that expense.

God has given us a Bible filled with stories, accounts, experiences, parables, miracles and many other things. Each of them have two things that are true of them. They are each filled with many facts and one basic biblical principle. Most of them have dozens of facts.

Usually there is one underlying principle. When David killed Goliath, we see a boy, a giant, a sling, five stones, a Jew, a Philistine, and many other facts. The principle in this account is that a little nobody, humanly ill equipped, but with the touch of God can handle a giant problem.

Our giant will not be a nine and one half Philistine, but maybe cancer, betrayal of a mate, death in the family, tragedy, and such.

Each time we are exposed to that account the principle is subconsciously reinforced and strengthened in our philosophy and action.

The more our faith is increased by exposure to the account the more our natural is replaced by the supernatural.

DECEMBER 29
92 Year Old Preacher

An old preacher was being recognized for his longevity in the ministry. They asked him to give his secret for his personal victory and faithfulness in the ministry. He explained that when he asked his congregation for a favorite hymn to sing in the Sunday night service, it was always an adult who suggested "Jesus Loves Me."

They all sang hardily the words we all love. "Jesus loves me this I know. For the Bible tells me so. Little ones to Him belong, We are weak but He is strong. Yes, Jesus loves me. The Bible tells me so."

The old pastor then said, "I have come up with some new words that are more fitting for us older folks, so we can continue to enjoy this old classic. Here for you now is a Senior version of Jesus Loves Me":

Jesus loves me, this I know,
Though my hair is white as snow.
Though my sight is growing dim,
Still He bids me trust in Him.
(CHORUS)
Yes, Jesus loves me,
Yes, Jesus loves me.
Yes, Jesus loves me,
The Bible tells me so.
Though my steps are oh, so slow,
With my hand in His I'll go.
On through life, let come what may,
He'll be there to lead the way.
(CHORUS)
When the nights are dark and long,
In my heart He puts a song.
Telling me in words so clear,
"Have no fear, for I am near."
(CHORUS)
When my work on earth is done,
And life's victories have been won.
He will take me home above,
Then I'll understand His love.

(CHORUS)
I love Jesus, does He know?
Have I ever told Him so?
Jesus loves to hear me say,
That I love Him every day.

DECEMBER 30
Bible Reading This Year

"And beginning at Moses and all the prophets, he expounded unto them in all the scriptures the things concerning himself" (Luke 24:27).

It will take seventy-two hours to read the Old Testament and eighteen for the New Testament. Ninety hours out of 8,760 hours that the Lord has given us in a year doesn't seem like too much. A tithe of our time would be 876 hours.

The Bible is given to us in two basic ways, principles and facts. In the story of David and Goliath, there are fifty or sixty facts. In the first exposure to the story, one will remember several facts. After reading it several times, hearing a Sunday school teacher present it, and maybe a sermon preached on it, we will know most of the facts from memory.

Then there is a basic principle in the account. A little nobody, with God's help and blessing can handle a big giant problem in his or her life. Every time we are exposed to the story, that principle will be more deeply imbedded in our outlook.. We become spiritual by becoming scriptural. The more scriptural we are the more spiritual we will be.

The Bible is filled with history, geography, science, engineering, music, philosophy, poetry, religion, drama, politics, struggle, suffering, prophesy, warnings, direction, helps, encouragement, examples, and covers every conceivable area of human knowledge and experience.

The Bible has the answer to the crime problem the divorce tragedy, the moral slide, the evolution debate, the liberal drift, the pornography blight, the AIDS epidemic, the abortion question, the teen delinquent problem, the illegitimate birth situation, the world energy problem, the world hunger problem, the birth defect burden, the pollution fear, the alcohol plague, the drug disaster, and the terror threat.

DECEMBER 31
The End. What Now?

Here we are, at the end of another year. This is it! What is to come? In like manner we shall all come to another end. The writer of Hebrews spoke of it, *"It is appointed unto men once to die, but after this the judgment"* (Hebrews 9:27). What will it be like?

Ray Comfort in *The Evidence Bible* has recorded the last words of some well known's:

—Princess Diana—"My God. What's happened?"

—Phillip III—"What an account I shall have to give to God! How I should like to live otherwise than I have lived."

—Elizabeth the First—"All my possessions for one moment of time."

—Anne Boleyn (Executed by her husband King Henry VIII)—"O God have pity on my soul."

—Socrates—"All of the wisdom of this world is but a tiny raft upon which we must sail when we leave this earth. If only there was a firmer foundation upon which to sail, perhaps some divine word."

—James Dean—"My fun days are over."

—Cardinal Borgia—"I have provided in the course of my life for everything but death, and now I am to die unprepared."

—D.L. Moody—"I see earth receding; Heaven is opening. God is calling me."

—Martin Luther—"Into thy hands I commend my spirit! Thou hast redeemed me Oh God of truth."

—Daniel Webster—"I still live."

—Henry Ward Beecher—"Now comes the mystery."

—William Shakespeare—"I commend my soul into the hands of God my creator."

—Patrick Henry—"Doctor, I wish you to observe how real and beneficial the religion of Christ is to a man about to die."

—John Milton—"Death is the great key that opens the palace of eternity."

ABOUT THE AUTHOR

Dr. Wallace was born August 22, 1930, in Odd, West Virginia, the second of six children. His parents were Lonnie and Reba Wallace of Toughkenamon, Pennsylvania. He was married to Janith May Farr of Kennett Square, Pennsylvania, from 1950 until her death in 2002. They have four children: Debbie, Tom Jr., Tim, and Donna. Dr. Wallace remarried on August 7, 2004, to the former Mary Cluck of Athens, Tennessee. Dr. Wallace and Mary are living in Murfreesboro, Tennessee, and travel together in the ministry.

Dr. Wallace was saved at General Motors Assembly Plant in Wilmington, Delaware. He began preaching in the noon services at the plant and preached there until leaving for Bible College. He served on the Staff of Highland Park Baptist Church, Chattanooga, Tennessee, with Dr. Lee Roberson for two years. (1953 and 1954)

Education and Honors:
1948 - Graduated from Kennett High School, Kennett Square, PA
1954 - B.A. Degree - Tennessee Temple University, Chattanooga, TN
1971 - Doctor of Divinity Degree from Bob Jones University
1994 - Doctor of Divinity from Louisiana Baptist University
2003 - Doctor of Divinity from Canadian Baptist Bible College

He pastored 3 great churches:
Baptist Bible Church of Elkton, Maryland, 1954 to 1971
Beth Haven Baptist Church of Louisville, Kentucky, 1971 to 1986
Franklin Road Baptist from September 1, 1991, to January 2000
Pastor emeritus of FRBC, Murfreesboro, TN, from 2000 to present

Other accomplishments:
Active in radio work for over 30 years
Published two church papers, "The Visitor" and "The Beam,"
Founder of Elkton Christian Schools, Elkton, Maryland, (K-12)
Founder of Beth Haven Christian Schools, Louisville, Kentucky, (K-12)
Pres. of Franklin Road Christian Schools, Murfreesboro, TN, (K-12) 1991 to 2000

Established a Bus Ministry of 18 routes in Elkton, Maryland,
Expanded Bus ministry in Louisville, Kentucky, to 42 routes.
Tripled attendance at Louisville Church in first 2 years.
Led Baptist Bible Church, Elkton, MD, through eight building programs.
Led in building a 3300-seat auditorium BHBC, Louisville, KY.
Led FRBC, Murfreesboro, Tennessee, in building a new educational building.
Led in purchase of two additional properties.
Past president of International Fellowship of Fundamentalists.
Served as president of Board of Directors of BIMI for 8 years.
Vice-President of the "Sword of the Lord," Murfreesboro, TN
Vice-President of Beacon World Missions.
Executive Board of Frontline Fellowship